Gospel Light's

PRETEEN MINISTRY SMART PAGES

The essential guide to understanding and ministering to teens

ages 10 to 14

Provides comprehensive, practical guidelines for creating a ministry that meets the needs of preteens

Gives a complete model for developing a preteen youth group

Helps pastors, ministry leaders and teachers understand the mind and emotions of 10- to 14-year-olds

Includes a variety of fun, kid-tested activities, service projects and missions to engage preteens and their families

reproducible

gordon and becki west

Gospel Light

HOW TO MAKE CLEAN COPIES FROM THIS BOOK

NOTE

Because church liability laws are inherently complex and may not be completely free of doubtful interpretations, you are advised to verify that the legal rules you are following actually apply to your situation. In no event will Gospel Light be liable for direct, indirect, special, incidental or consequential damages arising out of the use, inability to use or inappropriate use of the text materials, forms or documentation, even if Gospel Light is advised of or aware of the possibility of such damages. In no case will Gospel Light's liability exceed the amount of the purchase price paid.

Gospel Light in no way guarantees or warrants any particular legal or other result from the use of *Preteen Ministry Smart Pages*.

While Gospel Light attempts to provide accurate and authoritative information regarding the subject matter covered, *Preteen Ministry Smart Pages* is sold with the understanding that Gospel Light is not engaged in rendering legal or other professional services, and is sold subject to the foregoing limited warranty. If legal or other expert assistance is required, the services of a competent professional should be sought.

Forms are shown for illustrative purposes only. They should not be relied on for any legal purpose or effect until they have been reviewed by a competent attorney in your state who is experienced in laws relating to churches.

Editorial Staff

Founder, Dr. Henrietta Mears • **Publisher Emeritus,** William T. Greig • **Publisher, Children's Curriculum and Resources,** Bill Greig III • **Senior Consulting Publisher,** Dr. Elmer L. Towns • **Product Line Manager,** Cary Maxon • **Senior Managing Editor,** Sheryl Haystead • **Senior Consulting Editor,** Wesley Haystead, M.S.Ed. • **Senior Editor, Biblical and Theological Issues,** Bayard Taylor, M.Div. • **Editorial Team,** Debbie Barber, Mary Davis, Becky Garcia • **Art Director,** Lenndy McCullough, • **Designer,** Zelle Olson

Scripture quotations are taken from the *Holy Bible, New International Version*®. Copyright © 1973, 1978, 1984 by International Bible Society. Used by permission of Zondervan Publishing House. All rights reserved.

Library of Congress Cataloging-in-Publication Data

West, Gordon, 1959-
[Dynamic preteen ministry]
Preteen ministry smart pages / by Gordon and Becki West.
    p. cm.
Originally published: Dynamic preteen ministry. Loveland, Colo. : Group, c2000.
Includes bibliographical references.
ISBN 0-8307-3711-1
1. Church work with preteens. I. West, Becki, 1955- II. Title.
BV1475.9.W47 2005
259'.22—dc22
                                        2004030104

Dedication

We would like to dedicate this book to our mentors in early adolescent education, Dr. Donald C. Clark and Dr. Sally N. Clark, middle level education pioneers, who gave us the principles and concepts behind it all, and to Robin Welsh, our partner in ministry, who walked alongside us as we learned to apply those theories in the creation of sound, practical tools for ministry to early adolescents in the local church.

We would also like to express our love and appreciation to our own two wonderful daughters, Ashley and Emily, who have allowed us to learn and grow and to experience again the ups and downs of the preteen years as we have had the privilege of walking alongside them through this incredibly important period of life. They have given us the most awesome privilege of all, to parent—allowing us to lead and shepherd them and returning our love, even in the hard times.

Acknowledgments

We want to express our deepest appreciation to the many volunteer teachers, early adolescents and parents who gave of their time to share with us their experiences and their needs and who allowed us to look into their lives for a glimpse of reality. We also are indebted to the following leaders of early adolescents for sharing their successes and challenges with us in the writing of this book. None of us is in this vital ministry alone!

Keith and Nancy Braun

Terry L. Buxton, Sr.

Stephanie Caro

Judy Easson

Dee Engel

Randall S. Floyd

Ben Freudenburg

Susan Grover

Corey Hooper

Sharon Hovanic

Kordell Kennemer

Paul Klassen

Roger Phelps

Walt and Diane Pitman

Bill Russell

Jeanne Scheetz

Lois Sherwin

Dale Torry

Robin Welsh

Contents

Section Three—Nuts and Bolts:
Issues for Preteen Ministry

*These chapters are recommended for use in preteen parent education classes.

Introduction

Our friends say we must be crazy to work with fifth and sixth graders or that we must have been tricked into being part of the junior high staff. They can't comprehend why any normal adult would work with these crazy, high-energy, awkward, unpredictable, hard-to-understand young people. We can't imagine investing our lives in anything better than these incredible preteens.

Why such contradictory views of ministry to early adolescents? The key is understanding—or should we say the lack thereof. Few people understand or take time to understand preteens. With this book we hope to help you and the preteen teachers and leaders with whom you work to better understand and more effectively minister to these special young people whom God dearly loves.

Research shows us that early adolescence, that period of life from 10 to 14 years of age, is the second most important developmental stage in the human life (birth to 3 years of age being the most influential time). But experience tells us that kids in this age level are dropping through the cracks in our church ministries. Some have called them "tweenagers," but they're not really. It's not that they are between two stages; they are in their own identifiable stage of life.

Unfortunately, many public schools and most churches find it difficult to meet the needs of young people in this stage of life. Consequently, both schools and churches too often approach preteens as either children or as teenagers, without recognizing their unique developmental challenges and emerging social needs. Preteens need and deserve more than this.

How to deal with early adolescents has been a major focus in our public school systems for almost 20 years. "Throughout the 1980s, middle level schools were changing. While programmatic changes were gradual, many schools, in an effort to recognize and respond to the earlier onset of puberty, changed grade-level configurations."[1]

And now, because of changes in our public schools and changes in our kids, ministry to late elementary and junior high kids is perhaps one of the hottest issues facing many ministries today. Pull together a group of children's ministers or junior high pastors and the issue of what to do with sixth graders is bound to come up. Talk to a group of parents and they are understandably concerned about whether their child will make the jump from the church's children's program to its youth program. Talk to the kids and too many of them are just bored and turned off by their experiences at church.

In section 1, "Firming Up Your Philosophy: Understanding Preteens and Preteen Ministry," you will discover who these kids really are—according to them and according to educational researchers. It will help you design needs-based programming specifically for those characteristics and decide how your church might best group and grade early adolescents, without dropping them through the cracks. You will also be provided with ready-to-use outlines for talking with your church board, staff, parents and kids as you transition your ministry into one that will be more effective and more exciting for everyone! This section concludes with important tips for sharing your vision with key volunteers as you recruit, motivate and manage your ministry team.

In section 2, "Implementing Your Vision: Making Your Preteen Youth Group Work," you will get practical ideas for your early adolescent ministries that will work for your church, no matter how you decide to group and grade your 10- to 14-year-olds. We will start with "The Big Picture—A Model for Preteen Ministry," which presents a model that is ready to be implemented in your church. Then we'll provide numerous tips and great ideas for how to make your church's preteen ministry a place that preteens will call home, where they feel loved and included. The rest of this section is jam-packed with specific, tried-and-true activities recommended by successful leaders from around the country, including fun things to do, service projects and ways to get kids involved in ministry inside and outside of your church.

Section 3, "Nuts and Bolts: Issues for Preteen Ministry," will deal head-to-head with the hottest issues for those in preteen ministry that we identified after talking with people from all over the country who work with preteens. These issues include handling the unique discipline problems of early adolescents, creative ways to nurture the early adolescent's whole family,

how to get the most out of your curriculum, tips for mentoring preteens in ways that will make a long-lasting impact on their lives and leading preteens to salvation.

We want you, as someone involved in ministry to early adolescents, to know that you are doing one of the most essential works of ministry in the church today. We are excited that you are involved in the same adventure that we are, partnering with us in a ministry that will affect some very special kids for all eternity. We hope that this book will be helpful to your ministry. And we thank the many people who allowed us to share their stories and experiences, especially those brave, humble souls who were willing to admit that they didn't "have it all together" yet. In this ministry, all of us are very much learners and adventurers!

And what a wild, fun adventure it is. Working with early adolescents can be exhausting at times. It can be painfully discouraging at times. But it can also be the most exciting ministry that any of us ever have the privilege (and responsibility) of being a part of. What you are doing is of vital importance! Hang in there and keep ministering to those kids that you love. Because God loves them, too.

Note

1. Sally N. Clark and Donald C. Clark, *Schools in the Middle* (Reston, VA: National Association of Secondary School Principals, 1992), p. ix.

Firming Up Your Philosophy:

UNDERSTANDING PRETEENS and PRETEEN MINISTRY

Who Are These Preteens?

"Upon entering the world of the early adolescents, the observer immediately faces what seems like an unfathomable array of differences and discontinuities. The early adolescent is at one moment coordinated and awkward, shy and aggressive, astute and absent-minded, attentive and distracted, loving and 'squirrely'."

—Michael A. James, "Early Adolescent Ego Development"[1]

"It was the best of times, it was the worst of times, it was the age of wisdom, it was the age of foolishness, it was the epic of belief, it was the epic of incredulity, it was the season of Light, it was the season of Darkness, it was the spring of hope, it was the winter of despair."[2] So said Charles Dickens, and so say many of us who have survived early adolescence, that period of human development now identified as occurring for most kids between the ages of 10 and 14 years. Which of us does not look back at our own early adolescent years and wonder how we ever made it through them?

Preteens are filled with uncertainty. Everything is changing and all at one time! No wonder we have ambivalent feelings about our own early adolescent years. No wonder our students sometimes seem like they are on a roller coaster of emotions. And no wonder we, as leaders, teachers and parents of early adolescents, have a difficult time understanding who these students are!

Early adolescence is perhaps the most misunderstood period of human development in our society today. Even professionals are finding this age group to be a difficult one to research and define. Piaget neglected this transitional period, jumping from childhood to adolescence. Freud and Erikson did not recognize the period of early adolescence because "there was no well defined set of developmental, social, and behavioral characteristics" for this age level.[3]

In fact, only in the past 20 years have psychologists and educators recognized the existence of this specific, identifiable period of human development. We now understand that early adolescence is that period of transitional development that exists between childhood and adolescence. It typically lasts from age 10 to age 14. And it involves the transition from concrete thinking to abstract thinking, from a child's body to a young adult's body, from emotional dependence to independence, and from primary focus on parents and family to interaction with peers.

For too long, we have treated preteens as immature high school students or hard-to-handle elementary kids. This developmental period does not belong to either childhood or adolescence. These kids are not between two stages of life. They are traveling through a specific, identifiable, wonderful period of transitional growth and maturation.

Early adolescence is unique—it is different from childhood and from later adolescence. To try to make it part of one or the other is a mistake that creates problems and ignores the incredible potential of these great kids!

Kids Are Growing Up More Quickly—Or Are They?

The casual observer will conclude that preteens and young teens are maturing faster than they used to. Their bodies seem to be blossoming at an earlier age. They are involved in far more sophisticated activities, social interactions and issues than previous generations. Their world is confronting them with much more serious problems and questions than we had to address at their age. They know more than their preteen predecessors did.

But are they truly maturing, or are they being forced to grow up before their time? While their bodies are advancing at earlier ages, are their emotions and cognitive arenas keeping pace?

Watch movies or TV and you'll quickly see that various media are capitalizing on these physical changes. Younger kids are more interested than ever about their appearances and the look of their peer group. Early adolescents are "big game" for advertisers and moviemakers. They are being drawn in as never before as consumers.

Socially, emotionally and mentally, kids are being exposed to more mature material but may be no more ready to deal with it than we were at their age. David Elkind, in *The Hurried Child*, warns us that children are being forced to grow up more quickly than they ought to be. Through the media and other sources, society is exposing our kids to more mature concepts and visuals than ever before. Any evening of TV watching exposes young children to more than most of our parents ever saw in the movies. "Children and adolescents are . . . subject to impulses, desires, and behaviors not previously encountered by this age group. In part, this new awareness is due to social processes. They are involved in a wider range of social contact, through peers, school, media, and more diverse family structures."[4]

The fact that they are being forced to deal with all of this does not mean that it is good for them or that they are ready for it. Society has forced kids to be more sophisticated. In some ways they are maturing; in others, they are encountering things they are not equipped emotionally to face. The world of the early adolescent is more complex and they are more socially aware. But what many do not realize is that the preteen's skill development does not match this level of sophistication. Their social contacts have pressured them to act like adolescents before they become adolescents.

The Changes in Early Adolescents Are Having an Impact on Our Ministries

Even as researchers grapple with how to transform education to meet the unique needs of this age group, churches have to adapt ministry for them as well. Children's pastor Terry L. Buxton, Sr., from Dallas, Texas, tells us, "There seems to be an increasing lack of interest in what we are doing in our ministry; it is viewed as too 'kiddy' for them. They desire more relationship-building activities. It's hard to keep current with their age-group culture."

What Do Early Adolescents Really Need?

◉ **The needs of early adolescents—according to them.**

What do preteens want? We can learn a lot about their perceived needs by listening to the questions that they ask us at church. Here's a top-10 list of the questions your students are most likely to ask:

The Top 10
Questions Fifth and Sixth Graders Ask at Church

10 Are we going to have a snack?

9 Who's coming?

8 What are we going to do now?

7 Are you sure?

6 What are we going to eat?

5 Really?

4 Is it time to go yet?

3 What did you say?

2 Do we have to?

1 When are we going to eat?

We may wish that preteens would ask:

◉ "What Bible verse can we memorize today?" or

◉ "Is there a needy person in our group that we can show love to right now?"

But these aren't the issues foremost on most preteen minds. Their questions show their felt needs:

◉ Food! As mentioned once or twice above, food is both a felt need and a real need! Kids are a lot easier to work with when their stomachs are full.

◉ Friends! Preteens want to know "Who's coming?" because relationships are central to their existence. They want to be around peers by whom they feel accepted. Friends are a must. Our style of ministry needs to maximize development of relationships.

◉ Fun! They want to know what they're going to do, because they want to have fun playing and being active with their friends. They also want to be sure that they won't be embarrassed by an activity that makes them feel awkward. Preteens demand fun, so a certain amount of our ministry must be devoted to entertainment.

◉ Focus! Early adolescents want to be the center of attention—but only in certain ways. They desire to be noticed by their peers and the significant adults in their lives. So some of the things they say and do at church may simply be to get the attention they desire.

Although it is important to be sensitive to the likes and dislikes of our students, we must avoid building our preteen ministry solely on what the kids say they want or on what we assume they want. Just as we would not consider parenting children by meeting the children's every whim, we should not design our ministries with only the desires of the kids in mind. We must provide bold leadership in our ministry and carefully craft our preteen ministries according to the desires of the kids along with what we know kids need and what we know will help them grow spiritually—needs that even the kids may not be able to express or understand.

◉ **The needs of early adolescents—according to the experts.**

Young adolescents have seven key developmental needs according to research done by Peter Scales of Search Institute:

1. Positive social interaction with adults and peers.

2. Structure and clear limits.

3. Physical activity.

4. Creative expression.

5. Competence and achievement.

6. Meaningful participation in families, schools, and communities.

7. Opportunities for self-definition.[5]

Each of these developmental needs may be understood better in light of the physical, emotional, social, intellectual and spiritual characteristics of the preteen student.

The Physical Characteristics of Early Adolescents

⊚ **The rate of growth and changes in preteens vary widely.** This variation is seen between individual preteens and between the genders. In general, girls will grow more quickly and oftentimes will be taller than boys during the early adolescent years. Although the timing may differ, the experience is similar. Growth in each individual rapidly accelerates before pubescence and decelerates after pubescence. At some point after the body reaches sexual maturity, the growth hormone seems to stop its work.

⊚ **Growth comes in spurts.** Sudden spurts of growth cause the preteen to be awkward and clumsy. Bones grow faster than muscles, leaving the child's new bigger and better body uncoordinated. Hands and feet mature before arms and

legs. While mom and dad are running to the shoe store every week, the child's feet are causing big troubles. They are simply too big for the rest of his or her body, and the extra three inches (7.5 cm) inevitably trip up the child! Legs and arms grow faster than the trunk and are often the source of growing pains.

⊚ **Sudden growth causes fatigue.** Just as in younger children, this sudden growth creates fatigue in early adolescents. Their bodies are working overtime to grow and change and they are left with low energy and a greater need for sleep.

A few years ago, we gave an 11-year-old friend of the family his own copy of Dr. James Dobson's book *Preparing for Adolescence* (see p. 183). This boy had always been an early riser. Even on a Saturday, when he could have slept in, he was up and going before 5 A.M. In the book, he read Dr. Dobson's explanation of this growth process and the preteen's need for sleep. Dobson suggested that the preteen share with parents that he or she truly is tired. The next Saturday the boy slept until 11 A.M.!

⊚ **Early adolescents are very physical.** They like to be active and move about constantly. Outside activities are popular at this age, because this environment allows for large-muscle movement and loud, boisterous activities.

It is difficult for early adolescents to sit still for long periods of time. Their growing bodies need to be active and moving. Although they are easily tired, they also have surges of energy that need to be burned up. Growth spurts make them need more food, yet eating more gives them more calories to burn. Exciting activities or competition can overtire early adolescents, since their stamina and endurance are not adequate to match their love for activity. They are poor self-regulators when it comes to balancing fun activities and rest or sleep.

⊚ **The preteen is bombarded with hormonal changes.** The early adolescent's life is complex. The onset of puberty causes a flood of hormones into the body. New hormones affect the child physically, by causing dramatic growth and physical changes. They also affect far more than the child's body. The raging hormones dramatically affect the early adolescent's emotions.

The Emotional Characteristics of Early Adolescents

Erik Erikson wrote, "In no other stage of the life cycle are the promises of finding oneself and the threat of losing oneself so closely allied."[6]

◎ **Early adolescents are subject to tremendous mood swings.** These sudden changes are often confusing for the parent or teacher, as well as for the child. The preteen's mood jumps suddenly and dramatically between love and hate, happiness and fear, interest and boredom. These mood swings influence every area of the preteen's life, from relationships to the desire to attend church.

One mother of a 10-year-old girl put it this way: "It's hard to get her involved in anything right now. It's like she feels as if she's already got so much going on. And she's so confused and so mixed up emotionally. One minute she's happy and the next . . ."

As significant adults working with early adolescents, we need to remember that these kids have little control over their emotions. We must be patient with preteens who seem to overreact emotionally to any given situation. They may laugh one minute and cry the next. It is not their fault that their changing environment and changing chemistry collide and create wide swings in how they feel about themselves, their peers and their leaders. Our job is to help the preteen learn to respond or act appropriately *in spite* of his or her emotional state.

◎ **Early adolescents can, however, control their actions and words.** It's possible, but it's not easy! They need consistent training from loving, calm, patient adults to learn to react appropriately in spite of how they are feeling. Those who lead early adolescents must be able to deal with their own emotions in such a way that they can model appropriate behavior and true Christian maturity. The teacher or parent who has trouble handling frustration or anger constructively will not get very far helping early adolescents with their own emotional turmoil. This is a very real part of discipling early adolescents.

We recently overheard a group of parents at a soccer game sharing their struggles with their children who were all going through this roller-coaster ride. The parents were taking great solace in hearing that they were not alone. A laugh now and then emerged from the group as others could identify with a particularly vexing anecdote. It reminded us that part of our ministry to preteens involves getting their teachers and their parents together to compare notes with one another and recognize their common challenge.

◎ **Preteens are angry.** Anger is one of the most common emotions that emerge in the life of the early adolescent. They are often quick-tempered. This anger comes from a variety of sources, including fatigue, feelings of inadequacy, rejection or uncertainty.

One preteen student at church had to be stopped from repeatedly hitting another boy with a flat kickball. He inflicted enough pain to cause the other boy to cry. The teacher who stepped in to break it up described the event by saying that the offender seemed to have a need to beat up on someone. There was no clear reason for the angry outburst. Later that day, the same boy tripped and later hit another youngster.

In a private session with the boy's mother, a series of negative issues in the boy's life was uncovered. These were understandable sources of anger for the boy. In the midst of this emotional period in his life, though, he had few skills and no good patterns for releasing or appropriately expressing his frustration. This boy required ongoing counseling and training to provide him with practical ways to avoid the inappropriate reactions.

There is always a reason for anger and for anger being expressed inappropriately by early adolescents. They must be taught skills and have modeled for them patterns for processing feelings of anger positively.

Preteens are fearful. Their fear comes in the form of worries. They have increasing demands upon them in every area of life, and they have anxiety about being able to perform to an acceptable level, as they desire to please both their peers and their parents or teachers.

Nonacceptance and rejection are the early adolescent's biggest worries in life. The preteen is constantly evaluating whether he or she is fitting in and receiving approval. Things like report card grades and peer criticism are vital to the preteen's self-evaluation process.

Now, if you ask an early adolescent about fears, he or she will most likely deny them. Especially when those fears seem to be identified with younger years, like being afraid of the dark. The fears, however, are real.

Because they don't want to admit their fears, maybe not even to themselves, preteens may be somewhat of a mystery to adults. Preteens will protest against having a babysitter stay with them, but then they'll lock themselves in a closet when they hear a scary sound outside and no one is there to protect them! They don't want a baby's nightlight, but they will hide a flashlight under their pillow in case they hear a sound in the night. As adults, we must not discount these very real fears, because the preteen may well feel discounted.

Preteens are often threatened by competition. This is another area of seeming contradiction for preteens. One day, they will seem to love competition; the next, they hate it. We believe it has a lot to do with whether or not they win! Almost everyone loves competing if they are so good at something that they are assured a victory, but not many of us like losing.

Recently, Deann, one of our fifth-grade girls, shared with us that she didn't like attending her class when the teacher played *Jeopardy!* to review previous lessons. Deann is a very smart girl and a regular attender, so she can do quite well with the answers. However, she is also a perfectionist. Competition points out even the most minor of chinks in our armor, and preteens like Deann are already too self-critical.

Early adolescents have a love of humor. These kids will enjoy jokes and leaders who can see the lighter side of life. Humor should be included in every part of the ministry for preteens. Make your classrooms and programs fun places to be.

A few years ago we accidentally fell into a great activity for this age level. We had one leader who liked to tell jokes. Each week he arrived with a new joke to tell the rest of the staff members. One week we asked him to share his joke during the opening of our midweek youth group. Then a student had a joke to share. Then another one shared. Pretty soon, we had established a weekly tradition. Anyone there each week could tell a joke (as long as it was clean, put no one down, and was generally appropriate) to the whole gang. Sometimes the jokes were awful; other times they were hilarious. It was amazing how much we all looked forward to this time each week.

Humor must never be used as a weapon, though. It must be used in a mature manner. No child should ever be the subject of the joke. We may get a good laugh, but we will lose the child. Even those kids who seem to be able to handle it and who laugh along with us are not normally laughing inside.

Sarcastic humor directed at someone can make your whole youth group an unsafe place for preteens. Any child may feel like he or she could be the next victim of a joke. But good, positive humor and lightheartedness should be the flavor and tone of our ministry to preteens.

🌀 **Preteens are private.** Although at times it appears that they will never stop talking, during the later years of early adolescence, kids will develop private areas of their lives that they do not want to share with anyone else, especially not with authority figures. These private areas include their fears and questions about themselves and their peers. Great care must be taken during group discussions to show respect for the privacy of preteens. Teachers should allow some freedom in choosing discussion topics and never pressure preteens to divulge personal information.

🌀 **Preteens need encouragement, support and unconditional love.** We need to give kids strong, frequent affirmation. Because the preteen is constantly changing and experiencing conflicts and emotional upheavals, he or she needs to be reassured over and over that at least one significant adult loves and accepts him or her.

Unconditional love, according to Ross Campbell, M.D., means "loving a teenager [or preteen] no matter what. No matter what the teenager looks like. No matter what his assets, liabilities, and handicaps are. No matter how he acts. This does not mean that you always like his behavior. Unconditional love means you love your teenager, even when you detest his behavior."[7]

🌀 **Preteens need to be needed (and to get positive emotional feedback).** This is why preteens, both boys and girls, are frequent volunteers for the church nursery. They truly enjoy caring for small children, because they get to feel needed and loved by the little ones.

In answer to the question, What's your favorite thing to do anywhere, anytime? one seventh grader responded: "To babysit little ones . . . infants and toddlers." Having young teens and preteens work with other people's kids for a few hours a week gives the teens and preteens some positive emotional strokes. It also gives them an appropriate and serious look at the long-term commitment of becoming a parent.

Preteens benefit greatly from being placed in positions to extend care and to know that they are making a difference in the lives of others.

The Social Characteristics of Early Adolescents

🌀 **For the preteen, peers are incredibly important.** One 12-year-old junior high girl told us her favorite thing about church is "the kids, my age and little ones."

Early adolescents are greatly influenced by their peers. As kids begin to break away from their families and express individuality and independence, they immediately reach out to surrogate families to fill the void. These substitute families may take the form of the church youth group, an athletic team, a small group of friends—or a gang.

Their fear of nonacceptance leads them to want to look like, act like and talk like others their own age. The group is all-important! Failure to achieve a certain status of belonging in the group can result in an introspective self-pity for the preteen.

Real Kids Say

"How do you feel about school?"

"I like it."

"What's the best part?"

"Recess!"

—Jeff, 10 Years Old

⊚ **Early adolescents are self-critical and critical of others.** Early adolescents feel awkward. They often wonder if they are good at anything. They wonder how their intelligence and athletic ability compare with others. Failure or poor performance in any area, whether it be sports, academics or other observable indicators of intelligence or physical prowess, is sure to cause a crisis. A facial blemish, big feet or wearing the wrong brand of clothes can cause a crisis. In addition, the fact that they are surrounded by critical peers who are typically quick to point out these differences causes preteens to become increasingly critical of themselves (to fit in with what others say about them) and others (to get the critical glare off themselves).

Because of this tendency toward being overly critical, the preteen leader must set a positive example of being accepting and nonjudgmental. Perfectionism and a critical attitude have little to no place in the leadership of early adolescents. The wise leader will also look for activities, sports or ministries in which preteens can feel competent. This will help them balance out the harsh criticism they levy against themselves. It's important to help kids find activities and areas of interest in which they can excel.

⊚ **Preteens need good friends of the same gender.** Early in the preteen years, kids often do not like members of the opposite gender. We asked a 10-year-old girl what she thought about boys. Her response was classic: "They need help." We asked, "Do you mean mentally, or with their behavior?" Her answer: "Both."

This is the age of buddies and best friends. It is not only normal for preteens to feel close to a same-gender peer, but it is also a must for building a foundation for positive relationships with members of the opposite gender later in life. Any fears about such a relationship being a precursor to a homosexual orientation are completely misplaced. This is a natural, healthy stage of the preteen's development toward social maturity.

⊚ **Later in early adolescence, friendships develop with members of the opposite gender.** This is one more area of transition for the preteen. Because of this change, we believe it is important to make at least some of your small-group activities coeducational so that leaders can help kids learn how to relate appropriately to the opposite gender.

An ideal plan for preteens is to have a couple lead a coed group. Then both boys and girls get to interact with and observe the interaction between a mature Christian man and a mature Christian woman. If the leaders are married, the students benefit from seeing a healthy Christian marriage relationship. And having a couple as leaders guarantees same-gender leadership when dividing the boys from the girls is more beneficial for the activity or the discussion.

⊚ **Early adolescents are seeking independence and autonomy from parents.** Although preteens want to feel separate and independent from their parents, they still need and truly desire adult guidance and emotional support. This is why staffing our ministry programs with people just like mom and dad works so well. The church is at its best when one parent is supporting another by being that significant adult for a child who is searching for independence from his or her own mom and dad.

How successful an early adolescent is at achieving successful autonomy during this stage will have a lot to do with how he or she was parented during the early childhood years. As a young preschooler learns to be independent, the child's experiences will have a great impact on this next major stage of independence seeking. Michael James tells us, "If parents recognize the young child's need to do what he or she is capable of doing at his or her own pace and time, then the child develops a sense that he or she can control muscles, impulses, self, and significantly, environment . . . . An autonomous child enters early adolescence with a willingness to be him- or herself, to follow through with his or her own potential or abilities. The child also has feelings of self-certainty or self-confidence that reassure him or her as the child faces the challenge of identify formation."[8]

As leaders and teachers, we need to provide experiences that allow gradual acquisition of the desired independence. Giving preteens too much freedom will result in chaos and insecurity. Discouragement and depression may be the outcome. We need to give appropriate ways for kids to be in charge and to experience success in standing on their own two feet.

◎ **Preteens are increasingly concerned about their physical appearance.** Preteens are typically overly aware of their own bodies and the changes that may or may not have begun to occur. In fact, one could say they are obsessed with their physical appearance. It takes nothing more than a zit to cause a bad day! Because of this obsession about their own looks, early adolescents are very vulnerable to the expectations and perceived expectations of their peers and society as a whole as observed through the media. The magazine, movie and TV industries serve up a constant parade of desirable, admirable images with which these awkward young adolescents compare themselves unfavorably.

This is another area in which preteens feel they must do anything in order to fit in. Externals, like clothing and physical beauty, become a measuring stick that they believe will make the difference as to whether or not they are accepted.

◎ **Early adolescents become more reflective.** In striving to preserve their self-identity and emerging sense of individuality, preteens need privacy and time to just be alone with their thoughts and their interests. They will sometimes choose to read alone in order to have the privacy and quiet to think. Although this may seem very different from other characteristics of this age group, it is still an important part of their makeup, and we must attempt to provide these quiet, reflective times, too.

◎ **The preteen does not enjoy anything that seems like work.** This is especially true at home and especially during the earliest years. This seems contradictory at first, since they love to be needed. If the task is presented correctly, washing cars, doing dishes and babysitting will all seem like exciting challenges. It's when they become routine tasks and take on the drudgery of a job that preteens tend to lose enthusiasm.

Schoolwork can be particularly challenging for some preteens. We asked several early adolescents, "How do you feel about school?" The answers frequently sounded just like 11-year-old Frank's: "I don't really like school, 'cuz it's hard." When asked, "What would make school better?" he responded, "If we could play all day."

The Intellectual Characteristics of Early Adolescents

A 12-year-old who says she likes attending the worship service at her church was asked, "What do you like least about church?" She answered, "The big words that the pastor uses." Here again, preteens are in transition. The student is able to sit through the service and enjoy it, but she is certainly not at an adult comprehension level.

◎ **Preteens are very curious and, therefore, also quite distractible.** Attention span continues to increase with all of the preteen's activities, but the most impressive advances are in problem-solving activities. Preteens are capable of making judgments and are quickly developing the ability to use hypothetical reasoning, a product of formal or abstract thinking. Their brains function best when they are stimulated enough to cause the child to focus on the issue at hand.

◎ **Preteens are beginning to move from concrete to abstract thinking.** They are able to reason much more than ever before, but they still may have trouble with symbolism. At church, kids who have attended for years will start to question their beliefs as they continually seek to understand and personalize their faith on deeper cognitive bases.

While the brain and neurological system are almost fully developed at this point in life, the preteen's practical experience is lacking. The child is, therefore, unable to solve adult problems in appropriate, mature ways. He or she simply lacks the experience necessary to acquire and evaluate the data needed to process the situation. This is one reason that preteens must still have adult guidance and should not be given more responsibility than they are ready to handle.

◎ **Early adolescents have little concept of time.** When a teacher tells a preteen that a report is due in a month, this has little meaning to the child. The knowing teacher will help set short-term subordinate deadlines to help accomplish the big project. At church, it's no wonder that deadlines for deposits and registrations are not heeded unless the communication somehow gets to the parents. The preteen worker needs to be prepared for kids to be late!

◎ **Preteens' interests are in the present and in the real and the practical.** In large part because preteens lack the concept of time, they are most interested in what they can see, touch, hear, taste, smell and do—here and now. Our learning activities and lesson applications need to focus on what the preteens can experience and put into practice immediately in order for them to be relevant to our early adolescents.

◎ **They are prone to daydream.** If what you are doing is not exciting and meaningful, kids won't stay with you! Their entire world has opened up with so many new experiences. Their relationships have changed dramatically. They are beginning to realize they have a future and that they will one day grow up. This, joined with their growing ability to think abstractly, creates fertile soil for daydreams. The more involved we get the kids (mentally and physically), the less likely they are to daydream.

◎ **Preteens enjoy activities that include writing, drama or painting.** These kids enjoy expressing themselves in creative ways. Each may choose his or her own medium for expression, but finding ways to communicate individuality is a common theme among preteens.

It is profitable for early adolescents to be exposed to a wide variety of creative arts so that they can experience a number of different means for self-expression. With some training, kids who have specific talents can blossom at this age.

◎ **Preteens want to be challenged, but they have limits.** Although they want to be challenged intellectually, they are ambivalent about having to do the work if it seems hard or unfair. It is common to hear them say that their teachers ask too much of them at school.

One preteen girl told us, "I don't like school because you have to do lots of work." What would make it better? "No homework."

An 11-year-old boy answered the question, What don't you like about school? by telling us, "All the homework we have to do. You don't get that much free time."

The Moral and Spiritual Characteristics of Early Adolescents

Spiritually, early adolescents are very open to a personal relationship with God. As the student shifts from a parent-given faith to a personalized faith, it may appear that he or she has become interested in spiritual things for the first time. This transition sometimes causes the casual observer to assume that children cannot make significant spiritual decisions. In reality, children can make incredible decisions for God, but they must rethink them and reown them as they transition through early adolescence.

During early adolescence, students' consciences become more fine-tuned—especially about the behavior of others. They are extremely aware of the fairness and honesty of the adults around them. They will constantly evaluate the values of their parents and teachers. However, they may be more relaxed about their own behavior. For example, their own cheating in school or shoplifting is rationalized and makes sense to them while they are quick to condemn others who do the same things.

Fairness is extremely important to preteens. When adults are inconsistent, they are quick to point out, "That's not fair!" They have a sense of justice that must be satisfied, especially by the teachers and parents in their lives.

The Egocentrism of Early Adolescents

Egocentrism is the lack of ability to differentiate between one's own responses and the responses of others and between one's own thoughts and reality.

God wires a two-year-old child to define the world in terms of him- or herself, and we understand this to be a normal developmental process for the young child. We need also to understand the egocentrism of a preteen to be a natural characteristic of the emerging adolescent. The 10- to 14-year-old also sees the world in terms of "me." In fact, some have said that early adolescents are two-year-olds with hormones!

The preteen's brand of egocentrism may be identified most clearly in two mental constructions known as "imaginary audience" and "personal fable."

◉ **Preteens create for themselves an imaginary audience.** The early adolescent cannot differentiate between a preoccupation with him- or herself and what others are thinking about him or her. The preteen assumes that others are as obsessed with his or her behavior and appearance as he or she is, so the preteen is always anticipating the reactions of other people. The child is constantly constructing an imaginary audience and then reacting to it. For example, a preteen with a new pair of athletic shoes may walk by a crowd of peers and imagine that they all are looking at him or her.

As you can imagine, all this makes the preteen very self-conscious. The preteen assumes that everyone is focusing on him or her. This explains the early adolescent's desire for privacy and his or her obsessive drive to wear the currently popular brand of clothes. This explains the increasing amount of time the preteen spends in the bathroom each day getting hair and face just right. This self-consciousness is also why so many preteens have difficulty staying plugged into church programs when they do not feel that they belong to the group. The self-conscious preteen walks into your classroom assuming that everyone in the room is wondering why he or she is there and why in the world he or she wore that outfit!

Self-admiring also becomes common at this age. The preteen boy can convince himself that the image in the mirror will cause a girl he admires to drool, when in reality the girl will be so concerned about her own appearance and her own imaginary audience, that she won't even notice the two hours of grooming that he went through to make himself presentable.

Because preteens are so self-absorbed, they do not give the same emotional support and positive feedback that they are looking for in others. Unfortunately, both parties tend to be takers looking for this support to come from the other person but not offering it in return. This is why it is imperative to staff preteen ministry with adults who are mature and trained to focus on others instead of themselves. These people will effectively encourage the kids and be emotionally supportive to them.

You've probably heard stories about preteens who plan and carry out ways to hurt others because they believe people are ridiculing them. These incidents show the incredible power that the imaginary audience can have over the early adolescent. For some, the importance of self is so high that the value of others cannot even be understood.

◎ **Preteens tell themselves a personal fable.** This intellectual construct dovetails with the previous one. Since the child believes him- or herself to be so much the center of attention to so many people (the imaginary audience members), the preteen's feelings and life become very special and important. The preteen believes his or her experiences are unique. Only he or she has ever experienced such pain. Only he or she can truly understand the situation. And because he or she is unique, the dangers that might hurt someone else would never affect him or her.

A personal fable is a fictional (untrue) story that an early adolescent tells him- or herself. Personal fables may include these ideas:

◎ The preteen's feelings are special and unique.

◎ No one else understands how the preteen feels.

◎ The preteen is invincible. Accidents or bodily harm only happen to others, not to him or her.

A few years ago a motion picture released in the United States depicted a game in which participants lay down in the middle of a busy highway. In the movie, the kids engaged in this incredibly risky activity were never hit by the passing automobiles. The movie's suggestion that kids could do the same and not get hurt struck a chord with preteens who already believed that bad things happen only to other people, and several early adolescents from around the country were killed or injured trying this game. The motion-picture maker finally cut this portion of the movie.

Knowing what preteens are like and what they need and want, we need to design our programs to fit those characteristics. We can no longer do preteen ministry the way that we've always done children's ministry, nor can we attempt to throw preteens into traditional youth ministry. It's time for the church to design programming and ministry opportunities specifically for preteens—and their friends!

Notes

1. Michael A. James, "Early Adolescent Ego Development," *The High School Journal* (March, 1980), p. 244.

2. Charles Dickens, *A Tale of Two Cities* (1859; reprint New York, NY: Alfred A. Knopf, Inc., 1993), p. 1.

3. Hershel D. Thornburg, "Early Adolescents: Their Developmental Characteristics," *The High School Journal* (March 1980), p. 216.

4. Thornburg, "Early Adolescents: Their Developmental Characteristics," p. 215.

5. Peter Scales, *Portrait of Young Adolescents in the 1990s* (Minneapolis, MN: Search Institute, 1991).

6. Erik H. Erikson, *Youth: Change and Challenge* (New York, NY: Basic Books, 1963), p. 10.

7. Ross Campbell, M.D., *How to Really Love Your Teenager* (Wheaton, IL: Victor Books, 1981), p. 25.

8. James, "Early Adolescent Ego Development," pp. 247-248.

Designing Ministry for the Needs of Preteens

> *I have become all things to all men so that by all possible means I might save some.*
> 1 Corinthians 9:22

Several years ago, in the first year at a new church, we met with the leaders of the fifth-and-sixth-grade ministry to discuss summer programming. The leaders were distressed because, in a church where 80 fifth and sixth graders came to Sunday school, they could only get 5 or 6 to attend Vacation Bible School. They wanted to know, "What's the matter with these kids?"

We asked a different question: What's the matter with VBS? Perhaps the program was not meeting the needs of the fifth and sixth graders. We should be quick to review and evaluate the quality of the program when we hear of problems like this. The fifth and sixth graders obviously did not want what we were offering them in VBS as it had been done. We wondered if they did want something different.

So we decided to experiment and do something like VBS for the fifth and sixth graders only. We wanted to see if redesigning the program with their needs and desires in mind would change their willingness to attend. Some of the changes we made included these:

◎ Only fifth and sixth graders were invited. It was special for them.

◎ Although we saw it as a VBS for fifth and sixth graders, we never told them that. We created a brand-new name just for this program. (VBS sounded childish to these preteens.)

◎ We designed more team activities that allowed kids to build relationships.

◎ We told the kids that we would take them somewhere in town each night but that they would never know where we were going until we got there.

Once we had the week planned, we sent out brochures and registration forms and asked kids to preregister. Our leaders asked us how many kids we thought would end up attending. We said, "Probably 45 to 50." Their looks told the story: They thought we were crazy.

On opening night of this new program, 45 kids had preregistered, and we were ready for them. We even had the staff, the supplies, the food and the vans to handle an additional 5 or 10 kids, just in case. To our pleasant surprise, 95 kids showed up that night. We were off and running, even though we had to scramble the next day to get ready for the additional numbers!

Rather than throw up their hands in defeat and wonder what's wrong with kids, the leaders of preteen programs should instead carefully investigate the unique needs and desires of preteens and redesign their ministries to meet these needs and desires. The leaders have the responsibility for making programming attractive to early adolescents.

So what do preteens need and want in their church's ministries?

Ministering to the Preteen's Physical Needs and Desires

⊚ **Preteens want to be active.** We asked a number of preteens to tell us about their very favorite activities (in any area of life). Their responses were revealing and consistent. Almost every one of them gave an answer that had to do with playing in some form and almost all of those wanted to play active, physical kinds of games.

"Play volleyball." (Seventh-grade girl)

"Playing Nintendo." (10-year-old boy)

"Sports. Bowling and baseball." (12-year-old boy)

"i like bowling, too. We're in a league together ... and the computer." (Seventh-grade boy)

"Playing basketball." (12-year-old girl)

"Ride my dirt bike." (11-year-old boy)

"Play outside." (Fifth-grade girl)

"Skateboard." (Seventh-grade boy)

Preteens are in constant motion and they like to play. This is one of the areas where we see some childhood characteristics still existing in the life of the early adolescent. This means our programming needs to allow for kids to move around and change activities.

In educational settings, preteens need to have a variety of activities and the freedom to move frequently. Although their attention spans are longer at this age level, their bodies require movement. If your curriculum does not already provide for these needs, it would be best to find one that does. However, if you are unable to make that change, use idea books to come up with additional games, experiences, activities, art projects, music and more, that shift the children's attention and allow for them to get up and move.

Try having a different leader prepare each segment of your lesson. For example, one leader prepares and gathers all materials and does everything else required for your opening activity, another leader handles the Bible study section, and a third leader handles the closing activity. If you have a small class, simply put materials in different areas of the room, and have the kids get up and move with you for each section of your lesson.

Make sure that every program includes some form of playing or recreation. We asked a 10-year-old girl, "What would you change about church?" Her response was classic: "That we'd have a little more free time to play around before the lesson starts."

These kids love to roller-skate, swim, play basketball and just run and play. More than ever before they can understand and engage in team games, but they still require supervision and demand fairness and compliance with the rules. As leaders, we must have the wisdom of Solomon as we ensure that games are perceived as fair and that we ourselves play fairly. Have you ever wondered why the old standby Capture the Flag is so popular at this age level? It's because there are so few rules and restrictions and lots of running and yelling. Preteens' bodies are screaming for activity!

🌀 **Early adolescents need to rest. They tire easily.** Although (or because) they are always in action, preteens will eventually crash physically. Our programming needs to schedule quiet, slow times. Allow for kids to use up their energy in a fast-paced game, and then engage them in a Bible study and small-group discussion time while their bodies rest and their minds are more focused.

In general, don't plan programs for early in the morning! Preteens have a hard time getting themselves out of bed and dressed. We asked one preteen, "What would make church better?" She answered that the group should meet later (second service instead of first) because "it's hard to wake up in the morning and it would be easier and more convenient that way." It's natural for them to feel tired, so try not to compete with their physical needs.

🌀 **Their bodies are growing rapidly.** They need nourishment! Therefore, they are *always* hungry! Most food activities will also appeal to their increased desire for social contacts. A wise leader will remember the Four Ps of preteens—peers, pepperoni pizza and Dr. Pepper.

Food needs to be included much more frequently now than ever before. Any program, at any time of the day or night, will be more attractive to preteens if food is included.

Here are some quick and easy snacks that preteen kids enjoy:

🌀 Soda in the can. (It's "cooler" than in a cup). For outreach events, go the extra mile and buy name-brand sodas.

🌀 Make your own trail mix and serve it in paper cups. Try mixing minipretzels, small chocolate candies, raisins, butterscotch chips, peanuts and cereal. (Save some for the kids!)

🌀 Have a pizza party. Many national chains will donate pizza for church groups. Ask for the pizzas to be double-sliced so that you can give kids twice as many pieces!

🌀 Hand out packaged snacks and bite-sized cakes for a easy, quick and cheap snack.

🌀 Purchase popped corn and serve it in paper cups.

🌀 Make nachos by heating up canned cheese or nacho cheese sauce and pouring it over tortilla chips. Use foam bowls and paper napkins and your cleanup is a breeze!

🌀 Prepare large quantities of hot dogs in Crock-Pots filled with water. They can sit until you are ready to use them.

🌀 Serve individually wrapped ice-cream sandwiches.

When you have the time to do it, have the kids make their own snacks using one or more of the ideas above. Anything they are involved in making will be popular!

Snacks for Bigger Events!

☉ Use ice-cream sandwiches to make sundaes by letting the kids put their own whipped topping, chocolate syrup, nuts and cherries on top. It's easy and they love helping themselves.

☉ Pancakes are very filling and, therefore, very popular. Bring an electric griddle to class and make them there. Provide various toppings—syrup, fruit, whipped cream—for an extra treat. Try a pancake breakfast on a holiday Sunday or at the end of a major unit of study.

☉ Root beer floats are a little messy but much appreciated. Scoop the ice cream into plastic cups ahead of time. Let a small group of kids each take a 2-liter bottle of root beer and their cups and enjoy!

☉ Bake cupcakes in flat-bottomed ice cream cones (using the regular baking instructions) and frost them with canned icing!

☉ Make mock-Black Forest cake by covering a chocolate cupcake or a brownie with cherry pie filling and whipped cream.

Ministering to the Preteen's Social Needs and Desires

Friends are so important to preteens that they must be accounted for in our ministries. One seventh-grade girl told us that her favorite thing about church is "being together with friends."

Recently a Sunday School teacher approached us at a convention and asked how she could get her sixth graders to stop talking while she was presenting the lesson. Our answer was that she couldn't, at least not completely. And the more she tried, the less everyone would enjoy the class. It's like telling a two-year-old not to squirm. You can do it, but why bother? Who will it benefit?

☉ **Preteens need to talk.** One preteen at our church who claims to "love church and hate school" told us that her favorite thing to do in all the world is "talk to people."

Instead of trying to keep preteens from doing what comes naturally, try channeling that social need into productive ministry. When you are planning your lesson, make sure that there are regular, meaningful times of interaction for the students. Plan times for them to turn to a friend and discuss their answers to questions like these:

☉ How do you think the main character in today's Bible story felt when trying to follow God?

☉ When do kids your age feel like this?

☉ What will you do in situations like this to show that you want to follow God?

This approach is called "interactive education" and is of critical importance to preteens. Help your students experience the point you are trying to make through firsthand exploration of Bible truths. Then allow them the time they need to discuss their discoveries with their peers. The discussion that leads them through the cognitive comparison of the known to the unknown using the application of the Bible truth will be significant in helping them enjoy your class, identify the principle and follow through on life-changing application.

Social events are important to your ongoing ministry. Plan a variety of ways that kids can have fun and build relationships with other kids. Some preteen leaders may believe that just having fun is a waste of church time. We must get over this idea and realize that these kids must feel like they have friends at church. Social activities can help build relationships by providing significant talk time. (See chapter 10 for fun, creative ideas to help build relationships among kids.)

◎ **Early adolescents have a need to feel connected with peers.** This means that our lessons and other activities should involve kids working with other kids in groups whenever possible. Unless preteens feel connected with other kids and accepted by them, they won't come back. If they don't come back, we've lost our impact with them.

Whenever a new student comes through the door, hook up him or her with a mature, kind, regular attender of the same gender who will sit with the visitor for the morning. Challenge your regulars to be good hosts for guests. Wouldn't it be great if the adults in our church would do the same? It doesn't just benefit the guest, either. One 10-year-old girl told us that her favorite thing to do at church is "helping out the other kids in my class."

Walt and Diane Pitman work hard to create a youth group atmosphere that helps with the socialization of early adolescents. Once they created "Hot Shots," a Wednesday night youth group for fifth and sixth graders, their attendance mushroomed from 30 to 100 preteens.

At Hot Shots, Diane tells us, the kids are handled with respect. They are involved in youth-type activities and get to experience being treated like teenagers. They walk into the gym with popular music playing like DC Talk or other upbeat music. Here they begin with active games. Next they gather for a large-group time of singing, crowdbreakers, music videos, a message and testimonies. Guest speakers specially selected to appeal to this age level often lead devotionals.

Then the kids gather in small groups called "huddles" for prayer requests, discussion of the lesson and Bible memory work.

Early adolescents want to be where early adolescents want to be!

◎ **Preteens may be ambivalent about relating to the opposite gender.** As kids are going through so many physical and hormonal changes, their feelings about being grouped with the opposite gender will change from positive to negative and back again numerous times. Unlike the teen years, when many youth pastors form single-gender small groups, the preteen years are good for having a variety of groups.

Allow your kids some time to hang with the guys (or gals) and other times to learn to relate as young ladies and gentlemen in coed groups. Less intimate settings, like Sunday mornings, make for good coed groupings. Try single-gender groups for clubs or weeknight programs when more time is typically spent discussing issues and praying for personal needs. (See more on this topic in chapter 9.)

◎ **Create safe places for preteens to be together to talk.** Whenever you have gaps in your programming, provide a safe environment in which kids are given time to stand around and talk before the next event. For example, if you have a two-session program on a Sunday morning with a passing time in between, play a Christian music video during this transition time, provide a few snacks and let the kids stand around and socialize. Be sure that adults are giving the preteens space but also standing by to help the quiet child or a guest. Leaders should facilitate, not dominate, this time.

◎ **Kids want to feel like they have freedom, but they still desire safe boundaries.** When we first started in preteen ministry, we took a large number of fifth and sixth graders to a public park for an hour of competition and games. The evening had mixed results, but it was a baptism by fire that we will never forget!

Our first activity was to make huge banana splits in plastic rain troughs. Each team of 15 kids got several half-gallons of ice cream, bananas and all the toppings. We challenged the teams to see who could make the most beautiful and creative banana split in the limited amount of time we offered them.

As soon as we yelled go, the kids began breaking open jars of cherries, squirting whipped topping on one another and fighting over serving spoons for the ice cream. By the time we were done, the banana splits were unsafe to eat (not knowing how much glass or other debris had fallen in) and the picnic tables were covered with glass, goo and gunk!

The next activity at the park was a series of relay races. Pretty tame, huh? One relay had a student from each team sit on a block of ice while another pushed him to the finish line. Another was the old-fashioned run to the baseball bat, place your forehead on the end of the bat, turn around 10 times and run back to your team. It's a game kids play at very young ages. And it worked well.

Here's what we learned about freedom and limits with preteen kids:

◎ The kids want to feel like they are being given freedom, so taking them off campus to a park was a good thing.

◎ Preteens are still kids in many ways, so expecting them to cooperate in large groups without much adult supervision was a mistake.

◎ Activities that are beyond their skill levels (like opening new jars or cooperating with a large group to accomplish a multistep project) are an invitation for failure for both the kids and their leaders!

◎ Preteens want the security of the known. While kids' games (like the relay races) at church might be too childish, kids' games in the park are just right. A sense of freedom is gained from the location; a sense of security is provided by the known activity.

◎ **Although preteens are seeking independence from their parents, they are also looking for connection with other significant adults like their parents.** Our inclination is to try to be like the kids to whom we seek to minister. Although some identification is positive and preteen kids may seem like they want the adults in their lives to "lighten up" and be more like kids, what they're really looking for is the security of being led by a loving, mature adult who is, in reality, a whole lot like their own moms and dads—but isn't related to them.

A number of years ago, Larry, a preteen student, asked the new children's pastor at his church if he could serve as a junior teacher at VBS. Over the following few years, Larry and his family developed a close relationship with the pastor.

One day, Larry popped in to see his pastor friend. He had a heavy look on his face and asked if the pastor had time to talk. He had a serious question to ask: Should I be dating a non-Christian girl? Larry said, "I know that you'll say the same things that my dad would say, but I'd rather hear it from you."

It's not that kids don't want direction. They are simply trying to define themselves separate from their parents. Early adolescents are in one leaving stage of the leaving-and-cleaving cycles we all go through throughout life. (Other leaving stages occur around two years of age, five years of age and in the late teens or early 20s.)

◎ **Preteens are in the process of internalizing and personalizing values.** One of the challenges of transitioning kids from childhood to the teen years is to ensure that we are not just controlling them but that we are truly passing on internalized values to them. *Merriam-Webster's Collegiate Dictionary* tells us that to internalize means "to incorporate (as values or patterns of culture) within the self as conscious or subconscious guiding principles through learning or socialization."[1] The examples set by loving adults in our programs have great impact on the continuing formation of values in these kids.

While preteen kids are looking for adults other than their parents to provide boundaries and direction, the church leader has a powerful opportunity. Like a surrogate parent at this point, he or she can help preteens learn values. As the adult shares appropriate examples from his or her own life about ways of following God in everyday life, the preteen is mentored in what it means to be a Christian in practical ways.

Ministering to the Preteen's Emotional Needs and Desires

◉ **Preteens need routine structure and clear limits.** One of the most common questions preteens ask is, "What are we going to do?" They have some anxiety about the unknown. They want to know what's coming.

One church we observed noted a disturbing problem with so many kids dropping out between the children's ministry programs and the junior high group. After observing how each program was organized and talking with some of the dropouts, we discovered that the problem was in this area of need.

The children's leader provided kids with a great amount of structure and clarity of expectations. They knew what to expect and found a place of security on a weekly basis. The same leaders were in place every week. The classes started with meaningful, age-appropriate activities as soon as the kids arrived. Rules, although few, were clearly outlined and posted in the classrooms.

Once these same kids moved to the junior high group, however, they experienced a startling shift in philosophy. The junior high program gave the kids too much freedom for their age and too little direction. Various young leaders came and went, and none was assigned to specific students. The opening time had no structure whatsoever, and the kids were left to find their own friends or activities to fill about a half hour of time. The anxiety these situations created in the kids was too much for the kids and many chose not to subject themselves to what seemed to them like dangerous chaos. The worst part of this situation was that solid, leadership-potential kids were the ones that most disliked the lack of direction and chose to drop out.

No matter how cool preteens act, and no matter how much they may deny it, these kids need (and want) direction. (See chapter 13 for more on this topic.)

◉ **Let students participate in classroom decisions.** Our students need to feel included, and one way to do this is to provide choices. For example, we can allow preteens to make decisions about

◉ types of social activities;

◉ missions or service projects (from a list of options);

◉ classroom decoration;

◉ T-shirt or ministry logo design;

◉ topics for lessons or retreats (from your guided selection); or

◉ choices between art or music, writing or speaking, or drama or games in the learning activities.

Preteens are learning to be individuals and to stand on their own two feet. Offering them choices, within limits, allows them the practice and experience of making decisions and living with the consequences.

◉ **Preteens need to feel competent and able to achieve.** We need to program into our ministry challenging experiences in which students will gain a sense of accomplishment and success. These will help them feel better about themselves as learners and open them to further exploration and discovery.

At one camp for fifth and sixth graders, the leaders took the kids on a two-mile hike into a national forest. There they came to the end of an uphill trail at the mouth of a dark, dry cave. The kids were helped down a long, slanting wall of rocks to enter the cave. Without flashlights, there was no light at all. The combination of the hike with the challenge of the cave's unknown was stretching for some of the preteens. The leaders told us that there was a fair amount of complaining and whining about the whole experience. One boy had to have an adult stand next to him and touch his arm the entire time he was in the cave to help him handle his anxiety about the darkness. But when the campers finished their hike out from the cave, their faces were beaming—they talked for hours about how cool the cave was and how they were never afraid of it at all. They were proud of themselves for accomplishing something that stretched them.

A bigger challenge happened at another camp we observed. The camp offered a very challenging high-ropes course that culminated in a 100-yard-long high-speed fall. Though the campers were securely harnessed into safety cables at all times, this didn't remove the fear of the course. Watching kids work their way through this challenge was tough at times. Some became upset, some took what seemed like hours to get through, but every student was encouraged and helped by a nurturing leader who was trained in making this a success for each participant. At the camp where we observed this activity, every fifth and sixth grader was successful and the sense of accomplishment will last a lifetime for each!

◎ **Preteens want and need to be involved at church in meaningful ways.** If you've ever had to move and look for a new church, you will remember how difficult it was to enjoy a new church when you were comparing it to the last one in which you were so involved. No church experience can compare with the one that we were actively involved in (until we settle down and get involved again, of course). The same is true for preteens. They enjoy church more when they are doing something meaningful at church.

Charlie was a seventh grader who wanted to help out at Vacation Bible School. He wasn't sure that he wanted to do the usual—being an assistant in a classroom—but he was willing to work. The leader of the opening and closing music portions of VBS asked him to run the sound and light boards for her. Something clicked. Charlie saw this task as a meaningful and important way to serve. He insisted upon knowing every detail. He

wanted specific notes on when he was to do what so that he wouldn't miss a single cue. He loved his role and he felt important. He now sees this tech ministry as a special way for him to serve the church at other times, too. He knows that he has a way to make a unique contribution to the success of something bigger than himself. (See chapter 11 for more on this topic.)

Real Kids Say

"What don't you like about church?"

"It's pretty long. I don't know. It's pretty fun, but it's kind of long!"

—Juan, 11 Years Old

◎ **We must meet their need to feel needed.** Many of us use kids as helpers in classrooms or workers in other ministries. But we must be careful when doing this. Our program design must allow for the preteens to be successful in what we ask them to do. We need to give them responsibilities that fit their age, experience and abilities.

We must also make sure that they are actually used. If they are placed with another adult, make sure that the adult understands what the student is responsible for. Our own daughter, a preteen, volunteered to be an assistant in the kindergarten Sunday School room at church. She loved doing this at first. The room leader she first worked with had no time to prepare and gave our daughter lots of jobs when she showed up. She felt needed.

Soon, however, this teacher resigned and a team of two adults took over. All of a sudden, our daughter, Ashley, was inadvertently demoted to an extra pair of hands. No one intended to hurt her feelings, but her need to be needed was no longer being satisfied.

We must be very clear in preparing kids to serve, explaining to those supervising them how this should happen and then keeping in touch with the preteens through the duration of their service to insure that the experience continues to be a successful one.

◉ **Preteens need to be nurtured emotionally to be their best.** The hormonal changes in early adolescents cause them to be emotional beings. They need our help in maintaining equilibrium and in filling up what Ross Campbell calls their "emotional tanks." Parents and teachers serve an important role in providing emotional support and "fuel."

> There are several reasons why this refilling is so important.

◉ Teenagers [and preteens] need an ample amount of emotional nurturing if they are to function at their best and grow to be their best.

◉ They desperately need full emotional tanks in order to feel the security and self-confidence they must have to cope with peer pressure and other demands of adolescent society. Without this confidence, teenagers tend to succumb to peer pressure and experience difficulty in upholding wholesome, ethical values.

◉ The emotional refilling is crucial, because while it is taking place, it is possible to keep open lines of communication between parents and teenagers.[2]

Our students often arrive at church or at a social activity completely drained. We have no idea whether they had a fight with their best friend, got grounded by mom or dad, didn't get to eat the kind of cereal they wanted, or just flunked a test. They come looking for a safe adult who will listen to how they feel and communicate love and acceptance.

One activity that helps kids work through their emotional turmoil is drama. Being involved in skits or plays allows the child to step outside of him- or herself for the moment and to temporarily step into someone else's shoes. Drama helps preteens to release tension and anxiety in a constructive way. It also can help them achieve something cool in the eyes of their peers. Playing different roles assists kids in understanding themselves and other people.

Ministering to the Preteen's Intellectual Needs and Desires

Early adolescents are in the process of transitioning from concrete thinking to abstract thinking. Like many of their other characteristics, however, the kids in your group will be changing at different times and at different rates throughout the period of ages 10 to 14. Therefore, leaders of preteens need to recognize that we are dealing with kids at a variety of intellectual levels and with a variety of needs.

◉ **Preteens need to be challenged with abstract thinking in a nonthreatening way.** We need to help challenge our kids' thinking ability by exposing them to more abstract processes while not overwhelming them or threatening them. Most kids want to be challenged intellectually as long as they don't have to worry about failing.

Asking good questions is one of the best ways to challenge a child's thinking. Bloom's Taxonomy (see p. 32) is an excellent guideline for planning your questions to help move your kids to "higher orders" of thinking.[3]

HELPING KIDS
USE HIGHER ORDERS OF THINKING

(From Bloom's Taxonomy)

◎ The teacher asks the student to judge, compare, choose, estimate, evaluate, score, predict, rate, value, assess, select or measure.

◎ The student makes judgments about quality and quantity.

◎ The teacher asks the student to compose, propose, formulate, assemble, construct, design, arrange, collect, organize or prepare.

◎ The student solves a problem by putting information together that requires original, creative thinking.

◎ The teacher asks the student to translate, apply, employ, practice, demonstrate, interpret, operate, schedule, illustrate or dramatize.

◎ The student solves a problem by using knowledge previously known or just learned in this lesson.

◎ The teacher asks the student to distinguish, debate, question, solve, differentiate, compare, diagram, inventory, contract, experiment, test, analyze, criticize, relate or calculate.

◎ The student breaks down information into its parts.

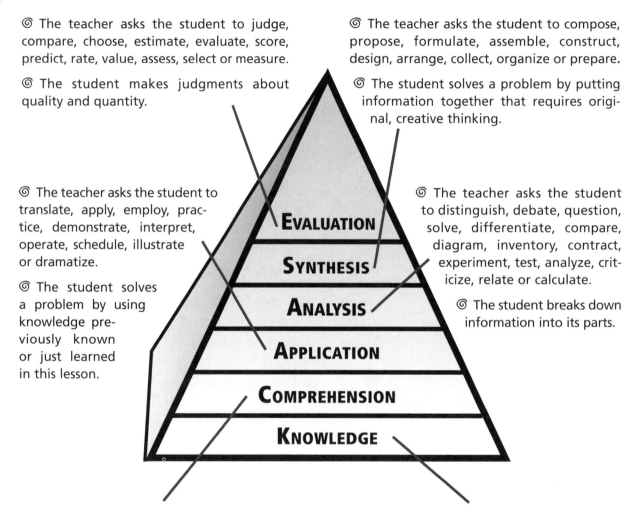

EVALUATION

SYNTHESIS

ANALYSIS

APPLICATION

COMPREHENSION

KNOWLEDGE

◎ The teacher asks the student to restate, describe, explain, identify, report, discuss, recognize, express, locate or review.

◎ The student retells the information using his or her own words.

◎ The teacher asks the student to distinguish, recognize, list, memorize, name, label, record, recall or relate.

◎ The student remembers information and can repeat it or recognize it when presented to him or her.

We are prone to asking questions from the bottom levels of the pyramid. To stretch kids' minds, practice moving to the higher orders of thinking represented in the upper layers of the pyramid.

QUESTIONS
TO CHALLENGE KIDS' THINKING

Sample Lesson: The Good Samaritan (Luke 10:30-37)

Start by asking the foundational questions that show a student's knowledge and comprehension. Then move on to the more complex modes of thinking. We have provided examples of a biblical information question and a personal application question for each level of reasoning.

KNOWLEDGE

- What did the Samaritan do to be a neighbor to the hurt man?

- Have you ever been a neighbor to someone? How? Explain.

COMPREHENSION

- How do you think the hurt man felt when he was helped by the Samaritan and not helped by the priest or the Levite?

- How could you be a neighbor to someone who wouldn't expect it?

APPLICATION

- If this story happened today, how would the Samaritan show he was a neighbor?

- If there was a kid at school who you didn't like but who was being picked on by some other kids, what could you do to be his neighbor?

ANALYSIS

- Which person in the story was most like Jesus—the priest, the Levite or the Samaritan?

- When it comes to being a neighbor, which one of the characters in the story are you the most like?

SYNTHESIS

- What might have happened if the Samaritan didn't stop to help?

- How does it affect people when they need your help but you are not willing to give it?

EVALUATION

- Would it make Jesus happier to see the hurt man follow the religious teachings of the priest or Levite or the actions of mercy of the Samaritan? Why?

- Which is God more concerned about in your life, the things you say or the things you do? Why?

Connect new information with what is already known. As you move the concrete thinker into higher orders of reasoning, it is helpful to start with known areas and then relate them to new concepts.

One creative team of fifth-and-sixth-grade teachers decided to throw a special Sunday School breakfast to help kids understand the Trinity. The team members served pancakes poured on the skillet in triplets (three pancakes connecting), to represent the unity of the Godhead. They demonstrated the three parts of the egg and the three forms of water (liquid, steam and ice) while they were cooking in order to show the three separate roles of the three persons of God. They even served a side dish of chili with meat, otherwise known as chili con carne, and placed carnations on the tables to help the kids remember the very difficult and unknown word "incarnation." Now that's a fun, memorable lesson!

Starting with the known and moving to the unknown makes preteens feel more confident about learning new material, because it validates their previous experience and gives them a firm foundation of understanding, a common ground upon which to build the new concepts and material.

Preteens need to be motivated to learn through their curiosities. If we truly desire to maximize the amount we are able to teach early adolescents, we need to learn to use strategies and techniques that increase their curiosity about learning.

Active learning experiences are one way to raise a student's curiosity. The concrete thinker needs the concrete experience to truly understand, and the abstract thinker will be challenged to go beyond the concrete activity if his or her interest is captured by it.

One preteen boy told us how he felt about school and his favorite teacher: "School's awesome. You get to learn stuff. [My science teacher] brought in like a bunch of hearts and one was an elk heart. And like he let everybody pick it up and hold it and feel all the parts and the aorta and stuff." Interactive learning provides students with unforgettable experiences.

A Word About Competition and Preteens

In our own church, the fifth-and-sixth-grade teachers have long used a *Jeopardy!* game format as a review tool every month or two. It's a big day in the classroom—kids are very excited. When we interviewed some of the students and asked, "What do you like best about church? "Jeopardy" was the enthusiastic first response of several students.

On the other hand, we were told that students who attend irregularly ask if they could go to a different classroom on Jeopardy Sundays. They are uncomfortable because they don't know all the answers and don't want to take part in what will undoubtedly be an embarrassing situation for them.

Do we really want to put kids through this at church? Some would say we should help kids learn to live in a competitive world. But do we do that by teaching them to be losers?

Just because competition is a natural tendency in our kids does not mean we want to promote this kind of behavior. Although our society and our school systems breed competition into our kids, research clearly shows that competition is at best not helpful for kids and at worst a detriment to their growth and learning. Alfie Kohn, in his fascinating book *No Contest*, tells us that 156 separate studies done on children from

1924 to 1980 revealed that cooperation among kids enhanced achievement 69 percent of the time, while competition only helped 4 percent of the time.[4]

"To say that an activity is structurally competitive is to say that it is characterized by what I call *mutually exclusive goal attainment*. This means, very simply, that my success requires your failure," says Alfie Kohn.[5] When we program kids into competitive situations, they want to do well because they want to win or because they are afraid of losing. Cooperative goals require that the group work together for the mutual success of all of its members. Which is the more biblical concept to teach kids?

Galatians 6:4-5 says, "Each one should test his own actions. Then he can take pride in himself, without comparing himself to somebody else, for each one should carry his own load."

Instead of superiority and competition, Jesus' challenge to His disciples was to become servants: "If anyone wants to be first, he must be the very last, and the servant of all" (Mark 9:35).

Consider the effects of students who are motivated to learn primarily through competition. The goal of the learning (understanding a key Bible truth or concept) is often lost in the emotions surrounding the competition. While too often we spend time creating competitive programs and learning situations, the experts tell us that there are more productive ways to get kids to store truths for the long term:

◎ While kids remember 10 percent of what they hear, they retain 90 percent of what they do. Active learning increases retention.

◎ Learning increases when truths are repeated at various intervals over a period of time. Interval reinforcement is valuable for its success in increasing retention, even though it takes some time out of your class session.

◎ Finally, creating a desire to learn is the most important way to help students retain the lesson. Make sure your lessons are compelling and relevant to the life of your preteens. They'll retain much more because the information is meaningful and useful.

In designing programming for preteens, be sure to avoid, or at least minimize, competition. This means games should be played for the sake of having fun, not winning. When you play games that require scorekeeping, move on to the next activity without announcing the score or the winner. If the next activity is fun and compelling, most kids will never notice the omission.

The April 1997 issue of *Sky* magazine ran an article entitled "Sideline Saddams," which talked about how parents put pressure on their kids to be competitors. The author, Timothy Harper, reminds us of how often we hear the message, either subtly or not, that winning isn't everything, it's the only thing. "Over the past two decades, surveys of children consistently show that the No. 1 reason they play sports is to have fun. Also ranking high: getting exercise, learning a skill, being with friends. Winning is always far down the list. A *USA Today* survey found that 7 in 10 youths wouldn't care if no one kept score at their games. Four in 10 wished their parents were not allowed at games."[6]

Probably the most harmful form of competition comes from personal one-upmanship. It is natural for insecure, egocentric kids to do this to one another (and to themselves). But too often, we're the ones who set the bad example!

Be sure that your adult leaders are modeling servant leadership and are not being overly competitive themselves (either with the kids or with each other). Leaders need to care about other people more than themselves and more than their own reputation. We cannot teach about servanthood nearly as well as we can model it!

Ministering to the Preteen's Spiritual Needs and Desires

Recently, a junior high pastor shared with us his excitement that one of his best and brightest students had asked him, "Am I saved?" The pastor was thrilled with the student's concern about his spiritual condition but puzzled over why such a bright kid didn't understand this concept already.

The same scenario often leads youth workers to conclude that nothing much was taught in the children's program. If this boy had attended faithfully for his entire life and still didn't understand his own salvation, what were those children's leaders doing?

Is it that children can't make any significant decisions or that they are not yet ready to understand something as complex as the gospel? To find the answers to these questions, we must understand the changes that the early adolescent must go through in how he or she thinks about God and faith as the student transitions from concrete concepts to abstract ones. The preteen's faith may look new, as in never before existing, but in reality it is simply different, as in existing on a new plane.

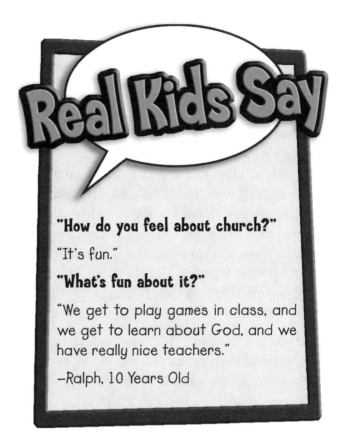

"How do you feel about church?"

"It's fun."

"What's fun about it?"

"We get to play games in class, and we get to learn about God, and we have really nice teachers."

—Ralph, 10 Years Old

◎ **The preteen needs to personalize his new understanding of the faith from the point of view of an abstract thinker.** The answer lies in the normal developmental processes of childhood and early adolescence. The child is faithfully taught—and to the best of his or her ability understands—lots of biblical content and spiritual truths on a concrete level. The student's faith is real but based on concrete concepts and experiences. Matthew 18:3 confirms the genuineness of childlike faith: "I tell you the truth, unless you change and become like little children, you will never enter the kingdom of heaven."

Then the early adolescent goes through an individualized transition to abstract thinking that includes advances and plateaus in development. During these stages, the early adolescent must rethink and reown all of the concepts he or she has previously embraced. The preteen must understand him- or herself and God on a more abstract level. This process does not negate the reality of childhood faith anymore than multiple subsequent reaffirmations of faith in teen and adult years negate the reality of teen faith. They are progressive, not mutually exclusive.

Bill Russell, a junior high pastor in Riverside, California, says fifth and sixth graders are asking questions: "Is God real? How do we know if the Bible is true? Why is Christianity the only way to heaven? I guarantee that questions like these are lurking in the backs of their young minds. And if those questions aren't explored and solid answers found, then you're running the risk of giving your kids the impression that the Bible is irrelevant—and that Christianity is unimportant."[7]

Preteens are searching for a personal relationship with God. Secular educators like Diane Long, David Elkind and Bernard Spilka, tell us that part of the child's personal fable is a search for a personal relationship with a powerful God. What an exciting step of development in the early adolescent! Instead of minimizing this characteristic as a "personal fable," we should capitalize on this time of special, spiritual openness and interest in a higher, relational power. This may well be a God-given longing for connection with Him. We know that God has made Himself knowable for even the non-Christian to discover: "Since what may be known about God is plain to them, because God has made it plain to them. For since the creation of the world God's invisible qualities—his eternal power and divine nature—have been clearly seen, being understood from what

has been made, so that men are without excuse" (Romans 1:19-20). The new ability to think abstractly allows the child to renew his or her search to understand the unfathomable God!

Early adolescents need to feel unconditional love in order to understand the love of God. In *How to Really Love Your Teenager*, Ross Campbell tells us that "to lead a teen to the close relationship with God which they possess, parents [or teachers] must make sure that a child feels unconditionally loved. It is extremely difficult for teenagers who do not feel unconditionally loved by their parents to feel loved by God."[8]

And when our students do not have a loving home led by Christian parents, we become their best hope of learning about that unconditional love from God. Our ministry must be highly relational. These kids need to experience unconditional love from at least one adult at church before they will understand that they are truly loved by a personal God. Each child needs to experience "Jesus with skin on" as a regular part of his or her church experience.

In order to have a truly relational ministry, we must do the following:

Recruit enough staff to give each student the attention he or she needs. One adult for every six to eight kids is recommended.

Choose staff members who are secure enough and mature enough to give unconditionally. Preteen ministry is no place for leaders who are looking to have their own needs met. Searching for popularity or love or significance from early adolescents will leave everyone wanting.

Young adults will add energy and enthusiasm, but they may be short on wisdom and authority. If you choose to use younger leaders with preteens, select ones that you are confident will be able to protect kids emotionally.

Play together. Social times allow adults opportunities to build relationships with kids that can help kids feel comfortable in getting more involved, perhaps even in joining a small group.

⊚ **Meet regularly.** Small groups need to meet often enough to develop intimacy. Kids need to feel known before love will feel real. (See chapter 9 for more help in this area.)

⊚ **Early adolescents need to see the Christian life as vital and exciting.** Henrietta Mears, a pioneer in Christian education, once asked these questions that we should each ask of ourselves: "Are you proving that the Christian life is a joyful, happy thing? Do you look glad that you are a Christian? Does your life radiate joy and enthusiasm? Check yourself carefully on this before you teach it. Make the Christian life contagious."[9] All we do in the name of the Lord should be attractive to others, but especially if we want to win early adolescents.

Ross Campbell notes that "if religious training is a degrading or boring experience for a young person, he is likely to reject even the best teaching, especially if morality and ethics are involved. It is from this type of situation that a teenager develops a bias against religious matters, and tends to consider church people as hypocrites. This attitude is difficult to rectify and can continue with him for a lifetime."[10]

The child who is bored with church is in spiritual danger. Although we never want to forsake the gospel and the foundations of faith for fun and games, we need to remember that fun and games have a lot to do with faith for preteen kids. It's not an either-or proposition; it's a both-and package for early adolescents!

Conclusion

The ways we program for early adolescents (10- to 14-year-olds) must be different from the ways we have traditionally ministered to elementary-aged kids and different from how we have programmed for high school students *because these kids are traveling through a wonderful period of human development that has its own unique set of needs and desires, different from any other period of life.*

Notes
1. *Merriam-Webster's Collegiate Dictionary,* 10th ed., s.v. "celebrate."
2. Ross Campbell, M.D., *How to Really Love Your Teenager* (Wheaton, IL: Victor Books, 1981), pp. 29-30.
3. Benjamin S. Bloom, ed., *A Taxonomy of Educational Objectives* (New York: Longmans, Green, 1956).
4. Alfie Kohn, *No Contest: The Case Against Competition* (New York, NY: Houghton Mifflin Company, 1992).
5. Kohn, *No Contest: The Case Against Competition,* p. 4.
6. Timothy Harper, "Sideline Saddams," *Sky* (April 1997), pp. 21-22.
7. Bill Russell, "Kids Quest," *Children's Ministry* (July/August 1998), p. 51.
8. Campbell, *How to Really Love Your Teenager,* p. 113.
9. Earl O. Roe, ed., *Dream Big: The Henrietta Mears Story* (Ventura, CA: Regal Books, 1990), table of contents.
10. Campbell, *How to Really Love Your Teenager,* p. 114.

Chapter 3

Grouping and Grading—Where Do Sixth Graders Belong?

> "The middle school movement is, more than anything else, a reorganization of people and the ways in which they work with each other.... A reorganization which is perceived as primarily a grade change, a different building, or redesigned curriculum will achieve very little."
>
> —Paul S. George, "Ten Steps Toward Implementing Effective Middle Schools"[1]

Where do sixth graders belong? Should they be a part of the children's ministry or the youth ministry? Should they be mixed with fifth graders or seventh graders—or should they be in a separate group? These may be some of the most hotly debated issues in our churches (and our communities) today. One church is completely at peace with its answer while another (perhaps even in the same community) is in turmoil. So what is the best way to group early adolescent kids?

A Brief History of the Junior High Movement

Sometimes it's helpful to have an historical perspective to understand where we are now and why we do things the way we do.

The junior high school model in American public education arose between World Wars I and II when educators decided that there was a need for a better transition between the style and expectations of the common K-8 (kindergarten through eighth grade) school and the high school. Junior high schools were designed to give seventh and eighth graders something different from both elementary school and high school.

Unfortunately, over time, the junior high school lost its unique mission. According to Ted Beranis, "As junior high schools became the standard for middle level education in more than 70 percent of our nation's school districts, many programs became tradition-bound and, frequently, imitations of high schools."[2]

The name "junior" high school, tells the whole story. Rather than continuing the original purpose of transitioning early adolescents, junior high schools have almost universally become little high schools.

Unfortunately, the Church has followed suit by making junior high ministry less of a transitional phase and more of a mini-high school ministry. In both public schools and church ministry, this trend has once again caused a need for a transition between elementary school or children's ministries and junior high or youth ministry.

Just Because It's Called "Middle School" Doesn't Mean It's Educationally Sound for Early Adolescents

Philosophy and rationale are essential to guiding our choices of grouping and grading early adolescents. Both in public schools and the Church, we have too often been guilty of grouping children the way we do for all the wrong reasons. One church's in-house evaluation of its own middle school ministry concluded that "while we think we are modeling the middle school concept . . . in reality, we are not!"

Why Do Public Schools Group Kids the Way They Do?

Although an abundance of excellent research has been done on the characteristics and needs of children in the middle level educational category, many of our public schools have, unfortunately, made their grouping and grading decisions based on two other factors:

⚙ overcrowding of elementary schools, and

⚙ lack of finances necessary to build new schools.

Because these schools have not considered the philosophical reasons to support the changes, many public middle schools have achieved very little (as the opening quote of this chapter suggests) in the way of addressing and meeting the needs of these very special kids.

Why Do We Group Kids the Way We Do in the Church?

Are we doing what's best for the kids? One would hope that as the church decides how to group early adolescents in ministry, it would use better motives than just handling overcrowding or a lack of finances. Unfortunately, many of the reasons we do things the way we do them in the church are no more student-focused than the public schools' reasons; for example:

⚙ "We don't have a large enough room to put all the sixth through eighth graders together."

⚙ "Our fifth and sixth grade department is too crowded. We need somewhere to put the sixth graders."

⚙ "The sixth graders are hard to handle. We don't know what to do with them. Let's move them to the junior high group."

⚙ "The sixth graders are hard to handle. We don't know what to do with them. Let's move them back to children's ministry."

⚙ "Our denomination doesn't print curriculum graded for that grouping of kids."

⚙ "Our budget won't stretch that far."

⚙ "Our volunteers aren't trained to work with that age group."

⚙ "Our current programs—Wednesday nights, Sunday mornings, camps, retreats—all would have to be changed. That's too much work and no one likes change, anyway."

⚙ "We don't want to do it that way!"

Three Methods of Grouping and Grading Are Commonly Used

There are several different plans that churches around the United States are now using to handle sixth graders in their ministries.

⚙ *The Traditional Method—Sixth Graders in Children's Ministry*

Many churches are still using the plan that has been most common over the past several decades. This traditional structure places fifth and sixth graders in the church's children's ministry and seventh and eighth graders (sometimes ninth graders also) in the junior high program.

The size of the group normally determines whether fifth and sixth graders are grouped together (or with even younger kids). Also, larger churches usually separate junior highers from high schoolers, while smaller churches may keep them together to have what they believe to be a large enough youth group.

A megachurch in the Phoenix area combines several hundred junior highers, senior highers and college kids for a contemporary youth worship service. Afterward, students may attend age-graded small groups. One of the church's struggles is with the early adolescents who get lost in the crowd, overwhelmed by the numbers and broad age span of the group. Some kids do not survive this multiage approach that crosses several developmental groups.

The Middle School Method—Sixth Graders in the Youth Ministry

Most, but not all, middle schools are made up of sixth to eighth graders. In some school districts, however, middle schools include only seventh and eighth graders, in others seventh to ninth graders. And a few schools even add fifth graders.

With the rise of middle schools across the country, many churches have moved sixth graders into the youth group and have renamed their junior high programs as middle school ministries. But that is often the extent of the adaptation. Again, renaming and regrouping a school or a church ministry does not necessarily make it a model that meets the needs of early adolescents. No matter how we group the kids, we need to be concerned that the programming meets their unique needs and equips them to navigate their developmental challenges.

The Transitional Year Method—Sixth Graders Ministered to Separately

This alternative plan is one that some churches are now using in order to give sixth graders the special attention they need. The key to this plan is not who owns the sixth grade ministry but rather that the sixth graders have their own separate, unique program. This transitional year may fall under either the children's leadership or the youth department.

A number of children's and youth ministry leaders surveyed have chosen to have a special program handling sixth graders all by themselves. This approach seems to work well for leaders, parents and the kids.

What's the Best Grouping for Our Students?

Christian educators around the country were asked how they are grouping early adolescents (10- to 14-year-olds) in their church ministries. Here is a compilation of their responses:

Are your sixth graders included in your children's ministry or in your youth ministry?

- Children's Ministry—70 percent

- Youth Ministry—18 percent

- Separate from Either—12 percent (although under the leadership of one or the other department of the church)

Are your sixth graders grouped with other students for ministry?

- Grouped with fourth and fifth graders—6 percent

- Grouped with fifth graders—53 percent

- Grouped alone—24 percent

- Grouped with seventh and eighth graders—12 percent

◎ Different groupings throughout the week—5 percent

Does your grouping of early adolescents at church match your schools?

(These are responses from churches in communities in which all of the schools follow the same grouping pattern—either all were junior highs or all were middle schools.)

◎ Yes, we follow the schools' grouping—89 percent.

◎ No, our church is different from the schools—11 percent. Almost all of these churches commented that they are currently in the process of preparing to switch to the same grouping as their local schools.

(These are the responses from churches in communities in which the schools follow a variety of patterns—some sixth graders attend elementary schools, while others attend middle schools.)

◎ Sixth graders are exclusively in children's ministry—50 percent. Most of these churches commented that they are currently evaluating their structure.

◎ Sixth graders are exclusively in children's ministry, but some or all programming is for sixth graders only—25 percent.

◎ Sixth graders are officially in children's ministry, but middle school sixth graders are allowed to attend junior high ministries—12.5 percent.

◎ Sixth graders are officially in youth ministry, but some or all programming is for sixth graders only—12.5 percent.

It is also significant to note that almost every church leader surveyed stated that parents of the children in their programs were either accepting or very accepting of their current grouping method. A few mentioned problems they had in the past that led them to choose their current structure in order to correct those problems.

The vast majority of churches are grouping their early adolescents according to the same system that the majority of their local schools are using. Those that are not are concerned enough about being out of sync with the schools that they are reevaluating their system. And many of those churches that have a variety of school patterns to match are finding creative ways to help kids by either designing programs solely for sixth graders or letting sixth graders attend some children's programs and some youth programs.

Susan Grover, a children's director in California, reminds us of some key considerations we should use when deciding how to group preteens: "I think it boils down to what is in the best interest of the children within the church. Once we are able to identify the specific needs of our students, we then need to do everything in order to meet those needs to the best of our abilities, given our time, talent, energy and resources. This does, however, require an openness to try new avenues and a willingness to get out of the box."

For the sake of simplicity, most agree that the best grouping plan is to maintain consistency with local schools whenever possible. With this comes a caution: Remember that the buildings or the name do not make the program responsive to the needs of the students. Your grouping and grading system is a secondary issue to what you do in the ministry for early adolescents as you program and plan to meet their needs and desires.

Creative Alternatives for Placing Sixth Graders

Community Baptist Church in Alta Loma, California, has worked out a system to help kids fit in both at church and at school. The schools in the area are mixed: Some are seventh and eighth grade junior highs, and some are sixth through eighth grade middle schools. Although officially fifth and sixth graders are together in the children's program, the leaders of the children's and youth ministries have agreed to allow sixth graders who attend middle schools to attend some of the junior high activities and special events. In this way, the kids are able to maintain relationships with older kids they meet at school and to be a part of the middle school social group if they so desire.

Another church in Pomona, California, is able to program for the changing needs of kids through these critical early adolescent years (10 to 14 years of age) by placing fifth through eighth graders all under the same leader. Although fifth and sixth graders are ministered to in their own group, separate from seventh and eighth graders, the unified leadership allows for kids to be carefully transitioned from elementary programs to high school ministries. We found this model particularly intriguing, since so often early adolescents are split up between different ministries of the church. Why not redraw the lines and allow one person to oversee kids for their entire early adolescence?

Changing the Structure of Your Program Requires Parental Support

Should you sense that your church needs to make a change in the way it groups and grades early adolescents, it is imperative that you prepare and enlist the support of your parents. (See chapter 5.)

The children's leaders and youth leaders at Ocean Hills Community Church in San Juan Capistrano, California, have been preparing their parents and researching the factors involved in transitioning sixth graders from children's ministry into a middle school format for many months. The schools in their community group kids in a variety of ways, and there are also a number of kids in their congregation who are homeschooled.

These leaders knew they were not prepared to make a decision without feedback from the parents of the children in their program. One way they gained feedback was to conduct a survey (see p. 44) of the parents involved. This survey was very helpful for their evaluation. In tabulating their results, they found it helpful to separate responses from parents of each grade level of student:

◎ Parents of fourth and fifth graders were much more resistant to the idea of moving sixth graders up to junior high. Perhaps it was hard for these parents to imagine their young children being almost ready for the junior high group.

◎ Parents of sixth graders were the most supportive of moving kids up. They may have the best current understanding of the needs of sixth graders.

◎ Parents of seventh and eighth graders voiced some negative responses toward combining sixth graders with their seventh and eighth graders. Of course, it must be noted that when this survey was conducted by the church, parents were asked to discuss the issue with their seventh and eighth grade children and reflect the students' feelings in their responses. This may explain some of the negative responses of the older kids in their summaries. This is also why we recommend surveying parents and kids separately. (See chapter 5 for a discussion of the differences in helping parents through change versus helping their kids through change.)

Notes

1. Paul S. George, "Ten Steps Toward Implementing Effective Middle Schools," *NASSP* Bulletin (September 1977), p. 98.
2. Ted A. Beranis, "Reorganizing Middle-Level Education: What to Consider and How to Proceed," in Sally N. Romans Clark and Donald C. Clark, *Schools in the Middle: A Decade of Growth and Change* (Reston, VA: National Association of Secondary School Principals, 1992), pp. 157-158.

Dear Parent,

As you may know, some of the school districts in our area have gone or are planning to go to a middle school structure. This change involves adding the sixth grade student to seventh and eighth grade campuses. At our church, the sixth grade student is currently part of the children's ministries area. This change in the school districts has prompted us to review our ministry structure.

We are in the beginning stages of researching this issue. As part of this research, your thoughts as to whether or not our church should move sixth grade students into the junior high area are very important to us.

Circle the number that best describes your thoughts. 1 = Strongly Agree; 5 = Strongly Disagree. If needed, use the back of this survey for additional comments. Please return the completed survey in the envelope provided.

1 I support adding the sixth grade students to our existing junior high ministry.

Strongly Agree		Agree		Strongly Disagree
1	2	3	4	5

2 I would like my child to have the option of going to either the sixth grade program or the junior high program.

Strongly Agree		Agree		Strongly Disagree
1	2	3	4	5

3 I would favor the development of an additional youth group for sixth graders only.

Strongly Agree		Agree		Strongly Disagree
1	2	3	4	5

4 The current programs meet the needs of my child(ren) and should remain as is.

Strongly Agree		Agree		Strongly Disagree
1	2	3	4	5

5 My child(ren) is (are) currently in the following grade(s): (check all that apply)

☐ fourth grade ☐ fifth grade ☐ sixth grade ☐ seventh grade ☐ eighth grade

Optional:

_____   _____
Name   Phone Number

Thank you for your time and consideration of this issue.

Bridging the Gap—The Transition to Youth Ministry

"We experience shock, a feeling of sudden and overwhelming anxiety, whenever we are confronted with something that is both unexpected and seemingly unmanageable. In many ways, moving from the culture of childhood to the culture of adolescence is like moving from one society to another. The abrupt change in the language as well as the rules and expectations regarding conduct can lead to another variety of shock-peer shock. On entering the culture of adolescence the young person is thrust into a world . . . for which . . . childhood did not prepare the emerging adolescent."

—David Elkind, "All Grown Up and No Place to Go"[1]

A considerable number of children's ministers surveyed reported that transitioning kids from the children's ministry, where they are the leaders, to youth ministry, where they are the youngest and least mature, is one of their biggest struggles in ministering to preteens.

Often children's leaders and the ministries they design are so completely different from youth leaders and their programs that kids have a difficult time making the leap from the children's ministry to the youth group. Not only is the early adolescent going through his or her own physical, mental and emotional changes, but now we throw a major social change at the preteen, too, by moving him or her into a completely different setting at church.

What Are the "Seams" Between Children's Ministry and Youth Ministry?

From the child's viewpoint, what differences does he or she see? What would the kids say? Think about being a preteen and trying to adapt as you experience these changes:

◎ "In children's Sunday School, they told me where and when to sit down, and I listened to the teacher talk a lot. In the youth group, no one seems to tell anyone what to do. I like the freedom, but sometimes I wish I knew what was expected, and I wish someone would control the bigger kids. They can get rough and sometimes they're mean."

◎ "My fifth grade Sunday School teacher was really old, but she was there every week, and she was so nice. My youth leader is in college. He's a lot of fun, but sometimes he gets mad if he doesn't win. Sometimes I feel like I've let him down or upset him."

◎ "My parents don't always come to the same church service. Last year, there was a class for me during either service. Now if my parents want to come to the early service, I miss youth group and have to sit in church with them. Then I don't see my friends and the youth leaders for a few weeks at a time. I feel out of it when I finally go back."

☉ "I used to know everyone in my Sunday School class, all six of us! Now there are tons of kids in youth group—all different ages and from different schools. We spend most of our time in a large group, so we don't really get to know anyone new. It's fun to have more kids in the group, but I wish I had more friends. I don't know if there are other kids my age in the group or not."

☉ "Last year, in the kids' classes we sang dumb songs—when we had music. I really like the CDs we use now. And they play them loud enough for us to hear!"

☉ "My parents have always let me go to camp with the church, but now they say they can't afford it anymore. It used to cost a lot less when I was younger and there are a lot of other activities now, too, that they say I have to use my own money for."

☉ "I'm glad that I don't have to check in with someone when I get to the youth room. I didn't like being treated like a little kid last year. Sometimes, though, I wonder if anyone notices when I don't come. I used to get postcards or telephone calls from my teacher if I missed even a week!"

These comments may seem insignificant to the adult leaders, but they are huge changes for the child who must learn the new system. With all these seams, is it any wonder that we lose some kids?

Kids Are Slipping Through the Seams

No matter where we divide the ministry to early adolescents between children's ministry and youth ministry, we know that kids are slipping through the seams and getting lost during this critical transition.

Normally when we address this subject, we are thinking about how to hand off kids between two different phases of ministry as though it can all happen on one weekend of the church calendar called "Graduation Sunday" or "Promotion

Weekend." However, when we truly recognize early adolescence as a developmental stage, we will understand that this bridge—the transitional developmental stage in the child's life—is a long gradual process that truly extends from fifth through ninth grades.

Whether your sixth graders are part of the elementary ministry or the youth ministry, they are neither children nor youth. If we're going to bridge the gap, both the children's ministries leaders and the youth leaders need to recognize that this period is different from the rest of children's ministries and different from the rest of youth ministry. When we lose kids in the gap, it's important that both the youth leader and children's leader recognize that it has much to do with the ways both do ministry. Both the youth and children's leaders must recognize and facilitate programming to meet the needs and characteristics of this very special period of life!

The Leaders of Both the Children's Ministry and the Youth Ministry Need to Work at the Transition

There must be cooperation, teamwork and trust between the leaders in the youth ministry and children's department of the church. We must be on the same page philosophically in our understanding of what these kids really need and on the same page when we program accordingly. If we are to bridge the gap between these ministries, we must take steps to become a unified team focused on what's best for our kids.

Unfortunately, it is very common for children's pastors and youth pastors serving on the same staff to have some friction and tension in their relationship. They must compete for classroom space, church vans, volunteers, budget monies, bulletin space and pulpit announcement time. They often have conflicting philosophies of ministry and/or education that must somehow be linked together.

If we are to bridge the gap between these ministries so that we don't lose kids by letting them slip through the cracks, we must begin by bridging the gaps between these key leaders. There are many things we can do:

◎ Have regular meetings to plan and discuss ministry.

◎ Attend conferences together to gain shared insight and experience (in this area and in broader ministry areas).

◎ Share information about kids and families as they transition over the years.

◎ Maintain and nurture a personal willingness to commit to working together. Sometimes this will involve a commitment to apologize to or to forgive the other party.

Think about your relationship with the youth leader or children's leader in your church. If you're a children's leader, think about how you relate to that youth leader. If you're the youth leader, what is your level of trust in the children's leader? And then consider 1 Corinthians 13:4-5,7: "Love is patient, love is kind. It does not envy, it does not boast, it is not proud. It is not rude, it is not self-seeking, it is not easily angered, it keeps no record of wrongs. It always protects, always trusts, always hopes, always perseveres." If the relationships between those working with children and those working with youth in your church aren't what they should be, pray for forgiveness, trust and unity.

Children's Leaders Must Prepare Kids for the Youth Group

There are some things children's leaders can do to initiate dialogue with the youth leader and help in the transition. For example, they can learn about the youth leader's philosophy, approach and programming. Then the children's leaders must ask themselves two questions:

1. What things do we do in our church's children's ministry that may not necessarily be age appropriate for our upper elementary kids? You may come up with these common answers:

◎ Tell Bible stories without an effort to relate them to the students' lives.

◎ Allow the teacher to do all the talking.

◎ Sit too much.

◎ Sing children's songs.

◎ Use flannelgraphs and other "low-tech" media.

◎ Use paper and pencil projects as teaching tools.

◎ Have small classes (rather than large classes and small groups).

◎ Recruit rigid or formal adults to lead the kids.

◎ Plan a structured environment with lots of adult controls.

◎ Lead sessions that don't have a good balance of fun interaction.

Children's leaders need to make upper elementary programs more like youth programs in order to prepare kids for this vastly different world. We need to prepare kids for the transition long before it happens by making smaller transitions in the children's ministry in preparation for the big day. Too often we think of this as a single event that we must accomplish. It's not—it's a long, slow transitional process.

2. What elements common to youth ministry can children's ministry leaders successfully incorporate into fifth and sixth grade programs to help prepare them for a move into youth ministry? Because we always want next year at church to be even more exciting than the current year, we don't want to steal any thunder from the youth program, but we do want kids to have a taste of youth ministry before they reach it. Help them get ready for the junior high or middle school group by adding some or all of these youth elements to your upper elementary program:

◎ Do Bible study (topical looks at issues of concern).

◎ Have interactive lessons in which students do a lot of the talking.

◎ Plan active lessons and games that get students to move.

◎ Play contemporary music.

- Use high-tech teaching tools (or at least videos).

- Implement discussion of what's being learned and applied.

- Use large groups for part of your teaching time and small groups for discipleship and discussion times.

- Make sure your leaders are fun adults.

- Create a casual atmosphere in the room and programs.

- Do lots of fun things such as social events, retreats and missions projects in which kids get involved.

What Do the Youth Leaders Have to Do to Help Kids Get Plugged In?

Junior high or middle school leaders should learn all they can about students of this age level and program accordingly. No matter how much preparation the children's ministry accomplishes for preteens, kids will still not be ready for a cookie-cutter "little high school" approach. The ministry needs to be different from the youth ministry designed for older teens. Here are several questions the motivated youth leaders should ask themselves to better facilitate the needs and program for preteens.

- **What things do we sometimes do in youth ministry that are not age appropriate for younger students?** There are some things that should be avoided in middle level youth ministry in order to help students get started. Whether they are entering as sixth graders or seventh graders, these elements can make the transition difficult for some and impossible for others:

- Too much freedom (responsibility that they aren't ready for nor truly desiring)

- Too little structure (therefore, a lack of security)

- Too many young leaders, not enough balance from more mature adults

- Not enough accountability (no attendance rolls and no "checking" on the kids by adults)

- Too little relational guidance (placed in a large group without being greeted and introduced)

- No sense of "protection" (placed with older kids and few adults)

What Can the Youth Leaders Do to Help New Middle Schoolers or Junior Highers Adapt to the Youth Program?

- **Don't put junior highers with high schoolers as a regular part of your youth ministry.** Seventh and eighth graders have a lot more in common with sixth graders than with high schoolers.

- **Continue to give guidelines that the kids need to feel secure.** Most of us can think back to our own insecurity in these younger years. Many of the kids are desperate to know what the rules are and to know that an adult will enforce those rules for their protection.

- **Provide structure.** Keep the newer students from having to experience the awkwardness of not being asked to join in or not knowing what to do. Tell how small groups or discussion groups will be formed. Decide for the kids what they are doing when and who will be in what group or van, etc.

- **Never use sarcasm or put-down humor.** Model respectful relationships, even with other adults who are "supposed" to be able to handle the sarcasm.

- **Make your youth group environment safe for everyone.**

- **Use fun, mature adults, with a mixture of enthusiastic young-adult or college-aged volunteers.**

- **Act like an adult yourself.** Early adolescents don't need buddies. They want guidance from safe, mature adults.

- **Use your small-group leaders to keep track of every student's attendance.** Just don't let them know you're doing it!

⑥ **Plan activities and situations in which incoming students (whether sixth or seventh graders) can do some things together without the older students.** This will allow students to build unity and relationships with their most-immediate peers.

A Model for Transitioning Kids

In order to better serve early adolescents, Red Mountain Community Church in Mesa, Arizona, has made a creative change in the timing of their transitions.

In Mesa there are no middle schools, only K-6 elementary schools and seventh to ninth grade junior highs. Therefore, the church has chosen to keep the sixth graders in the children's ministry within a youth group designed specifically for fifth and sixth grade preteens. The ninth graders remain in the junior high program.

The high school pastor, junior high pastor, and fifth- and sixth-grade ministry leaders worked together to develop a way to overlap their ministries at the transition points. It seems to be working very well. And it is an example of breaking down the walls between departments and the walls of tradition to think of better ways to transition kids from a children's program to a youth program.

Here's the way it works throughout each year:

⑥ September—Pastors meet with parents.

The children's pastor, junior high pastor and high school pastor meet together with all of the parents of sixth through twelfth graders to promote the ministry programs for the year and to specifically explain the transitions between these ministry areas.

⑥ Early January—Ninth graders are promoted.

The ninth graders are promoted to the high school group in January. They attend all classes and programs that the other high school students attend. Ninth graders begin their year's small groups at this time also. The absence of ninth graders in the junior high group clears the way for sixth graders to start transitioning into the group with a less threatening atmosphere.

⑥ Mid-January—Sixth graders are introduced to junior high events.

The sixth graders are encouraged to attend special events, such as junior high winter camp. The junior high camp is held with other churches that normally have sixth through eighth graders in a middle school ministry, so sixth graders fit in with the large group.

⑥ January through May—Junior high staff members join children's staff.

The sixth graders continue attending the fifth-and-sixth-grade youth group on Sunday mornings until the end of the school year. However, starting in early January, the junior high ministry's small-group leaders join the fifth-and-sixth-grade Sunday School team on Sunday mornings and lead sixth grade small groups.

⑥ January through May—Sixth graders attend junior high midweek program.

From January through May (when schools end for the year), sixth graders are invited to attend the junior high group on Wednesday nights, but they may also choose to stay in the children's ministry's fifth-and-sixth-grade club, which runs concurrently with the junior high ministry. This overlapping allows a few months of safety for the kids to drop back into the security of the children's program if they feel it is necessary.

⑥ Early May—Sixth graders attend one last event.

At the end of the school year, sixth graders attend their final children's event. For Red Mountain, this is a graduation campout with fifth graders and the children's staff plus the junior high staff and some seventh and eighth grade kids who exhibit leadership potential.

⑥ Late May—Sixth graders complete the transition to junior high ministry.

On the Sunday following the end of the school year, the sixth graders officially join the junior istry on Sunday mornings, making the ... n complete after five months of overlap- ... programs.

One of the serendipitous benefits that Red Mountain Community Church has seen using this overlapping transition is that for five months, two different ministry staffs claim the sixth graders, and both sets watch over these kids to make sure that they are doing well in the transition.

Help Kids Make the Transition: More Tips for Bridging the Gap

Remember that the transition is not a one-time event that happens at the end of a school year. Blend from one ministry to another over a period of years.

However, there are some individual things that churches have shared with us that have helped make the transition more successful. Here are their ideas:

◎ Have junior high leaders and several friendly kids visit fifth- or sixth-grade programs several times before promotion to tell them about the junior high program and to answer their questions.

◎ Have the junior high pastor or key teacher lead fifth- or sixth-grade Sunday School several times so that kids can get to know him or her.

◎ Ask older students to serve as mentors or guides. Ask seventh or eighth graders who are leaders in the junior high ministry to befriend new students and help them with the transition, telling them about the program and just being their buddies. Choose your guides carefully and then specifically assign them to two or three younger students. It's amazing the security this gives the younger kids and the positive challenge that it provides the older ones.

◎ Invite the children's leaders to attend some of the junior high programs after promotion is done.

The first few socials, retreats, activities and classes can be frightening for the kids who are moving into a new program. Having familiar faces in the crowd can really help. The children's staff will also be able to help the youth staff get to know some of the kids who might be most at risk of dropping through the cracks.

◎ Use summer ministries to help with the transition. Many churches use summer ministries to help transition kids from children's ministry to youth ministry. It is common to promote kids to the youth ministry at the beginning of summer. Then the fun summer events can be used to attract and get to know the new kids. With the sporadic attendance that some churches have in the summer, though, care must be taken to not lose kids during this same time period.

Bridging the Gap Must Be a Team Effort

The Astoria-Megler Bridge carries Highway 101 across the Columbia River from Washington to Oregon. It's a good example of a steel truss bridge. A truss bridge is one that is made up of supports that are formed as rigid triangles. These three-part building blocks give the bridge its strength. We need the same three-part strength in our partnership to minister to preteens—a trusting, cooperative team effort among the youth leaders, children's leaders and God.

Ecclesiastes 4:12 tells us, "Though one may be overpowered, two can defend themselves. A cord of three strands is not quickly broken." In the ministry to early adolescents, we need to build that same truss bridge, made up of units with unique strengths. Threesomes—the children's ministry, the youth ministry and God—are key to the strength of the ministry. As a team, we can see our kids safely across the rivers of life as they journey onward in the adventure of walking with God toward maturity.

Note

1. David Elkind, *All Grown Up and No Place to Go* (Reading, MA: Addison-Wesley, 1998), pp. 81-82.

Getting Your Ministry Started—Or Restarted

> "Make changes that focus people's attention on the vision."
> —Price Pritchett and Ron Pound, "High-Velocity Culture Change"[1]

Change may well be the most threatening aspect of ministry that any of us ever face. Some of us as ministry leaders don't like change. Many of the people we are responsible to—boards, senior pastors, parents, kids and congregation members—don't like change. But change is a necessary element of life. Correctly processing change is a necessary element of leadership. And, after evaluating your ministry in light of who preteens are (see chapter 1) and what they need (see chapter 2), you are probably seeing at least one or two areas of your present programming that require change in order for your ministry to preteens to become all that it should be.

What Are the Stages of Change?

Many models of change have been outlined by those whose careers involve helping to change life-threatening, addictive or unhealthy behaviors. From their research, we find that once we humans move beyond complete denial, change happens in several stages.

◎ Stage 1 is sometimes called precontemplation: Sure, we know there are problems, but things are not that bad. Unlike denial, we're aware of the problems. We have information that would help us to change. It just hasn't hit home yet and doesn't seem to be a top priority.

◎ Stage 2 is contemplation and preparation: This is where our thoughts reach "critical mass"—the point at which it would be more frightening to keep things as they are than it would be to change! We know we have to do something. It can't wait for another six months or until the new budget is completed.

◎ Stage 3 is action: We're committed to do something. Even if we make only small changes, this signals the start of new behavior on our part. Doing something differently requires the most effort and determination of these stages, which is the reason commitment is necessary!

◎ Stage 4 is maintenance: We feel we can breathe a little more easily and are able to construct ways to maintain the changes. However, this is the stage in which we need to be vigilant against our human tendency to relax a little too much (after all, the new program is in place). Unless we are vigilantly maintaining our own new ways of thinking, it's easy to fall into old patterns (and find the old problems rearing their ugly heads).

We must be open to the possibility of failure when we make any significant change. We may not get it right the first time. That's okay. Life and ministry are a learning process. View change as a cycle—and failure as the part of that cycle in which we get an effective lesson in our weaknesses and ways to improve. As we prayerfully consider any change, we need to recognize that risk and action are necessary ingredients in establishing a truly effective ministry to preteens.

Where Are You in This Process?

Remember that even if you can honestly say you are ready to take the courageous step of making some changes, you must also consider the other players in your preteen ministry:

◎ the leaders to whom you are responsible (the senior pastor and your church's governing boards),

◎ your volunteer staff (some of whom may also be parents),

◎ the parents of the preteens, and

◎ the students themselves.

In *High-Velocity Culture Change,* Price Pritchett and Ron Pound tell us that we must start by making "changes that focus people's attention on the vision."[2]

We started the ball rolling in one church by announcing to the kids (after securing staff approval and parental and worker support) that we would no longer have Sunday School for fifth and sixth graders. As we loaded the bus to return from a weeklong summer camp, we informed the kids that the next Sunday they would come to something new—with a new name. In reality, this name change was primarily symbolic, but it pointed kids and adults to the fact that we had a vision to implement a youth group designed specifically for early adolescents.

Of course, a name alone will not sustain the momentum of change. We had to insure that the newly named program was filled with people who were hand selected to work with preteens and who understood our vision. Sunday morning had to become, both suddenly and dramatically, the most exciting part of the preteen's week.

A wise businessman who is vice president of a major corporation in our city told us once that most change creates immediate excitement among your followers. This initial excitement eventually gives way to a "death" experience when the costs finally become reality. Leaders need to prepare their followers for the inevitable slump and then work hard during the downtime to help them come through to the other side. One way to do this is to talk constantly about the vision and the benefits that will result for the kids (and parents, church and volunteers). Focus on what you'll gain and show people your commitment to the vision.

If You Are Serious, Start with Prayer

Whenever we're hoping to help people work through a change in their lives, we need the assistance of the Holy Spirit. In your private devotions or in meetings with key leaders, review these verses and prayer ideas as you prepare to work out the details of revitalizing your preteen ministry:

◎ Ephesians 1:22-23—"And God placed all things under his feet and appointed him to be head over everything for the church, which is his body, the fullness of him who fills everything in every way." Pray that you and the other members of your team will understand what God wants for His church and His preteen kids!

◎ Romans 15:13—"May the God of hope fill you with all joy and peace as you trust in him, so that you may overflow with hope by the power of the Holy Spirit." Pray that your vision will be contagious, that your hope and excitement will motivate others to join your movement.

◎ 1 Thessalonians 5:16-18—"Be joyful always; pray continually; give thanks in all circumstances, for this is God's will for you in Christ Jesus." Pray that, even in the face of setbacks or opposition, you will not get discouraged and that you will faithfully follow God's lead both in content and timing.

There are certain aspects of change that are common to preteen ministry and need to be looked at carefully when transitioning early adolescents into either a new grouping and grading system or simply a new style of ministry.

Your Church Leaders May Have Concerns About the Changes

Your church leaders are likely to wonder about the cost of the change, the need for the change, and just how well you have thought through the transition. Do you have the support of parents and kids, or will this be a problem for the church board down the road?

Any youth or children's leaders not yet involved in this process will wonder how this will affect their ministries. Will you be competing for workers? Will you want the kids to use the youth space? Will equipment, such as sound systems, microphones and vans, suddenly become difficult to share?

Explaining the need for and benefits of change to your church leaders must be your first priority. If you do not have their backing, your plan is destined for failure and there is no need to get your volunteers, parents and kids excited about it.

Of course, much prayer must go into this process and you need to discern the dynamics of the power base at your own church, but the following can be tailored to fit your situation. You will need to present your ideas first to the key decision maker in this area or, possibly, to the senior pastor or the church board. You may need to make multiple presentations of the vision and plan.

Here are some guidelines of what you should share with the leaders of your church as you seek support in making a major transition in your preteen ministry:

◎ **The need for a change in preteen ministry at our church.** Highlight key points from chapter 1 and chapter 2 about the needs and developmental characteristics of preteens. Focus especially on those needs that your current program does not address.

◎ **The benefits of a change in this ministry at our church.** Share with the board or your pastor what problems you hope to resolve as a result of this transition. Will this help you increase attendance? Will it address specific complaints that you have been receiving?

◎ **Your plan for enlisting the support of parents.** Let the leadership know that you are aware of the need to have parental backing. Come with specific dates for informational meetings and plans for communicating with parents who are perceived by others as leaders and with parents at large.

◎ **Your plan for enlisting the support of volunteers.** Although you should not discuss this plan with all of your volunteers, it is wise to have selected a few church leaders (who may also be parents of preteens) with whom you have shared the vision prior to meeting with the church board. If possible, choose volunteers who have earned the respect of the board through their faithful service. Let your board know that you realize your need for board support before going forward, but that you wanted to be ready to tell them how excited church leaders and parents were about this idea.

◎ **Your plan for selling the kids on this transition.** Again, have specific dates and ideas for when you will announce the changes to the kids. Leave yourself plenty of time to prepare for this kickoff. Utilize a natural transition time, such as your annual promotion, to begin with a fresh batch of kids.

◎ **Your proposed budget.** The transition might include increased needs for items such as T-shirts, sound equipment or room decorations, but more money is not a necessity. Preteens are more concerned about fun and relationships than they are about fancy equipment. You may be able to request a reallotment of currently budgeted funds for the things you do need. Be upfront about what you are expecting, but don't let money stand in the way. If your program is successful, it will get more funding in the future.

⊚ **Your plans for necessary facility changes.** Like funding, bigger, nicer facilities are great, but don't let the lack of space keep you from going forward. Be creative with current space and be patient in waiting for more and better space.

Your Volunteers May Have Concerns About the Changes

Selling a paradigm shift or a new vision requires a lot of talking. Share your ideas with anyone who will listen as often as they will listen. Ted Beranis, a public school principal who has led such a transition, writes these helpful words in his article "Reorganizing Middle-Level Education: What to Consider and How to Proceed": "If the advantages of the change are articulately and realistically expressed, enthusiasm will be contagious."[3]

Many public schools and churches that have made this transition have failed in this area of staff support. A principal or a pastor cannot one day decide that the whole structure will change and not take into consideration the preparation of the workers.

Becki went through a change of format in a public school when middle school philosophy was just beginning to take root in the country. Her school changed from Air Academy Junior High School (with seventh and eighth graders) to Challenger Middle School (for sixth through eighth graders). The school followed a recommended three-year process of study, preparation and implementation. (At churches, this process may take far less time, but we offer this as an example of preparing for a successful transition rather than rushing to a failed one.)

During the second year of the transition, administrators worked closely with the teachers and talked frequently about the transition. Teachers were offered subsidized college-credit courses on middle level education. Faculty meetings regularly included updates on the process and involved the teachers in the changes. Teachers had input into forming staff teams, were given opportunities to do personality and leadership-style testing and were fully informed about the whole process.

In the third year of the transition, when the school became a middle school officially, teachers were ready to work out the bugs and they were on board with the administration and parents.

The same process must be put in place to prepare your ministry leaders. Help your volunteers become educated on the needs and characteristics of preteens. Perhaps use this book as a study guide for your volunteer ministry staff. Focus on the first two chapters to help explain the needs and benefits of making this change.

Look for a quality preteen ministry in your community and arrange to visit the church with your team of volunteers while the program is in progress. Take the ministry leader of the quality program to coffee or a meal afterward and let your volunteers pick his or her brain regarding the program and the process of implementing it. Consider having an outside consultant or speaker come to your church to address specific needs and issues and to take your staff members further in their understanding of preteen education.

Allow time for volunteers to ask questions, to do their own study, to observe and to think. Listen to their concerns and answer them truthfully. If you don't know something, say so and do more research, or enlist their help in finding the answer. If you're on the right track, if God wants you to make the switch, no honest question or concern will derail you permanently.

Your Parents Will Certainly Have Concerns About the Changes

Many of the leaders we surveyed who had talked with parents about making a grouping and grading change said that they received mixed responses from parents. Parents must be brought on board before the transition is made. If parents do not understand the transition, they are likely to stonewall it. This is a natural human reaction, especially if children are involved.

Communication is key to enlisting the support of parents. The problem is that it is so much more difficult to reach all of your parents. To do this right, you will need time and patience, and you will need to do so through a variety of means.

Early in the process, we recommend having a parents' meeting for current parents and the parents of the next group of kids who will be coming into your group. Hold it right after your church service while parents are already on campus. Offer something for the younger kids to do and provide refreshments to hold everyone over. Make it easy for your families.

In this meeting, let the parents hear directly from you—your heart and passion for this change. Understand that once you have this meeting, any negative sentiment will spread quickly. Parents whose oldest child is just entering the preteen years may be the most protective and hesitant about any change that seems as though young kids are being pushed into youth activities prematurely. If you have not gone through this period with your own kids, understand that parents are feeling like their "baby" is growing up too quickly. The physical, emotional and social changes in their own child may frighten them. The perceived dangers of older children and society definitely frighten them. If your school district has gone through a messy change in its approach to this age level, they may be convinced that the whole notion is wrong.

When you meet with the parents, be ready to be sympathetic and understanding, but be convinced that your plans are best for their kids. Be ready to state the vision and benefits of your plan both briefly and clearly. And always remember, these are the kids' parents you are addressing, so communicate honor and respect along with the facts.

Follow These Guidelines in Your Meetings with Parents

1. Start by casting your vision and sharing your plan with a small group of respected parents who have been supportive of your ministry in the past. Make sure that these parents understand exactly what you have in mind and that you address any issues or concerns they may raise. Do not proceed without first receiving a favorable response from this group. Ask this small group of parents to be very visible at your future meetings and, perhaps, to share their own feelings with the other parents. Having a peer stand up and say, "I was hesitant about this at first, but now I understand and support it" can go a long way in convincing other parents.

2. Call a meeting of all the parents of preteens. You may have to do this several times to allow for all parents to attend or for all of the material and questions to be covered. Don't rush this process.

3. Open your first meeting by having the parents tell you the needs and characteristics of preteen kids. They are, after all, the experts on their own children.

The next few steps should probably be spread across two or three meetings.

4. Be ready to show that you understand the needs and characteristics of preteen kids and that you have specific, identifiable ideas to meet the needs. Now is a great time to unveil two or three major changes that you are considering. Make sure parents hear these as concepts, not plans.

5. Share with the parents the same benefits that you shared with the board or senior pastor. What benefits are in this transition for their children?

6. Reassure parents that you are not trying to rush their children to grow up more quickly but rather are looking for better ministry to meet their children's unique needs. Help them understand that you know preteens are uniquely different from children and also from teenagers. This will resonate as wisdom and truth with your parents.

7. Be ready to listen to parents' concerns and to give honest, nondefensive feedback.

8. After the meetings, you may need to have a volunteer summarize what was presented and what issues or concerns the parents brought up. This would make an excellent newsletter to hand out to the parents of preteen kids. Some will never come to a meeting, so the printed page will help keep them updated. Others will need the newsletter to remind them of what was actually said.

Meetings with parents should be tools to open the doors of communication. Your desire should be for parents to see you as a transparent, approachable leader who will listen to their concerns and ideas. This will have much more fruit for your ministry than attempting to convince anyone that you have the answers or know what is best.

If you have proven yourself in the past to be someone of good judgment when caring for their children, most parents will accept the above information and trust you to proceed with the benefit of their child in mind. Beranis reminds us that "the comments of those relatively few individuals who withhold support and remain negative about the transition must, of course, be evaluated for substance, addressed when appropriate, but blunted with firm yet respectful response."[4]

Your Kids May Also Have Concerns About the Changes

Make sure that you have done your homework with the church leaders, your ministry leaders and the parents. And then hit the ground running with the kids. (After all, they're the ones at the center of all this!)

Pick a natural transition time for the kids to implement the changes you have planned. Probably the best time is at promotion from one grade to another. After the last Sunday of the "old" ministry, have a huge pizza party or pool party. Pull out all the stops. Then gather the kids and explain all the changes. Make sure you sound confident and excited. Make sure your staff does, too!

Then, all at once, change everything the next Sunday. Rename programs, redesign the room and add staff if necessary. If your budget allows, have T-shirts printed for the kids and staff with the new name and logo for your group. Have all of these pieces of the transition puzzle ready so that they may be implemented quickly and thoroughly. (More information on how to implement changes like these can be found in the next three chapters.)

Kids want action. They want to know you're serious about the changes. They want to follow an adult who is not afraid to lead. Our experience has always been that we cannot be too prepared for the implementation of a new program or idea. When we announce that change is coming, kids want it now. Be ready to implement major portions of your plan all at once when the time is right. As Pritchett and Pound say: "Start out fast and keep trying to pick up speed. Leave skid marks."[5]

Notes

1. Price Pritchett and Ron Pound, *High-Velocity Culture Change: A Handbook for Managers* (Dallas, TX: Pritchett Publishing Company, 1993), p. 28.

2. Ibid.

3. Ted A. Beranis, "Reorganizing Middle-Level Education: What to Consider and How to Proceed," in Sally N. Clark and Donald C. Clark, *Schools in the Middle: A Decade of Growth and Change*, (Reston, VA: National Association for Secondary School Principals, 1992), p. 164.

4. Ibid.

5. Pritchett and Pound, *High-Velocity Culture Change: A Handbook for Managers,* p. 44.

> "The spiritual nurture and care that volunteers give to students reflect the spiritual care and nurture volunteers receive from leaders."
>
> —Mark Oestreicher, "Help! I'm a Junior High Youth Worker!"[1]

What Motivates Someone to Work with Preteens?

Some of your friends may wonder why you would choose to work with preteens. (You may wonder yourself on some days!) So—why have you chosen to work with early adolescents?

Here are some responses to that question from people just like you:

◎ "I think they're the most exciting kids at church. They're fun and they're vulnerable. They need someone to teach them who likes them, and I do."—Mary, fifth-and-sixth-grade room leader

◎ "I like kids that are very verbal and that I can exchange ideas with. They already have a basis of stuff for us to talk about. Common ground. I guess I enjoy the exchange."—Sarah, volunteer preteen teacher

◎ "They have a lot of potential. It's exciting to see that they can make good choices. A lot of people doubt whether they even have any potential. Also that they are coming from an area of their life where they are dependent on their parents and they're starting to see that the choices they make now can be their own."—Bob, sixth-and-seventh-grade small-group leader

What's your answer to that same question? The passion that you feel for preteen ministry is the single most important tool you have for recruiting others to help with the ministry. Take time to think about what really excites you about working with these kids:

◎ Is it that you feel called by God? How much more compelling of a reason would anyone need?

◎ Is it because this was a difficult time in your own life? Many of us want to give to young people what we did not have ourselves.

✺ Is it because you think building the spiritual lives of kids is the most exciting investment you could make? That's what some would call a passion for this ministry.

✺ Is it because you never grew up yourself and you want a legitimate excuse to have more fun than any grown adult is supposed to have? This reason won't attract those adults who equate quiet classrooms with learning, but those aren't the ones we want to help with preteen ministry anyway!

Gather your story together and go out looking for the best possible workers that you can find. Convince them that they will have just as much fun and will feel just as significant as you do when they try working in this vital area of the church.

What Does a Successful Preteen Ministry Volunteer Look Like?

Who should you go after? Are there characteristics in common? Well, yes and no.

God has rightly placed us in a body of various parts and functions and gifts. "All these are the work of one and the same Spirit, and he gives them to each one, just as he determines. The body is a unit, though it is made up of many parts; and though all its parts are many, they form one body. So it is with Christ" (1 Corinthians 12:11-12).

This principle is too often forgotten. Too often church youth ministries fill up with rowdy, young, fun-loving people, when actually there are a number of other types of people who can minister to youth. Children's ministries tend to be staffed with people gifted in organization, administration and mercy. In both cases, the students we are trying to reach are so diverse in their temperaments, likes and dislikes, that we fall short of doing our best for them if we do not offer them a wide variety of adult role models. Each adult worker will connect better with certain students than with others, and each will connect differently.

There are, however, some key indicators for workers who will be successful in ministry to early adolescents. First of all, the worker must show a legitimate expression of the work of the Spirit in his or her life. This can be seen in the following characteristics:

✺ **The preteen leader must be loving.** "Greater love has no one than this, that he lay down his life for his friends" (John 15:13). Because the early adolescent can be demanding and needy, the leader must be willing and able to give of him- or herself in mentoring and discipling preteens. This is no ministry for someone with major needs of his or her own. The amount of love that the leader is able to pour out in meaningful, practical ways, in actual tangible involvement in the students' lives, will be directly proportional to the power of the ministry in those students' lives.

✺ **The preteen leader must be lighthearted and joyful.** The early adolescent leader doesn't necessarily need to be crazy or wild, but must be able to enjoy a laugh and a smile. People who are characterized by legalism or rigidity might best work in another area of the church or in a support role for the other workers. The preteen leader must be able to enjoy the kids for who they are. When ministering to these kids, "a cheerful heart is good medicine" (Proverbs 17:22) both for the kids and for the leaders!

✺ **The preteen leader must be calm and secure.** "I urge, then, first of all, that requests, prayers, intercession and thanksgiving be made for everyone—for kings and all those in authority, that we may live peaceful and quiet lives in all godliness and holiness. This is good, and pleases God our Savior" (1 Timothy 2:1-3). One mom told us that her best tip for working with early adolescents was to pray. Although some would say this to make a joke, she was serious. It takes prayer to give the volunteer the inner peace and serenity that is necessary for meeting the needs of preteens whose lives are in transition. It also helps the leader not get too uptight about whatever the ministry might throw at him or her. Preteen workers need to be able to roll with the punches.

The preteen leader must be patient. Early adolescence is one of the most self-focused periods of human development. The leader who does not understand this will see the preteen's self-absorption and forgetfulness as rude and obnoxious. With patience, the leader can see these as natural traits that need to be addressed, as the student is nurtured and discipled. We are to "Preach the Word; be prepared in season and out of season; correct, rebuke and encourage—with great patience and careful instruction" (2 Timothy 4:2).

The preteen leader must be kind. "A kind-hearted woman gains respect" (Proverbs 11:16). Being hard on kids is not usually a good idea at any age, but with preteens it's the beginning of the end. For the leader to maintain any kind of rapport with students, respect is essential. Kindness is a key indicator of respect.

When you like someone, it's hard to disobey him or her or do something that would upset that person. When kids respect their leader, what the leader asks them to do will come much more naturally to them.

The preteen leader must be a worthy role model for kids. "Follow my example, as I follow the example of Christ" (1 Corinthians 11:1). We all know it so well, but the old saying is still true: "More is caught than taught." Early adolescents are desperately seeking to distance themselves from their own parents and families. At the same time, they have a great hunger to belong to something just like what they are leaving. The church leader almost becomes a surrogate parent for the student who will watch every move the leader makes. The student wants to know if the leader's life measures up to his or her words.

Ross Campbell, in *How to Really Love Your Child*, tells us of the importance of loving, godly role models to help kids own their values. "A child first looks to his parents for direction that enables him to develop healthy values. Whether he finds what he needs from his parents depends on two things. The first is whether the parents have it themselves. The second is whether a child can identify with his parents in such a way as to incorporate and accept parental values. A child who does not feel loved will find this difficult."[2]

The preteen leader must be faithful. By faithful, we mean that the worker should be consistent in church and ministry attendance and true to his or her word in every respect. The leader must follow through or risk disappointing the students and damaging relationships. "Let your 'Yes' be yes, and your 'No,' no, or you will be condemned" (James 5:12). Early adolescents feel as though their whole world is coming unglued and they desperately want some stability from the adults in their lives. The church leader needs to be someone who is consistently there for the student, and the students must be able to count on the leader to do what he or she has promised. At this age, kids have already experienced too many adults who were not dependable; they are now skeptical and won't put up with someone who appears to be phony to them.

We have found it necessary at times to ask a leader to step down from a ministry to early adolescents on this point alone. A leader who does not show up or can't be counted on to do what has been promised makes a poor shepherd for an early adolescent. The child may not even show up regularly, but when he or she does come, the child is counting on the leader to be there and to be ready to call the child by name!

The preteen leader must be understanding and compassionate. The right person for the job will be able to see life through the eyes of the early adolescent. Sometimes having had a difficult time at this age level oneself helps a prospective worker relate to the insecurities and awkwardness of the preteen.

Henrietta Mears, a pioneer of Christian education, was fond of saying, "First I learned to love my teacher, then my teacher's God."[3] Our compassion in relating to middle level students is incredibly important in helping them build a new or renewed relationship with God. "Let your gentleness be evident to all. The Lord is near" (Philippians 4:5).

We once worked with a leader in our fifth-and-sixth-grade ministry who was super faithful; he had worked with the kids for many years. He was a hard worker; he would do anything from teach to load luggage. He was dependable; he was always the first person there, greeting the kids, and he rarely missed a Sunday.

However, he lacked compassion and understanding of other people. He had a critical attitude that showed through in jabs and jokes about people or aimed at people. He used sarcastic humor to communicate his frustrations or disapproval of others rather than being straightforward. Anyone could be his victim, either kids or other adult leaders, and he would normally jab when he had a crowd to laugh at him.

For all of his good qualities, he did much damage with his bitter humor. He made other adults defensive and brought out the worst in them. He made kids fearful and created an atmosphere in which no one felt safe. Hard work can be destroyed when we are not kind and compassionate in dealing with the fragile feelings of preteens (and our coworkers).

⊚ **The preteen leader must be mature.** "For this reason I remind you to fan into flame the gift of God, which is in you through the laying on of my hands. For God did not give us a spirit of timidity, but a spirit of power, of love and of self-discipline" (2 Timothy 1:6-7). It is important that the leader of preteens be mature enough to use his or her spiritual gifts and to have the power that is unleashed by God's Spirit.

Self-discipline is necessary for the mature leader, since it can be a temptation at times to become one of the kids, to joke when a joke is not loving, to compete when competition is not helpful. The prospective leader must be chosen for his or her maturity and Spirit-filled self-control.

⊚ **Finally, and most importantly, preteen leaders must show evidence of spiritual growth in their own lives.** After all, the nine characteristics above are the fruit of the Spirit: "The fruit of the Spirit is love, joy, peace, patience, kindness, goodness, faithfulness, gentleness and self-control" (Galatians 5:22-23).

Some might feel that weakness in any of these characteristics disqualifies them from the ministry, but this is not a standard of perfection. The characteristics described as fruit of the Spirit are ones that should be constantly growing in the maturing Christian. If these characteristics are increasingly evident in a person's life, with the help of the Spirit, the person will be a good model for the kids to follow.

How Do You Find Prospective Preteen Workers?

So you're ready to share your excitement about the ministry with someone who is increasingly living out the fruit of the Spirit, but where do you find prospects to recruit? Think of recruiting like fishing. Just as you would drop your fishing line in where you expect to find fish, drop your recruiting line into "recruiting ponds" where you know there are potential workers in your church. Try some of these:

⊚ The parents of your students

⊚ Past workers

⊚ Short-term workers in summer programs or special events who may be willing to take on newer, bigger responsibilities

⊚ Substitutes who may have enjoyed their experience with the kids

⊚ Single adult groups

⊚ New member classes

Remember that your job is to offer the opportunity to as many people as possible. Don't decide that someone is too busy or wouldn't be interested. That decision is between the prospective preteen worker and God!

Never Get Desperate About Recruiting

If the ministry to preteens at your church is God's ministry, there's no reason to get desperate. He will take care of His ministry in His own time. Besides, good people do not always respond to desperate pleas. If our message to the church is, "No one wants to work with the fifth and sixth graders," most people can figure out that there must be some good reason to avoid this duty!

Some churches have chosen to require parents to work with their child's classroom. This is the same as desperation. Not all parents are equipped personally or spiritually to work with preteens. You want workers on your team who have been gifted and called by God to be in the ministry.

Remember the Power of Prayer in Recruiting

We often forget the most important step in recruiting—PRAYER! Here are some passages for you to meditate upon and pray through before you go out looking for workers:

🌀 Matthew 9:37-38: "Then he said to his disciples, 'The harvest is plentiful but the workers are few. Ask the Lord of harvest, therefore, to send out workers into his harvest field.'" *Pray that the Lord of the harvest will supply His workers for His harvest. Praise Him that He considers it His job to bring the right people!*

🌀 Romans 15:13: "May the God of hope fill you with all joy and peace as you trust in him, so that you may overflow with hope by the power of the Holy Spirit." *Pray that your enthusiasm and hope will be infectious as you contact potential recruits. Praise Him that yours is a ministry not of desperation but of hope!*

🌀 Ephesians 4:11: "It was he who gave some to be apostles, some to be prophets, some to be evangelists, and some to be pastors and teachers." *Pray that God will help you quickly find those whom He has gifted and equipped for the ministry to preteens!*

🌀 1 John 5:14-15: "This is the confidence we have in approaching God: that if we ask anything according to his will, he hears us. And if we know that he hears us—whatever we ask—we know that

we have what we asked of him." *Pray that God will help us to know His will and allow us to be a part of it. Praise Him that He will bring His workers to the harvest, just as we have prayed for Him to do!*

Keep Your Preteen Staff Through Motivation and Management

Of course, the best recruiting of all is to keep the workers that you already have. You can do this through proper care and training of your staff! A wise person once said, "They don't care how much you know until they know how much you care!" The same is true with those we lead in preteen ministry.

🌀 **Train your staff members to do their jobs well.** Good people know if they're failing at their ministry. Volunteers who are struggling or feel like failures don't last long. Equip your staff to minister to early adolescents successfully. Train them to take risks for the sake of the kids and to know that most failures are not fatal!

🌀 **Build friendships with your team members.** We must establish personal friendships with our workers for a lot of reasons. One team benefit of this is that it also helps keep them vital and on the job for the long haul. Make ministering to preteens fun and personal.

Robin Welsh of Arvada, Colorado, finds fun ways to show her staff members how much they are loved and appreciated. When we visited her church, we met numerous people who said they wanted to be in her ministry more than any other because of the good care they receive from her.

Her staff members would arrive at planning meetings to discover little heart-shaped cups filled with red and white candies in February and plastic eggs filled with jellybeans in March. She never forgets a birthday, taking the time to send a birthday card with a personal note. At times in her years of ministry, she has found side rooms at nice restaurants to hold planning meetings. The atmosphere is more fun than meeting at church, anyone can order whatever they want to eat, and the waiters keep bringing the coffee and water for the duration of her meeting. Of course, the most important quality Robin brings to the ministry is that she is a good friend herself.

◉ **Listen to their concerns, questions and problems.** Our workers need to know that they aren't going it alone. If they have problems or concerns, they want to be able to talk to someone

> If you are willing to listen to what I have to say and my frustrations or if I feel like you've got a lot to do and yet you are willing to come and talk to me and listen and hear what I have to say, then I am motivated to continue ministering.—Tina, sixth-and-seventh-grade small-group leader

about them.

Leaders often assume that when workers bring a problem or concern to them, the workers expect the leader to fix it, but this isn't always the case. Many workers are perfectly capable of handling their own problems, but they would like to know someone cares enough to listen and empathize with what they are experiencing. Often all leaders really need to do is offer an encouraging word when a worker shares a problem or concern.

◉ **Build teams of coworkers.** When we asked some workers what the church leadership could do to help them be satisfied in their ministry for the long haul, one small-group leader in fifth-and-sixth-grade ministry said, "Give us coteachers who go over the material together and are able to exchange ideas. That's very helpful."

Working in teams helps workers stay motivated. Workers can back each other up and can share the load of teaching, planning and special projects; and they can debrief when something goes wrong in class.

Using multiple adults in classrooms is also one of

the best ways to avoid child abuse and accusations of wrongdoing, according to most authorities on child sexual abuse.

◉ **Give your workers the tools and resources they need.** There may be nothing more frustrating and time-consuming for the volunteer worker than not being given the appropriate tools for the job they've been asked to accomplish.

Curriculum that isn't age appropriate can be just as frustrating to the teacher as it is to the student. Most publishers will send out consultants to help train your workers to use their materials to the fullest advantage. Take advantage of this help.

Make sure your workers have quality resources that are easy to use and the supplies they need to make working with the kids as easy as possible. One preteen teacher puts it this way: "Just give me the tools that I need to do it."

◉ **Enrich your workers and the ministry with creative ideas.** One preteen leader voices the need of many: "I think anybody is going to run out of fresh ideas. Fresh things that I can bring to my class would really help me." There are lots of easy ways to provide creative ideas for your staff. Here are just a few:

◉ Subscribe to educational magazines, tear out helpful articles and pass them around.

◉ Attend conferences and send your workers to them as well. Budget funds for this sort of training. Look for regional Sunday School conventions in your area.

◉ Buy idea books. Consider establishing a resource library your workers can access easily.

◉ Conduct idea exchanges. One of the easiest training meetings we led for our own teachers recently also seemed to be one of our most popular. We pulled out all our different activity and game books, looking for Easter activities. We then took these ideas and demonstrated them for our staff. Volunteers want good ideas to jazz up their teaching ministry.

◉ Suggest that teachers observe another class or

program that is functioning well and suggest the following questions as a guideline for the observer to watch for: How did the leader involve the kids? How did the leader achieve the aim or goal of the lesson? How did the leader communicate interest and caring for the students? It is not necessary that the model class or program be perfect, as people can learn as much from weaknesses as from strengths.

◎ Work with leaders in several nearby churches to plan a training event together.

◎ **Motivate your team by letting them know you appreciate them.** Here are some quick and easy ways to show your appreciation for your staff members:

◎ Say the words "Thank you for working with the kids" or "Thank you for being here today." We often forget the most obvious!

◎ Give them chocolate bars with kind, personalized notes attached. You can never go wrong with chocolate.

◎ Create T-shirts for the youth group and give the staff theirs free. Tell them you are doing so because you appreciate all they give already.

◎ Find a substitute for a faithful worker who wants to take a week off. We recently gave a single mom a six-week vacation to attend an adult elective. The rest of the staff were encouraged because they found out they, too, could have a short break sometime.

◎ Send notes or postcards designed to encourage and motivate volunteer workers. Keep a supply of note cards or postcards handy. You can jot a quick note and put a stamp on in minutes!

◎ Have the kids write notes or bring flowers.

◎ Invite your team to your home for a game night or dessert. Too often we only get our volun-teers together to plan Sunday School lessons!

Walt and Diane Pitman have the students each write a "zap-o-gram" telling several things that they appreciate about their leaders. They are a "real boost for the leaders because, let's face it, these kids don't naturally verbalize praise." One of the Pitmans' leaders told them that when she gets home from work and is too tired to teach, she'll read those "zap-o-grams" and get reenergized!

◎ **Manage your team with the four Ps.** Make sure that you are regularly involved in your team members' lives and ministries. Here are four key things you should do with your team:

1. Plan together. Team members like to be included in the decision-making process. Listen to team members' ideas and use them.

2. Pray together. Focusing on God's will for your ministry together will help the team keep focused on the mission and will help each member know that he or she is part of a team.

3. Perform together. There's nothing like getting the job done! There's a deep satisfaction that comes from accomplishing ministry tasks, especially when you do them together.

4. Play together! When you have fun together, you build friendships. When your friends are in the ministry team, you aren't likely to quit the team!

Keep Your Preteen Staff Members Fresh by Nurturing Them

Whenever we can meet with our workers and give them a verbal hug—a word of encouragement, a spiritual challenge or a heartfelt thanks—we perform an important part of our role as leaders. We need to keep our staff fresh and motivated in order to have them filled up enough to nurture their kids.

Notes

1. Mark Oestreicher, *Help! I'm a Junior High Youth Worker!* (Grand Rapids, MI: Zondervan/Youth Specialties, 1996), p. 61.

2. Ross Campbell, M.D., *How to Really Love Your Child* (Wheaton, IL: Victor Books, 1992), p. 132.

3. Henrietta Mears, notes.

Implementing
Your Vision:

MAKING YOUR PRETEEN MINISTRY WORK

The Big Picture—A Model for Preteen Ministry

> "The early adolescent is like an improvisational jazz piece. Some is prearranged but it is constantly changed, adapted, manipulated by the players-people, places and things in the child's surroundings. The piece expresses all kinds of human emotion and can grow into a beautiful work if carried in the right hands."
>
> —An eighth-grade math teacher [1]

A Holistic Model for Ministering to Early Adolescents

Now that we have looked at numerous principles for redefining ministry to early adolescents, let's look at how to put it all together.

Our surveys of early adolescent ministries across the United States showed that there is a wide variety of programs being used with these kids. They range from the traditional—children's choirs, Sunday School, children's church and midweek clubs—to the more unusual and creative youth group programs that many have designed just for preteens. This chapter provides a comprehensive picture of a ministry model that works well for early adolescents, 10 to 14 years of age.

Keep in mind, however, that it's not a requirement that you recreate every aspect of the following program (in fact, it probably wouldn't even be a good idea). The important thing is how you think about and work with the early adolescents that God has entrusted to your care. The following ideas are offered to spark your creativity as you move forward to create a program for these wonderful kids living through this important and unique period of human development. Regardless of how large or small your church is, these ideas are transferable.

Step 1: Give Your Ministry a Name That Gives the Kids Something to Belong to

In our model, we have chosen to call the ministry to early adolescents "LiveWires." (For other creative program names, see p. 78.)

Step 2: Restructure Existing Programs

Making your church pro-preteen does not mean throwing out all of your existing programs and starting from scratch. Many of the wonderful things you are now doing can be tweaked to be more age appropriate.

The first step for restructuring existing programs is to create fresh new names. Look for ways to hold the whole ministry together by having each program's name somehow tie in with the theme you have created by the ministry's umbrella name (in this model, LiveWires).

Then redesign programs by focusing on how to minister to the early adolescent's unique needs and learning styles. Incorporate small groups into every aspect of the revised programming. Review all of the traditional structure and revise anything that is not age appropriate.

◉ Transform Traditional Sunday School to PowerPacks

The Shortcomings of the Traditional Structure

First of all, early adolescents do not want to go to school of any kind for a sixth day of the week. The very name is a turnoff for many early adolescents.

Second, calling the program "Sunday School" reminds the early adolescent of childhood. Sunday School is what little kids do. Early adolescents are doing everything within their power to distance themselves from things that are childish.

Finally, and most importantly, if the Sunday School program is truly traditional, meaning that it asks kids to sit still and listen for the entire program, the approach is not early adolescent-friendly at all. As we've mentioned before, early adolescents want and need to move, explore, experience and discuss what they are learning.

The New Design

PowerPacks is designed to be the key Christian education setting for early adolescents. This education should take place primarily in small groups, and the groups should encourage relationships between the kids and adults and the kids and their peers. This is an entry-level discipleship program for regular attenders and a primary evangelistic setting for visitors.

The Benefits of the New Program

The PowerPacks name gives the program a special identity. It tells kids that this is "just for early adolescents." It promises fun and activity and promotes enthusiasm.

The curriculum for PowerPacks should approach Bible study in a way that is significantly different from the approach used in the childhood years. Early adolescents desire topical studies that are focused directly at their life issues. Neil Postman and Charles Weingartner, in their book *Teaching as a Subversive Activity*, tell us, "There is no way to help a learner to be disciplined, active and thoroughly engaged unless he perceives a problem to be a problem or whatever is to-be-learned as worth learning, and unless he plays an active role in determining the process of solution. Unless an inquiry is perceived as relevant by the learner, no significant learning will take place. No one will learn anything he doesn't want to know. And if he is made to—that is, forced to act as if he does—he and his teacher will regret it. That's the way it is."[2] Teach preteens things they need for life.

It is important that the teaching style includes hands-on activities that bring the Bible truth of the lesson to life. Active education appeals to early adolescents because they need movement. Allowing

the kids to participate in activities in small groups provides an opportunity for them to discuss and apply the Bible truth while meeting their social needs. These small groups should be designed to promote deeper involvement in the ministry, encouraging kids to make personal decisions for God and to get involved in discipleship groups.

Here's an annotated schedule for a PowerPacked morning:

☺ Opening (10-15 minutes)

PowerPacks should open with a brief time that incorporates a discussion, game or activity that introduces the lesson and gets the kids' brains focused on the topic of the day. Depending on the size of your group and the kind of activity you choose, all students may participate in one activity together, or teachers may lead small groups of students in the activity.

☺ Interactive Study and Life Application (30-40 minutes)

The majority of the students' time in PowerPacks is spent in exploration of a Bible passage in either a small or large group, depending on the size of your church and the leadership skills of the teachers. Then students form small groups of six to eight kids with one handpicked adult leader to explore the relevance of the Bible passage to their lives. These groups might well be coed groups, since weekend services are less intimate in nature and include all those who attend at this age.

The advantages of small groups include allowing the kids to talk and to build relationships; both are important needs of early adolescents.

Small-group leaders should be ready to lead their kids in a learning activity that includes meaningful discussion questions that will help the small groups discuss what they have learned and how they will apply it to their lives. Have leaders ask questions and make comments such as, "How is what happened to (Paul) like what might happen to you? Compare the choice that (Joseph) made to a choice a kid your age might have to make. What can you do to follow (Esther's) example?"

☺ Closing (5-15 minutes)

Try varying your closing between large and small groups, depending on the lesson of the day. Use small groups for more serious or personal topics, large groups for more lighthearted or celebratory lessons. In either setting, use this time for prayer, application and summary of what has been learned. This is also the place for announcements and special elements, such as music.

☺ **Transform Traditional Children's Church to SuperCharge**

The Shortcomings of the Traditional Structure

As explained above, the name alone can send early adolescents running. Traditional approaches also do not take into account the early adolescent's need for relevance, activity and a youth-group feel. If our current children's church is grouping fifth and sixth graders with first through fourth graders, we're violating our understanding of developmental stages that show 10-year-olds have more in common with 14-year-olds than with 6- and 7-year-olds.

The New Design

The name SuperCharge not only fits with the LiveWires theme, but it also helps sell this time of praise and worship as something special, again designed specifically for early adolescents.

SuperCharge is an age-appropriate time of praise and worship designed specifically for the needs

A MODEL FOR

MINISTRY TO EARLY ADOLESCENTS
LiveWires Ministry

TRADITIONAL PROGRAMS CAN BE TRANSFORMED

SUNDAY SCHOOL BECOMES
PowerPacks—interactive Bible study on practical topics of interest

CHILDREN'S CHURCH BECOMES
SuperCharge—large group worship with live band, videos, drama, puppets and active/interactive education and topical themes

VACATION BIBLE SCHOOL BECOMES
Come Alive Week—high-energy nighttime program with off-campus excursions, small-group studies and lots of fun

CHILDREN'S CHOIR BECOMES
Wired4Sound—various fine arts experiences, special shirts and performances in senior centers, younger kids' Sunday School, and worship services

SUMMER CAMP BECOMES
L.I.F.E. (Living in Foreign Environments)—choice of friends, counselors, cabin names, and outrageous fun and exploration

NEW PROGRAMS CAN BE ADDED

YOUTH GROUP
W.O.W. (Wired on Wednesdays)—low-key evening of games, food, non-Christian friends, topical study

FNL (Friday Nite Live)—socials for kids to bring friends and have fun with loving adults in safe settings

SERVICE OPPORTUNITIES
S.O.S. (Summer of Service/Serving Our Savior)—training to be assistants in programs for younger children

MISSIONS TRIPS
Life2Life2Life—exposure to hands-on missions experiences

and desires of early adolescents. It should incorporate as much creative music, video and other technological tools as the church is able to afford and accomplish with expertise. It should involve the students in various support roles as they help lead and organize their own worship service.

Here's a plan for SuperCharging your preteen worship time:

◎ Preparation

Before the students ever arrive, have upbeat, contemporary Christian music or music videos playing in the worship room. Play these loudly enough to fill the silent void but quietly enough that kids can talk to one another as they arrive.

Adult leaders should be present before the first kids show up, but train specific students to serve as greeters, hosts for guests and attendance takers.

◎ Opening Music (10-30 minutes)

Use the best musicians you can find to put together a worship team for SuperCharge. Use students to help lead the singing, along with adult leaders. Put together the best accompaniment you can. This may mean having your one or two instrumentalists play along with a prerecorded soundtrack. Do what you can.

As financial resources and human talent become available, this time of worship can eventually include a live band, TVs suspended from the ceiling for video clips, colorful costumes and a platform for drama. But to begin, a boom box playing contemporary Christian CDs is good.

◎ Bible Teaching (20-40 minutes)

The majority of the early adolescent's time in SuperCharge should be in a large-group setting. This further develops the sense of belonging to something bigger than themselves that early adolescents need, and it does so in the context of corporate worship. It provides a sense of the Body of Christ. It also helps prepare students for the teaching style most commonly used in youth groups.

Select or create a Bible study that focuses on topics that are relevant to early adolescents and their experiences. Although SuperCharge is not designed to include as many games or activities as other settings (since it is more teacher directed), it should still not be a 20-minute lecture. Involve students by using brief learning activities and pair shares throughout the lesson to help students stay focused and to think through the Bible lesson.

Object lessons, up-front activities in which all the students are focused on the task assigned to a few (especially if the group can coach or cheer on the participants), and tasks that students can do alone or with a partner in their seats are all good ways of incorporating active learning into the large-group setting.

◎ **Transform Traditional Midweek Clubs to W.O.W. (Wired on Wednesdays)**

The Shortcomings of the Traditional Structure

Most club programs have similar shortcomings, including one or all of the following:

◎ They focus on competition, either physical or mental, incorporating highly competitive memorization tasks and recreation activities. Most early adolescents don't want to compete; they want to fit in. No early adolescents want to lose.

◎ They bribe kids with extrinsic rewards for attending, learning memory verses and various other accomplishments. Unfortunately, bribes do not create long-term, intrinsic motivation.

◎ They utilize pen-and-paper teaching styles and rote memorization learning techniques. Early adolescents don't want more schoolwork and they don't learn best through rote memorization.

◎ They lump early adolescents into the same programs as early elementary and, sometimes, even preschool kids.

The New Design

As the name implies, Wired on Wednesdays is a midweek program designed to give early adolescents a fun, rowdy, highly relational, informal evening in the middle of the week. W.O.W. includes small groups focused on service or ministry projects, games, food, youth group-type sharing, music and topical teaching. The kids will look forward to the fun break from school, time with friends, a place to bring non-Christian friends, and a youth group-type atmosphere.

◎ Opening Games (15 minutes)

Start the evening by pulling out all the stops with high-energy, low-competition games. Be sure your game leader has a touch of insanity! (See game ideas in chapter 10.)

Leaders should participate in the games to set the example. They should model having fun, being a little crazy and not being overly concerned about winning or losing.

◎ Music (10-15 minutes)

Just as in SuperCharge, use contemporary Christian music presented in the best ways your church can offer. Start out rowdy, and then transition into a quieter mood for a large-group study.

◎ Teaching Time (20-30 minutes)

This W.O.W. teaching time should be a creative blend of large-group presentations with small-group discussions and activities. A key leader should coordinate and direct this time. This is an ideal opportunity for a ministry leader who is normally spread too thin with administrative duties on a Sunday morning to focus on teaching this important group of kids.

◎ Ministry Groups (30 minutes)

In this part of W.O.W., students choose from a variety of service projects or ministry assignments. In small groups, they can work together to write "we missed you" cards to absentees, wash a church van, make snacks for fellow students, prepare a drama skit for later in the evening, create a puppet show or Bible story to present to a younger class next Sunday, or practice to lead worship for SuperCharge.

◎ Closing and Snack (10 minutes)

Preteens like food. Be sure to close the evening with a snack (prepared by other students) and a closing song or two. After the official end, play contemporary Christian music and keep the room open for kids to stand around and socialize with other preteens and staff members.

◎ **Transform Traditional Children's Choirs to Wired4Sound (Music and Fine Arts Program)**

The Shortcomings of the Traditional Structure

Early adolescents, especially males, typically do not want to sing. As anyone who has directed an upper elementary choir can testify to, it is difficult to keep boys interested in choirs at all. Children's choirs also frustrate action-oriented early adolescents by focusing too much attention on rehearsal and not enough on performance.

The New Design

Early adolescents gather together for a brief devotional before splitting up to various specialty classes. Specialty classes can be flexible and designed to meet student interest. These classes should be led by church or community members who have expertise in the specialty. For example, if someone with dramatic skills is available and willing to teach early adolescents, then drama becomes one of the specialties. Various music and fine arts specialties that work well include choir, drama, puppetry, painting, clay, dance and photography. The classes should run for a few weeks and are concluded

with an open house for parents to observe the students' accomplishments.

The Benefits of the New Structure

⊚ Boys and nonmusical girls are much more likely to become involved.

⊚ Kids are exposed to those in your congregation and community who have unique skills (and more people in your church will have the privilege of getting to know the kids in your group).

⊚ Short-term goals allow for more frequent accomplishments and completion and, therefore, a sense of success that early adolescents need.

⊚ This program allows students to express themselves creatively (another early adolescent developmental need) and to learn new areas of competency using creative arts.

⊚ Many of these fine arts can be used in other areas of ministry. This helps the early adolescent feel needed and offers a variety of new ways for the student to serve in the Body of Christ.

⊚ Transform Traditional Vacation Bible School to Come Alive Week

The Shortcomings of the Traditional Structure

Vacation Bible School has several perception problems for early adolescents:

⊚ VBS is what their little brothers and sisters attend, so it must be just for little kids.

⊚ The name implies something it's not. Who wants to go to school on their vacation? How many of us would spend our two weeks each year at Vacation Bible Work?

⊚ Past experiences with some published VBS curriculum may leave preteens with the attitude that this really isn't going to be fun.

The New Design

Come Alive Week is a weeklong evening program in which students are divided into coed teams of eight to ten preteens with an adult couple (or male and female coleaders). The setting and activities help kids know this is a youth-style event, while the high ratio of adults to kids gives the early adolescent the security he or she needs.

Look for ideas in your VBS curriculum that you can use to create a preteen-friendly VBS. For example, here's a plan for an evening of Come Alive Week using a spy theme:

⊚ 5:30 P.M.—Preparation

Upon arrival, spies (kids) check in. Detectives (staff) take attendance and listen to theme memory verses. Students choose their team name and team cheer to help create an identity for the team. This identity carries throughout the week as the group does virtually everything together as a team.

⊚ 6:00 P.M.—Opening: Large-Group Singing and Competition

Rowdy music welcomes the spies and detectives into the large-group "spy headquarters," a large room with a high ceiling and movable furniture. The upbeat contemporary music is occasionally interrupted for competition, contests in which teams are awarded spirit points for silly things like bringing up the first blue sock with a hole in it or a hair off the head of one of the male detectives! The team with the most spirit points at the end of the evening gets their snack first.

⊚ 6:20 P.M.—Surprise Activity

Each night there is a surprise activity, which takes place off campus. These surprise activities may include roller-skating, swim parties or games in the park. Use a short video clip to introduce the theme of the evening and to announce the surprise activity (for example, a James Bond car chase for a road rally).

⊚ 7:20 P.M.—Quiet-Down Music

Use music in a large-group setting to help calm the spies after their outing. Give the kids a chance to share the highlights and thrills of the event they just experienced. Then send them off to their "precinct" areas for small-group time.

⊚ 7:30 P.M.—Bible Study in Small Groups

Since so many visitors will come to Come Alive Week, small groups make an excellent setting for teaching and for sharing the gospel in personalized ways. Try working the spy theme through your teaching time (perhaps "Mission: Possible—Searching to Know God"). Use active lessons that involve kids in firsthand exploration of Bible concepts and provide opportunities for them to discuss the Bible concept of each lesson.

🌀 8:30 P.M.—Closing

Close the evening with a fun snack (like root beer floats, nachos with cheese sauce, ice-cream sandwich sundaes, or pizza), more music and competition, and plenty of time to socialize.

The Benefits of the New Structure

🌀 Placed at the start of the summer, this program helps build group identity and helps incoming students feel like a part of the group.

🌀 The fast-paced evenings are wonderful ways for kids to reach out to their friends and bring them to church.

🌀 As a transition between children's programs and youth ministries, activities are designed with the familiarity and security common to younger children but the excitement of being away from the church that is more typical of youth ministry.

🌀 **Transform Traditional Camp to L.I.F.E. (Living in Foreign Environments)**

The Shortcomings of the Traditional Structure

Camp is great, but too often the education portion is based on lecture-style teaching. Although pre-

teens love camp, the church must make Christian camps truly excellent in order to compete with the large number of sports camps and recreation programs now offered to our kids during the summer.

The New Design

L.I.F.E. (Living in Foreign Environments) is a restructuring of the traditional camp experience to ensure that every aspect is age appropriate for preteens and educationally sound:

🌀 Campers are grouped by friendships into small groups led by a handpicked cabin leader.

🌀 Cabin leaders give special attention to bonding relationships within their groups. The students work together to select their own cabin names, create a cabin cheer or song and decorate their cabin. Leaders create cabin T-shirts, pins or visors to help kids connect as a group.

🌀 Active elements such as games, hikes, skits and recreation are high energy and fun but minimize competition and the necessity for athletic skill.

🌀 Chapel lessons are taught with active and interactive education and appeal to the spiritual, intellectual, social and physical needs of students.

🌀 The mixture of rowdy recreation and quiet cabin activities appeal to a variety of learning styles.

Additions to the Ministry

🌀 **Friday Nite Live (once each month)**

Friday Nite Live (FNL) is designed to help kids transition from children's ministries to youth ministries. It provides a youth group-type activity once each month on a Friday night.

Students play large-group games and have upbeat music. In the large group, the Bible is taught by a youth leader focusing on contemporary issues that are of interest to the students, such as peer groups, drugs, parents, friends, guy-girl relationships, and death and dying. Then students divide into small groups with two adults (usually a married couple) for discussion and application.

FNL serves as a training ground for evangelizing

friends and for leading students into grappling with abstract concepts in practical ways.

Life2Life2Life Missions Trip

Missions trips are ideal for giving early adolescents hands-on experiences in serving others and sharing their faith. The name suggests the pattern of 2 Timothy 2:2: "And the things you have heard me say in the presence of many witnesses entrust to reliable men who will also be qualified to teach others."

Typically, preteens enjoy being involved in some kind of maintenance work at orphanages or with the elderly. They are able to spend time with people, play with other kids, sing, perform dramas or puppet shows and share testimonies. Those who want to go on the missions trip should be trained in the culture, goals of the trip and ministry before being approved to go. (See chapter 12 for more ideas on where to go and what to do with preteen kids.)

S.O.S. (Summer of Service/Serving Our Savior)

This is a training program designed to train preteens to serve in programs for younger children. It may be held concurrently with Vacation Bible School or at other times such as spring break or Saturdays during the school year.

The students meet for the first hour to receive teacher training from their adult small-group leaders in key teaching and leadership skills, including training in storytelling, drama, crafts, music, discipline and talking with children during guided play. If S.O.S. coincides with VBS or another program for younger children, have the kids practice what they have learned in the second hour. This requires preparation of your VBS teachers to have a vision for helping their student teachers.

Design Your Ministry on Principles, Not Other People's Models

Our desire in presenting this model is to give you one complete big picture of how to put an entire age-appropriate ministry together. It is not so that you will feel compelled to copy this pattern or to include all of the various elements in your ministry.

Over the past few years, conferences around the United States have drawn thousands of ministry leaders to see how certain successful churches are doing their ministry. In these conferences, participants are warned to study the principles and not to go home and try to copy someone else's ministry. After every conference, however, leaders return home and forget these warnings. All too often these same leaders become casualties in ministry.

We cannot copy other people's ministries. Please gain from this model and from the concepts in this book what can be done, *and why*, and then have a ball inventing your own approach to preteen ministry!

Notes

1. Michael A. James, "Early Adolescent Ego Development," *The High School Journal* (March 1980), p. 249.
2. Neil Postman and Charles Weingartner, *Teaching as a Subversive Activity* (New York: Dell Publishing Co., 1969), p. 52.

Creating a Group Identity— A Place to Belong

> "Adolescents are particularly vulnerable to alienation ... to be alienated is to lack a sense of belonging, to feel cut off from family, friends, school, or work—'the four worlds of childhood.' It is during this time that adolescents seek independence. But it is also a time when group identity is needed so that the individual will become socially integrated."
>
> —Joanne M. Arhar, University of South Florida[1]

All of us have a God-given need for relationships. We need at least a few good friendships and a place where we feel as though we belong. Early adolescents have a pronounced need for both of these things.

Observe your students. You will find that much of the way they behave has some relationship to these felt needs—friendships and belonging. In the next chapter, we will discuss ways to help preteens build friendships and find a meaningful place in the group, a group with an identity that they can be proud of.

Early adolescents want to be accepted by their peers. They need the security that comes with belonging to a group. This is part of the reason that gangs have such attraction to kids in these years.

Give Kids Ownership of the Group

To give kids ownership of the group, begin by finding out what they think is fun and meaningful, and then focus more energy in those directions, especially as it serves the goals of your ministry. Be sensitive to what you hear from the kids. Listen and take action when appropriate.

Lois Sherwin, a children's ministry director from California, surveys her preteens twice each year. She uses the surveys to find out what's going on in the lives of her kids. She asks questions such as these:

◎ Who are your best friends?

◎ What school do you go to?

◎ What musical groups do you listen to?

What are your favorite TV programs?

What do you like best about church right now?

If you could change anything about church or our youth group right now, what would it be?

Lois's staff uses two or three Sunday School sessions in the weeks following each survey to answer questions that the kids posed on their surveys and to give feedback to them about their suggestions. When necessary, the staff explains why some suggestions won't be able to be implemented.

Another aspect of group ownership is taking responsibility for the work of the group. How can we entrust increasing amounts of responsibility to kids? How can we get our students to be responsible group members? Kids need to be offered responsibility, but they also must be taught skills to aid them in following through on these responsibilities.

Here are some tips for working with preteens to help them take on responsibilities in their group:

Give kids specific, realistic assignments. Whether it's an article for the newsletter or a service project, preteens need to know exactly what you expect of them. What you assign also needs to be within their capabilities (which will vary from child to child). Allow them tremendous liberty in how they complete assignments, but be clear on your expectations. This is the first step in setting them up to succeed.

Remember that early adolescents have little concept of time and deadlines. It's just a fact of life. We noticed it with our studious preteen daughter who still needed to be reminded about school deadlines looming near. Preteen kids do not have a practical frame of reference for time and, therefore, must be repeatedly and kindly reminded about deadline dates.

Hold kids accountable for the responsibilities you entrust to them. The important thing is loving accountability. Life is a learning experience, and kids will learn from their failures and from their successes, from what they do right and from the mistakes they make. Some of the mistakes they make and failures they experience will be in the responsibilities you have entrusted to them. It's OK to point out when a child drops the ball, but it's also important to let the child know you still believe in him or her and the child's ability to accomplish what you entrust to him or her. Maintain an atmosphere in which failure is not fatal.

Remain steadfast in your desire to entrust responsibility to kids. It's important for kids to be involved, but it doesn't make your job easier—just different. Instead of doing all the work yourself, now you'll be working at explaining, training, guiding and reminding your students. It will take just as much time as doing it yourself, so you just have to remind yourself that your goal is getting students involved and helping them learn new skills and experience personal growth.

Make Kids Feel Part of the Group

It's important that we make preteens feel included in the group in whatever ways we can. Try one or more of these ideas:

Spotlight kids as "stars" of the week. Train kids to share their personal testimonies about their own faith journey. Then take turns giving students the center of attention as they present a three- or four-minute life story. Ask parents to collect favorite pictures or memorabilia with their child and send them in on the assigned

Sunday. This will help kids get to know one another and feel special.

◎ **Select several regular attenders to serve on a leadership team.** Meet regularly with these students to listen to them. Ask them what was good and what could have been better about recent socials or activities. Heed their advice when planning future events. Take time to mentor their special leadership potential.

◎ **Choose students to help plan socials.** You or another adult leader can meet with a group of kids to plan and execute upcoming events from start to finish. Let them decide what they'll eat, how you'll decorate, and other matters that affect the students' enjoyment of the evening. If your group is large enough, try choosing different kids for each activity.

◎ **Create service teams within your ministry.** These teams will serve the youth group itself. Some kids are great servants. Here are some great tasks for preteens to accomplish for the good of their peers:

◎ Setting up chairs or resetting for the next group that will use the room.

◎ Serving a snack.

◎ Taking attendance.

◎ Passing out classroom Bibles, pens or markers and any handouts.

◎ Cleaning chalkboards or dry-erase boards before and after class.

When you really put some thought into it, you will find there are many things adults in your ministry do that kids could be doing. And by doing these things, kids will gain an even deeper sense of belonging to the group.

Never Underestimate the Power of a Name

The name you use for your preteen ministry is important. It will be the first impression that many kids and almost all adults have of your min-

istry. Therefore, it is important that you carefully choose the name that will be your group's identity statement. Here are some factors to consider:

◎ **The name must be kid-friendly.** Names for preteen ministries need to sound fun. They can't be "geeky" or sound overly "churchy." Diane Pitman gives us this guidance: "Pick a name with excitement, that can be visualized and has some spiritual significance." The name you choose must, more than anything else, appeal to your students!

◎ **It must be usable as an identity.** Some names may sound good, but if they don't lend themselves to a visual representation, they will be hard to use in a logo. If they're too long or wordy, they'll be hard to remember and will end up getting shortened anyway. The name should be one that offers inspiration for spin-off names you may use to describe different aspects of your programming. In the example of LiveWires given in chapter 7, the name has many programs under its umbrella with names that relate to it, like PowerPacks (alternative to traditional Sunday School) and SuperCharge (large-group worship service).

◎ **Finally, the name must sell your ministry to the parents and potential adult workers.** Here's the balance: We can't turn off the adults we partner with in ministering to preteens. They need to be excited about the ministry name, too. Everyone associated with your preteen group should be glad to be identified with it!

Make sure your ministry name relates, for the adults involved, some of the most positive and fun-loving aspects of these kids. Also, whether the name specifically identifies the members of the group or just fits so well that it makes your congregation think of these kids, the name should have a logical connection with preteens to help parents understand who you're talking about.

Creating a Great Ministry Name

A number of church leaders shared with us their names for their ministry to early adolescents. Let's see what we can learn from some successful leaders who have created identity with names. Here are some of the most fun, creative names we ran across:

◎ "Slap Dog" was created by kids by spelling "God Pals" backward.

◎ "Hot Shots" came from Grace Church in Edina, Minnesota.[2]

◎ "Faith Corps" was used at Eagle Mountain International Church in Newark, Texas.

◎ "Club 56" is used in several churches across America.

There are some common strengths that make these names good choices for early adolescent ministries:

◎ They sound cool. For example, "Slap Dog" sounds similar to the currently popular Big Dog brand of sportswear.

◎ They are action oriented and give a sense of fun. Several names remind us of power and energy.

◎ Each one is broad enough to use as a theme throughout the ministry's various programs and each has visual potential for mascots and logos.

◎ All of the examples have a punchy, crisp sound that is appealing to the ear.

◎ Each connotes something positive to the kids.

◎ To varying degrees, each of the ministry names gives a brief vision of the ministry or identification for the adults involved as staff or parents.

How to Create a Great Logo

If you have the budget to handle it, a quick search of the Internet using the keywords "create logos" will unearth numerous professional agencies that will help you create a logo, and every imaginable support document using that logo, for varying fees.

A logo that incorporates a symbol or graphic element can be a strong focal point for your preteen ministry. When creating a logo, consider these choices:

◎ Illustrative logo—a logo that includes an illustrative representation of what your company does.

◎ Graphic logo—a logo that includes a graphic (or abstract) representation of what your company does.

◎ Font-based logo—a dynamic type treatment that is unique to your company.

◎ A combination of all of the above.

When designing your logo, consider these factors as well:

◎ **What's your budget?** If you have enough money, hire a professional. And if you do, expect the best. Be sure to ask up front whether or not you are purchasing the exclusive use of this creation. If you want the drawings to be your property, you will need to pay more.

Start out by telling the artist (whether paid or volunteer) exactly what you're looking for in a logo. The artist may have a better idea, but he or she needs to know what you are looking for and how you plan to use it. Don't be afraid to provide too much detail—right down to the color scheme you desire or a type of animal to depict in the logo. Every ounce of information counts.

Ask the artist to provide you with at least three different versions of your logo for you to evaluate and from which you can choose. Tell the artist what you like and don't like, and give him or her the opportunity to go back to the drawing board until you are satisfied.

If you're on a budget, consider browsing through a variety of computerized clip art books and discs to see if someone has already created something wonderful that you could use.

☺ **Is there a regional theme that would work well to identify your ministry?** A youth pastor at one church in the Southwest called his youth group "Oasis." It fit well with their need for water down there! And it was inviting to kids physically, emotionally and spiritually. Not having many lakes in his area, the graphics that included water, palm trees and camels were both fun and different from the norm, while still fitting into their desert lifestyle.

☺ **What colors are hot with your preteens this year?** It's good to be aware of what colors the kids are into right now, but be aware that if you choose to use these colors, you will need to recolor your logo every year or two. Several years ago, when fluorescent colors were all the rage, we created a logo that looked great. The next year, it didn't look great anymore, but it was simple enough that we could use the same drawing with different colors. Make sure your logo has that flexibility.

☺ **Does it look fun?** Your logo needs to be just as cool and fun as your ministry name is. Our suggestion is to show both your ministry name and the logo to at least 20 other people before you adopt it, and make sure half of these are kids the age of your youth group. Listen to their feedback. Make sure that you don't tip them off so that they say the things you want to hear. It's easier to hear criticism before you have 350 T-shirts printed up!

☺ **Is the logo simple enough to print attractively?** For most of us, the logo will be (at least occasionally) reproduced on a photocopier. Does it look okay in black and white and will the copier be able to pick up on its finer points and any gray scales? Try running a few copies to see.

Also, your budget comes into play again on this issue. For preteens, group logos will eventually show up on T-shirts. Can your logo be reproduced with one color on a T-shirt and still look attractive? If not, are you willing to pay the extra money for a multicolor silkscreen each time you make T-shirts?

In these ways and many others, you can help kids gain a sense of a group identity. You give them the clear sense that they are a part of something bigger than themselves. You give them a ministry they can be proud of.

Notes

1. Joanne M. Arhar in Judith L. Irvin, ed., *Transforming Middle Level Education* (Needham Heights, MA: Allyn and Bacon, 1992), p. 142.
2. Hot Shots Preteen Ministry developed by Jerenne Block, Associate of Youth Ministries, Arizona Community Church, Tempe, Arizona.

> A friend loves at all times, and a
> brother is born for adversity.
> Proverbs 17:17

Small Groups Help Preteens Develop Relationships with Their Peers

Relationships are key to long-term spiritual growth and involvement in church life for the emerging adolescent. Kids who do not have friends at church do not enjoy themselves and do not keep coming back.

John and Susan are brother and sister, adults now, but brought up by the same parents attending the same church in their younger years.

Susan found her friends at church. She continued being fulfilled by attending church, even through her teen and young adult years and today is in professional Christian ministry herself.

However, John met few people his age and gender at church. His circle of friends became the boys in the Boy Scouts and in the sporting events he enjoyed. Most of these kids were not Christians. Although John still claims Christ today, he left the church in his early teen years and stopped actively living out his relationship with God as his non-Christian friends drew him away from the church. Today, he rarely attends church and is not leading his own growing family in the ways of the Lord.

What made the difference? We can't know all the ins and outs for sure, but the effects of having or not having friends who encourage and support your walk with God is self-evident. No one wants to attend a church where they don't feel they have at least one or two close friends.

For preteen ministry to be successful, the ministry leader must account for the socialization needs of the preteen child that are central to this developmental stage. Preteens feel social acceptance is their number one concern. For leaders to accomplish their instructional objectives, the church program must provide for activities that meet students' socialization needs. Because of that socialization need, small groups must be incorporated into the preteen ministry in as many ways as possible. It is through small groups that early adolescents can get to know one another and build the friendships they need.

Small groups are a pivotal point between children's programs and youth programs and an essential ingredient to any complete preteen ministry. Although younger children certainly want to belong and to have friends, the need for relationships becomes central in preteen years. Within a small-group setting, it is much more likely that students will get to know a significant adult and a group of peers. Both are necessary to the healthy development of the preadolescent.

The great news about small groups is that any church can do them. They do not require finances or church facilities. They require only loving adults who are willing to give up a few hours each week to lead preteens.

For the small-group ministry to be healthy, it must be a positive and encouraging environment. The early adolescent longs for a group of peers in which he or she can develop trust and find caring. Where these elements are built, the small group will flourish. According to Karen Wood, professor at the University of North Carolina at Charlotte, involvement in small groups can increase in sensitive preteens "a greater acceptance of differences in peers" as they spend time together.[1] Once the relationships and trust are built, then the small group becomes a wonderful environment for teaching biblical truths.

For preteens, small groups are essential for both education and discipleship. Educationally, small groups lend themselves naturally to one of the most effective means of teaching preteens—cooperative learning. Spiritually, discipleship relationships within the context of the small group allow for several kids to be mentored at once and for deeper relationships than are usually created in the typical Sunday School setting.

Here are two ideas for incorporating small groups into your ministry:

1. In every educational setting, begin incorporating the use of small groups. This ensures consistency throughout your programming and immerses preteens in the small-group culture.

Even if you have only six or eight preteens, you can create two small groups.

2. Create affinity groups. Find adults who are willing to share their special skills or hobbies with kids. At a church in Tucson, Arizona, where we served for almost a decade, a group of preteen leaders started a hiking club, an arts and crafts club, a drama team and a leadership team. Each affinity group functioned as a small group but met with the stated purpose of accomplishing some shared activity or interest. Deep relationships often flourish around a shared interest.

A Key Educational Tool for Preteens Is Cooperative Learning

This technique is educationally sound since it involves all of the students in the learning and thinking process. It helps kids establish relationships and breaks down cliques as the kids work together to discover new truths. Through their interaction they discover similarities in their interests. They may be surprised at how much they have in common that they might not have discovered had they been simply an audience for a leader's presentation.

As part of the small-group interaction, cooperative learning can be used to involve students in the learning process. Preteens have a critical need to hear and appreciate other people's ideas and to communicate their own ideas to their peers. There are a number of reasons why small groups work well for preteens when they utilize cooperative learning.

◉ **Cooperative learning in small groups allows preteens to talk.** Discussion with their peers is far more energizing for early adolescents than listening to the leader talk. Think of it this way: For many preteens, the mouth must be moving for the brain to be working.

◉ **Cooperative learning in small groups motivates kids to learn**. According to David and Roger Johnson, cooperative learning promotes motivation to learn in several ways. Students have motivation, incentive to learn, high expectations to succeed and a high commitment to continue learning.[2]

🌀 **Cooperative learning in small groups allows kids to move.** Preteens need to move. Because active learning is involved, kids are up and moving around during the interactive learning activities, demonstrations and games. The informality of a small-group setting also helps the energetic preteen who can appropriately lean forward, stretch, get down on the floor or otherwise move those growing muscles.

🌀 **Cooperative learning in small groups helps kids develop values.** Discussion is also an important part of values development. Preteens are moving away from thinking concretely and taking the value statements of authority figures at face value. They are moving toward young adulthood, which involves thinking abstractly and rethinking and owning every value for themselves. Discussion with peers is a critical aspect of refining what the student believes about life, morality, God and himor herself. The experience of discussing their values publicly helps students strengthen their beliefs.

🌀 **Cooperative learning in small groups provides positive support for the student.** While all of the many physical, emotional, social and spiritual changes are taking place in the preteen's world (inside and out!), they need people around them who understand and support them.

David and Roger Johnson tell us that cooperative learning is built around positive interdependence,

which is an environment that encourages students to support each other. Students are supported by having mutual goals, dividing tasks and resources and having individual roles with their groups. "In order for a learning situation to be cooperative, students must perceive that they are positively interdependent with other members of their learning group."[3] This type of small-group learning typically results in bonding friendships with work partners.

🌀 **Cooperative learning in small groups also gives support and encouragement to low achievers.** This is perhaps the area in which cooperative learning has been most criticized in the public school system. It has unfairly been branded as a way to dumb down education, since the group must work with kids who are thought of as slow. This is not only untrue educationally, but it is an inappropriate attitude in the church.

When the students who "get it" or who just happen to be maturing a little faster find themselves helping or encouraging others in their cooperative learning group, they are taking on the roles of leaders and teachers. When we teach others, we actually learn more ourselves. This approach also gives everyone in the group an opportunity for further synthesis and application of the biblical lessons. In the context of the church, it also allows them to experience real ministry in serving others.

Meanwhile, your new students, nonbelievers, or those who aren't understanding the content as quickly, are not left to wonder what this is all about. They are given the opportunity, again in a secure environment, to ask questions, get help and make their own discoveries. Instead of dumbing down your Christian education program, cooperative learning ensures that everyone who wants to learn will be able to do so.

🌀 **Cooperative learning in small groups works because participants learn to respect the ideas and opinions of others.** Cooperative learning activities and discussions give students the wonderful experience of expressing their own ideas and listening to those of others.

However, to ensure the quality of this interaction, groups should be no larger than six to eight. This size will help students feel that their participation is necessary—and valuable.

Student leaders will discover that others have creative answers to questions. Also, quiet students will be happy to have an opportunity to share their thoughts in a smaller setting. It may be the first time that students have realized that others have legitimate, yet different, beliefs of their own.

As a leader, small-group discussions give you (and any small-group leaders you have enlisted) the opportunity to facilitate preteens' sharing and discussing ideas and learning to deal with differences. Kids must be taught these socialization skills. This is part of the big picture of Christian education: to prepare the preteen to deal well with his or her peers, even those with whom he or she may disagree.

◉ **Cooperative learning in small groups typically results in fewer behavioral problems in preteen classrooms and youth groups.** This is a wonderful fringe benefit. This occurs because students feel that they are somewhat in control of the direction of their own group. They are more involved in the learning process. And they know others are listening to their opinions and ideas.

In our summer camps, we used to have chapels in which Gordon spoke for 30 to 45 minutes with groups of 50 to 100 students. It was spellbinding—so spellbinding that eyes glazed and mouths dropped open. Some even uttered sighs of admiration (or were they snoring?). Then along came cooperative learning!

The first time that Gordon announced to our experienced camp counselors that we were actually going to have fifth and sixth graders turn to each other in small groups and discuss their answers to questions, the counselors almost mutinied. They were sure that nothing good could come of this technique! Reality proved them wrong.

After the first discussion period, Gordon took feedback from students and this time it was the adults'

mouths that dropped open. The preteens not only had stayed on task, but they also responded with deep insights. We were all hooked!

Keep Small-Group Discussions on Task

Once you have students in small groups, it is important to guide them in ways that will keep all of the students on task to accomplish the goals of each session. The way you set up a question or activity is essential.

Be sure that all students know they may have to report back to the group in one way or another and are, therefore, required to be involved in the discussion. David Johnson refers to this as "individual accountability."[4]

Here are some tools for keeping kids on task in small groups:

◉ **Have an adult or teen small-group leader oversee or facilitate each group.** Teachers with limited amounts of time to teach may find this helpful as well. The large-group leader or teacher can involve the whole class or youth group in a game or activity or share a short presentation. Then the leader can turn the students' attention back to their own small-group leaders who have been given curriculum with printed questions in advance. The small-group leaders can immediately launch into their own discussion of what just happened and can even shape the questions to better fit their students. The large-group leader should always float during this time to assist small-group leaders who are having trouble and to make sure that each group is on track regarding both the topic and the time schedule.

◉ **Number the kids in each small group.** Make sure that each member has a different number. Then ask a question or assign a task that requires all of the groups' members to work together and to listen to the other students' answers.

For example, you might say, "Put your heads together to respond to this question. Make sure that everyone in your group knows the answer. In a few minutes I will call on one member of each group to share your answers." After enough time has passed, call on all of the students with a specific number to stand and answer the question or further explain his or her group's findings.

This technique helps ensure all students stay connected since they never know when their number might be called to answer.

🌀 **Use the jigsaw puzzle technique**. Form small groups of three to six students (with each group being the same size); then number the students in each group. Be ready with three or more different learning activities that help reach the goals of your session. At the appropriate time, assign all students in each group with the number one to a specific task, led by an adult leader. Do this for each of the other numbers as well. With larger groups, you may want to have two kids from each small group participate in each learning activity. Then the kids in each number group will report the findings or results of their "piece of the puzzle" (part of the lesson) to the rest of the people in their original small group.

For example, in a lesson on faith and obedience in a non-Christian world, you might have one group of students (all the number ones) work on a skit to show the ways preteens must trust and obey in their lives. A second group (all the number twos) could watch part of a Bible video and look for three reasons to believe the account of Daniel's friends. The third group (all the number threes) might work together to read Daniel 3 and prepare a list of ways that Shadrach, Meshach and Abednego's challenges are similar to the faith-stretching events of life as a preteen today. Each activity may be led by an adult or by one of the students, depending on how you set up the project.

When these miniseminars are completed, the members of each group must return to their team and teach the other members all about their piece of the lesson. The skit group could conclude the session by presenting its application drama. This jigsaw technique maximizes involvement and peer mentoring. It also allows for a large amount of activity and a variety of approaches to reach the same learning aims.

Occasionally Mix the Group Members to Maximize the Small-Group Experience

There are several ways to purposefully expose kids to more potential friendships:

🌀 **Have assigned small groups that change quarterly.** Plan ongoing small groups for key elements of the session, like the opening activity, life application and prayer. Keep track of your students' attendance and evenly distribute regular attenders and infrequent attenders among the various small groups you form. This will help each group have a core of students. Three months will allow your small-group leaders to get to know the group members well enough to give you feedback on who should or should not be grouped together for the next quarter.

🌀 **Each month or so, offer kids an alternative affinity group.** We have successfully used affinity groups once each month, groups in which students are grouped according to their common interests or hobbies. They may choose from computers, service projects, discipleship, art and recreation activities. The leader of each group weaves Bible study into his or her specialty and the kids get to meet others who are interested in the same topic or activity but who are not necessarily in their regular small group. Also, have special activities so that kids can choose to do something different once each month or so.

🌀 **Have "upset basket" Sundays when no one is in his or her regular group.** As each preteen arrives, hand him or her a square of colored paper at random. Have each small-group leader dress in that color for the morning or wear a name tag made of paper of the same color. Kids will complain and ask if they can switch, but in the end they will enjoy the experience of working with a new adult and some peers they may not have spent much time with previously.

PRETEENS CAN BENEFIT FROM A VARIETY OF SMALL GROUPS

SUNDAY MORNING MINISTRIES

Coeducational small groups may be incorporated
into the regular educational and worship programs.

MIDWEEK CLUB MINISTRIES

Midweek clubs are a good time for single-gender small groups to
offer preteens a different type of relationship with an adult mentor.

AFFINITY SMALL GROUPS

Affinity small groups may attract preteens for shared interests
like hiking, drama, service, leadership team, or arts and crafts.

The Importance of Small-Group "Families"

The most important goal of small groups within your preteen ministry is to establish healthy relationships between students and adults in which mentoring and discipleship can take place. The small-group leader's goals must include helping each early adolescent feel significant and valued as a member of the group.

◎ **Emphasize the importance of small-group leaders being present to greet each member of the small group as he or she arrives.** This is true for Sunday School, youth group or any other ministry setting. Remember that preteens are very self-conscious. The first minute after they arrive in the room is critical. The more welcome and secure they feel, the better their whole morning will go.

◎ **Emphasize the importance of being genuine, real and transparent for the kids.** This may be the most important quality of the preteen small-group leader whose goal is to mentor and disciple their students. Neila Conners suggests that we "allow students to see the teacher as a real person with likes and dislikes, hobbies, and interests. . . . Students can meet with caring, sensitive, and informed adults who are prepared to help students learn how to make decisions and deal with their own personal development and self-concept."[5] Such positive and enriching contact with a d u l t s is priceless. "Every student needs to have a relationship with at least one adult . . . which is characterized by warmth, concern, openness, and understanding."[6]

Preteens are in the process of leaving the family and at the same time are desperately looking for another "family" to belong to. They need to build relationships with adults who can help them grow spiritually and help them learn how to live the Christian life. Consistency in both the leadership and membership of small groups is very important for providing an atmosphere in which strong bonds of friendship can be formed.

John was a fifth grader whose parents had divorced a year or two before he attended camp with us. Gordon got to know him in the context of a small-group setting. When asked how he felt about having to go back and forth between two homes and never having the attention of both his parents at one time, John said that it was cool. After all, he got "two bedrooms and two sets of everything!" It was about a year later, though, that the cool wore off and the reality of the loss set in. Because of the relationship built, John could come to Gordon and share his change of heart and look for comfort and guidance.

The adult who wants to disciple a small group of preteens must be willing to invest much of his or her time, encouraging them and supporting them. This preteen author (one of our personal favorites) tells it like it is:

Please Listen to Me

By Ashley West

Sometimes when you don't listen,

My body feels so small.

I feel as tiny as a mouse,

That has no voice at all.

Whenever you interrupt me,

I blow up like a bomb . . .

Especially when you're an adult,

Just like my dad or mom.

If you would take one second,

I'd give you all I've got.

If just one time you'd listen to me,

You'd see what I've learned and thought.

The leader must invest in genuine, caring relationships with the kids. The leader can build relationships with kids in so many ways. Just do things with the kids that are important to them:

⊚ Attend their sporting events.

⊚ Be there when they receive awards at school or badges in scouts.

⊚ Let them telephone you to tell you about hurt feelings or bad grades.

⊚ Take them to McDonald's for sodas when they do well on tests.

⊚ And maybe easiest, but most effective, invite them to hang out with you at your house, doing what you would be doing anyway, seeing you in action with your family, eating your food, watching your TV and learning what differences being a Christian makes in your everyday life.

Of course, in today's world, the preteen leader must be smart about the ways he or she chooses to spend time with kids. Make sure that you take necessary precautions to keep yourself above reproach. That means, don't be alone with a child, and avoid being too touchy. While with a group of kids and adults, just spend some one-on-one time with kids.

Even with all the time preteen leaders should spend with kids, to remain socially healthy, they should also spend quality time with other adults. Mark Oestreicher gives us this precaution: "If junior highers [or preteens] replace your adult friends, you've got a problem on your hands. Either you're allowing young teens' admiration of you to cloud your judgment, or you're a bit overzealous about your calling, or you're in need of therapy. Take a break. Catch your breath. Hang with people your own age. Work at building relationships with peers. It will keep you fresh in ministry."[7]

Jesus was the master of letting His followers hang out with Him while He went about His business. Robert Coleman explains, "Having called His men, Jesus made it a practice to be with them. This was the essence of His training program—just letting his disciples follow Him. ...One living sermon is worth a hundred explanations."[8] Just as Jesus chose a few men with whom He would work most closely, the preteen small-group leader must be selective about his or her time as well.

Many debate whether a small group should focus on the select few—particularly kids with potential for leadership—or be thrown open to the masses. Popular wisdom from the most experienced small-group leaders is that all preteens should be given an opportunity to be involved in small groups. This may be their first chance to commit to their own, personal spiritual growth.

Coleman tells us that with the disciples, "Jesus was willing to put up with a lot of those things which issued from their spiritual immaturity. He knew that they could master these defects as they grew in grace and knowledge. Their capacity to receive Revelation would grow provided they continued to practice what truth they did understand."[9] How much more should we be patient and accommodating to preteen kids who are even more of a work in progress?

What we teach preteens in small groups is not nearly as important as what we live in front of them is. Like Paul, we should beckon kids to "follow my example, as I follow the examples of Christ" (1 Corinthians 11:1). Long after our "disciples" forget everything that we tried to teach them, they will remember how we lived.

"As apostles of Christ we could have been a burden to you, but we were gentle among you, like a mother caring for her little children. We loved you so much that we were delighted to share with you not only the gospel of God but our lives as well, because you had become so dear to us. For you know that we dealt with each of you as a father deals with his own children, encouraging, comforting and urging you to live lives worthy of God, who calls you into his kingdom and glory" (1 Thessalonians 2:6-8,11-12). When the lesson is done, we should be able to be satisfied in telling our preteen students, "Whatever you have learned or received or heard from me, or seen in me—put it into practice. And the God of peace will be with you" (Philippians 4:9).

Should Parents of Preteens Lead Small Groups?

Yes and no.

One preteen pastor in Portland, Oregon, uses parents of the kids primarily for small-group leaders. The groups are short-term so that parents can rotate in and out and the kids get to draw close to a network of significant adults. Others avoid using parents, often based on the preference of their preteens.

Although they are starting to not want to hang out with mom and dad (at least not in public and around their peers), they do want relationships with people just like mom and dad. Preteens are not looking for grown-up friends as much as they desire to be led by mature adults.

We must be selective in choosing volunteers to work with preteens, but if a parent is otherwise appropriate for the ministry to this age group, the fact that he or she is a parent should be seen as positive, not negative. While you may not want to place a parent as the leader of his or her own child's small group, the parent can be an effective leader of another group of his or her child's peers.

Parents make great preteen small-group leaders for the following reasons:

🌀 They have already received months (or years) of real-life training on the characteristics of preteens.

🌀 They have a more vested interest in the spiritual health of the students in our ministry than even we do.

🌀 They have the wisdom and maturity that younger adults may not have.

🌀 They can benefit from seeing their own child interact with his or her peers.

🌀 They gain further wisdom in how to nurture their own preteen, thus furthering and deepening the potential ministry to our students.

🌀 Finally, the best benefit of all is what happens to a parent's stock in the eyes of his or her own child when a fellow student walks up to the leader's child and says, "Wow! I wish my dad were as cool as yours!"

Small Groups Create an Excellent Environment in Which to Evangelize Kids

In the context of a fun family group that does things together, the leader and other students are able to build friendships with the non-Christian preteen who might be coming along with a friend or just be new to the church. Out of that friendship, the preteen will start wanting to know more about what makes the other members of the group tick. This will eventually give an opening for reaching out to the non-Christian student to share the specifics of the gospel.

As the small-group leader gives of him- or herself for the kids, the preteen will also respond spiritually to that love. This is the example that Jesus left for us. God is love and love gives. "For God so loved the world that he gave his one and only Son, that whoever believes in him shall not perish but have eternal life. For God did not send his Son into the world to condemn the world, but to save the world through him. Whoever believes in him is not condemned" (John 3:16-18). The best way for a preteen to understand love is to see it lived out through the sacrificial living and giving of a loving adult leader. Think of the many ways that Jesus denied His own comforts in order to love people and help them understand the gospel. We need to be just as willing to serve our kids.

Should Small Groups at This Age Be Coed or Single Gender?

The debate rages on. Here are the advantages of each approach.

The Advantages of Separating Boys and Girls for Small Groups

🌀 In single-gender small groups, young men or young women are able to develop close relationships with role models of the same gender.

🌀 Preteens have a developmental need to have close friends of the same gender.

🌀 Same-gender groups may initially be easier to bond, since some activities will be naturals for each gender.

🌀 Since preteens are only beginning to show interest in the opposite gender and girls generally reach this point earlier than boys, many kids would initially prefer to be with only their own gender.

🌀 Some hot topics can be discussed more appropriately in single-gender groups, like physical changes and sexuality, which are so much on the minds of some early adolescents.

The Advantages of Combining Boys and Girls in Coed Small Groups

🌀 Young men and young women both need male and female role models. Coed groups led by a married couple are ideal because they also show preteens a picture of the value of Christian marriage and family life.

🌀 Preteens are becoming aware of the opposite gender and need healthy guidance in developing appropriate friendships. The small-group context is ideal for this training.

🌀 Coed groups allow for activities that may be considered traditionally male or female to be shared and experienced by both genders, allowing for a broader appeal to nontraditional kids!

🌀 Oftentimes in coed groups, boys tend to be less aggressive and girls tend to be friendlier. The mixture seems to bring out the best in both genders.

🌀 Some spiritual topics can be more fruitfully discussed in coed groups because a variety of opinions might be shared.

The Experts Confirm All That We Observe About Early Adolescents

They need relationships! "Early adolescence, especially in the United States, is a vortex of change. Concurrent with individual transformations, youth often experience dramatic shifts in school environment, the peer group, and the family. How well young people cope with these changes and demands and how they deal with the tasks of adolescence will significantly influence the course of their lives. The ability of young people to respond to new challenges depends on their personal capacities coming into the transition and the degree to which they are supported by a network of caring relationships."[10]

As leaders in the church, we want to make sure that the caring network of supportive relationships is a Christ-centered and faith-nurturing one so that the answers that the preteen comes up with for coping with adolescence are healthy—physically, psychologically and spiritually.

Notes

1. Karen Wood, *Transforming Middle Level Education* (Needham Heights, MA: Simon and Schuster, 1992), p. 316.

2. David W. Johnson and Roger T. Johnson, "Motivational Processes in Cooperative, Competitive, and Individualistic Learning Situations" in Carol Ames and Russell Ames, eds., *Research on Motivation in Education: The Classroom Milieu* (San Diego, CA: Academic Press, 1986), p. 276.

3. Ibid., p. 252.

4. Ibid., p. 253.

5. Neila A. Connors, "Teacher Advisory: The Fourth R" in Judith L. Ervin, ed., *Transforming Middle Level Education* (Needham Heights, MA: Allyn and Bacon, 1992), p. 163.

6. Ibid.

7. Mark Oestreicher, *Help! I'm a Junior High Youth Worker!* (Grand Rapids, MI: Zondervan Publishing House, 1996), p. 60.

8. Robert E. Coleman, *The Master Plan of Evangelism* (Old Tappan, NJ: Fleming H. Revell, 1963), pp. 38-39.

9. Ibid.

10. Anthony W. Jackson and David W. Hornbeck, "Educating Young Adolescents: Why We Must Restructure Middle Grade Schools," *American Psychologist* (May 1989), p. 833.

Games, Special Events and More!

"We treat the kids [with] respect . . . and expect much from them."

–Diane Pitman, Edina, Minnesota

How to Plan Kid-Approved Activities

Here are some helpful questions from toy industry insiders that you can use to help you as you plan special events, games or activities:

☉ **What activities have your kids really enjoyed in the past?** Think about the games and activities you know your kids love. What is it about them that the kids like? Consider doing a variation of one of the group's favorites as your next "new" game. Preteens seem to be able to play 101 variations of Capture the Flag.

☉ **Did you test the game or activity?** Get your own children together or the youth staff or your church staff, or at least talk through the game or activity with some other people to make sure it will work and to help you see things that you've overlooked.

☉ **Is the activity simple enough and planned out carefully?** The most wonderful game, activity or special event will fall flat if no one understands what he or she is supposed to do. Make sure that you've made the instructions easy and that you've thought of every detail, such as materials needed, safety issues and the goal of your activity.

☉ **Have you engaged your kids' imaginations?** "Capturing the imagination is what makes a game fun for older kids," states a former toy product designer.

☉ **Does the game or activity meet the social needs of early adolescents?** If the activity helps kids meet each other in a comfortable setting and allows them time to talk and to hang together, it will probably be pretty successful. Kids don't care too much about what they're doing if their social needs are being met![1]

Outrageous Games and Activities for Preteens

The ideas in this chapter intentionally present a range of options and ideas. In choosing games, activities and special events for your preteens, always determine the appropriateness of the

(for Smaller Churches)

Preteens exist for crowds of their peers. Unfortunately, you can't just manufacture more preteens for your event. Smaller churches might try appealing to the "crowded mall" mentality of their kids by

🌶 joining with other churches for special events;

🌶 advertising at the neighborhood schools to invite more preteens;

🌶 teaching your own preteens to invite friends;

🌶 including younger or older kids in the activity (but try to stay within the early adolescent period of 10 to 14 years of age);

🌶 making sure that your meeting room is not too big for the number of kids who will attend (make sure they "fill" the room, however small the group is).

theme or location for your church.

Ice Relay

When you gather your preteens for a swimming party, bring along an ice cube and several blocks of ice. (You can make these by freezing water in paper milk cartons.)

Have the kids line up in the swimming pool in straight lines as for a typical relay race. In the water, they will stay warm and enjoy the game much more than pool games where they must stand on the side and wait their turn. Also, you will be able to stand on the side and be seen as you give instructions.

Use the ice cube to demonstrate the relay you are about to ask kids to play: passing the ice cube backward between your legs to the next person in line behind you. Then bring out the ice blocks for the kids to use.

Tell the kids that they must pass the blocks back and forth, up and down their lines, until the ice is totally melted. This race is hilarious to watch, as

the ice cannot be seen from the side of the pool.

Mall Hunt

Games, kids and malls—this one is an automatic home run with preteens.

Recruit 10 to 12 adults or teens who do not normally work with your group. Ask them to arrive at the church at the beginning of your meeting, dressed in everyday clothes. Parade them up in front of the group and tell the kids to look closely at their faces and memorize them. Don't tell the kids why yet!

After a few minutes, dismiss the volunteers with instructions to go to the mall and change. The volunteers are to disguise their identities, but still blend in with the crowd at the mall. We have had young women put on wigs, glasses and padded maternity wear. One staff member portrayed a little old lady by dressing up with a hair net, cane and knitting needles. One man's costume was an empty cardboard box that he climbed into and shut the lid on. Give these volunteers 10 to 15 minutes of lead time by continuing on with your lesson, some music or presenting some other activity at church. Then explain the game to the kids.

The object of the mall hunt is for each group of five to six kids, led by an adult sponsor, to find as many of the volunteers as possible. When identified, the volunteers should give the team that found them a coupon. Coupons should be pieces of paper with a graphic or message on it. Each volunteer should have enough coupons to be able to provide each group with one if they are found.

Be sure to explain these rules:

🌀 Each group must stay with its leader at all times or else be disqualified.

🌀 No coupons will be issued to a group that is not together with all its members and leader.

🌀 No group may go into any store. All activity must remain in the main mall.

🌀 No volunteer will go more than about 5 to 10 feet into any store (to allow them to pretend to be shopping), but the volunteer will respond to any verbal request from the groups.

🌀 Since each group is competing against the others, each group must be discreet when it finds someone so that other groups are not tipped off.

🌀 Each group must be back at the designated meeting spot (a back mall entrance works well) at

Be sure to contact the mall's management office in advance to gain permission. Most malls are happy to allow this activity when they hear the rules and are asked in advance. All adult sponsors should carry the contact person's name in their pocket during the activity, because mall security may not have gotten the word!

the announced time or points will be deducted.

Surprise Water Balloon Volleyball

When the temperatures go up, try this game. Fill several hundred water balloons and place them in a plastic trash can. The more balloons, the more fun. If you don't use them all in the game, you can always end the event with a free-for-all water fight.

Have two volunteers hold up a sheet in place of a net, or if you have volleyball standards, hang several sheets over the net.

Divide your group in half, with one group on each side of the net. Throw one or more balloons into the game at a time. The kids must watch for the balloons coming over the "net" and must try to catch them without breaking them. If they are successful, they may lob them back over the net.

Keeping score is unnecessary. Everyone wins in this game, because sooner or later, everyone gets cooled off (including you)!

Raiders Run

Start your evening by showing a clip of an action movie or TV show in which the main character must triumph over a variety of physical chal-

lenges. Then divide the kids into teams of 5 to 10. Give each child except one on each team a rubber snake. You can make inexpensive snakes out of silicone tubing or buy them at a toy store. Be sure each team starts out one snake short. In order to be in play, the participants must have a rubber snake in their hands. The kids with no snake start out the game in the designated "jail." All of the players with snakes must stick together with their teams at all times during the game.

The object of the game is for a group of kids to travel from clue to clue that you have hidden. They will be looking for the treasure, which may be an actual prize or the focus of your lesson for the night.

Have several leaders on rooftops (if played outdoors) or on ladders or balconies (if played indoors), each with a can of Silly String to be used as "spider webs." Have another set of leaders with water balloon "bombs" to smash on the ground in front of kids. (Make sure not to drop the balloons on kids.) Finally, two or three staff members roll a large inflated earth ball "boulder" (available from various recreational resource catalogs) around on the ground chasing the kids.

If players get hit by any of the hazards—spider webs, bombs, or boulder—they must leave their teammates and go directly to the designated jail area. Here they turn over their snake to the first player in line, who may then return to his or her team.

This game can expand or contract to fill as much or as little time as you desire.

Bubbly Beverage Bonanza!

Have your preteens bring their favorite can of soda to your next gathering. During the event, find a grassy area and have the kids line up in teams as for a relay. Have the first person in each line get down on his or her hands and knees and use only his or her nose to roll the can of soda down the lawn to an insulated drink cooler with its lid off. When the participant reaches the cooler, he or she opens the can of soda (stand back!) and pours it in the cooler before running back to tag the next person on his or her team. Add ice and serve the Bubbly Beverage later in the evening. (For some reason, it almost always tastes like root beer!)

TP Tightrope

Buy enough rolls of toilet paper so that you have one roll for every two students in your group. Then go to a hallway or outside where there is plenty of room. Tell the kids that when you blow the whistle, they should back up from each other with one person holding the roll and the other pulling the end of the paper. See which pair can unroll the longest

As with any messy game, after the mess is made, have the kids work together to see who can pick up the most pieces the quickest.

piece of toilet paper in the shortest amount of time without breaking the "tightrope."

Hide and Seek/Hide and Don't Seek

When you are in a camp or retreat setting, this game is good for your staff and your students.

Play Hide and Seek with the adults doing the hiding on the first evening. Tell the kids they must stay together in their cabin groups (or teams of five to seven students). Only when they find an adult as a group does it count as a valid catch. Heighten the excitement by letting the teams that find adults bomb the adults with water balloons at the end.

The next night, repeat the game with the kids hiding (in pairs or trios). This time, however, have your staff start to look for kids and then discreetly slip back into some prearranged meeting place for a few minutes of refreshments, relaxation and relief from their leadership duties. The kids love the fact that they never get found and the adults love their few minutes of rest!

And don't worry about reusing this game. You can always wait a few years before recycling it, or you can reuse it in a fifth-and-sixth-grade camp every

year, and those students who have played it before will think it's cool to be one up on you!

Cold Turkey

For a special game at a preteen event around Thanksgiving time (or during those festive days of after-Thanksgiving leftover turkey), play Cold Turkey. Have kids sit in a circle facing toward the center. Play Hot Potato, but use a frozen, wrapped Cornish game hen as the "potato." With a smile and a twinkle in your eye, tell the kids that the hen is a baby turkey.

Play one of your students' favorite CDs as the "turkey" is passed. When the music stops, the one holding the turkey is out. Continue playing until only two players remain. The winner of the last round gets the grand prize—the turkey!

Turkey Bowling

This is another good November activity. Gather 10 empty two-liter bottles and a wrapped Cornish game hen. Have kids use the hen as a bowling ball in their attempt to knock down the two-liter bowling pins.

Super Scramble Bowling

Super Scramble Bowling takes the competitive edge off of the game and helps kids mix during your activity.

Have the same number of students (three or four work best) and/or leaders on each lane. Instead of writing names on the score sheet, write down player 1, 2, 3, and so on. Have each bowler in every lane bowl one frame and record his or her score.

After each frame, announce who will move using the following list (which should also be posted at each lane):

☺ Frame 1—Highest scorer for this frame moves one lane to the right and takes over the position that was left by the bowler who just moved from this spot.

☺ Frame 2—Highest scorer for this frame switches places with lowest scorer in same lane.

☺ Frame 3—Anyone who bowled a gutter ball

has to find another bowler who bowled a gutter ball and switch places with him or her.

🌀 Frame 4—Lowest score from this frame moves one lane to the left and assumes the position of the bowler who just left.

🌀 Frame 5—Super Scramble! On "go," everyone must find a new lane and the highest cumulative score goes to the first person to get there.

🌀 Frame 6—Lowest cumulative score in each lane adds 10 points to his or her total.

🌀 Frame 7—Highest cumulative score in each lane subtracts 10 points.

🌀 Frame 8—Anyone who has scored a strike in any frame of the game must find another strike bowler to trade places with.

🌀 Frame 9—Super Scramble! (Choose one or more of the above!)

🌀 Frame 10—Bowler who scored closest to seven in this frame wins!

Creative Arts and Performance Groups

Early adolescents need to be exposed to a variety of activities and be able to sample from a wide array of experiences. This helps kids discover their gifts, talents and interests. For this reason, most true middle schools will have students make several short-term choices of electives.

At church, we commonly have children in children's choirs and focus a large amount of their creative expressions in the area of music, with drama a close second in larger programs. For preteens, we need to rethink this approach and provide a variety of creative options. Here are a few that work well:

Developing Music and Fine Arts Electives

An excellent way to expose preteens to a variety of experiences is to create a music and fine arts evening. This can be done either at a time when you have other activities going on at church or on an evening just for preteens.

Enlist appropriate teens and adults from your church and community who have music or fine arts talents and are willing to spend a few weeks

"How do you feel about school?"

"I like school because it's fun."
—Robert, Seventh Grader

"It's challenging, kind of fun once in a while."
—Bill, 11 Years Old

"What do you like best about school?"

"The electives. Right now I'm in shop."
—Robert

"PE and the specials we get to do like music, library, art, computer lab and all that stuff."
—Bill

with your students. Have the students gather each week for a large-group opening session in which you can lead students in an interactive study, play a game together or sing a few songs. Then break into focus groups in which the students spend four to six weeks working on whatever specialty project for which you've been able to recruit a leader: writing poetry, sculpting clay, painting, playing the piano, drawing, making macramé, making origami shapes, playing percussion instruments, singing, choreographing, designing sets, using puppets, creating videos, photographing, or whatever!

At the end of each session, include your parents and families by having an open house at which students may show off their craft from the last several weeks.

A pattern similar to this has been very successful for Central Christian Church in Mesa, Arizona. This church's preteen ministry includes a music and fine arts program called Adventure Zone to occupy kids during the Saturday evening adult electives just prior to the Saturday evening outreach service. This church found the enrichment program to be a solid offering during an evening designed for outreach into the community, since so many parents would desire for their children to have more exposure to creative arts than most schools offer today.

Making Choirs Preteen Friendly

Several of the preteen girls we interviewed named singing as their favorite thing to do at church! But don't expect preteen boys to come out unless the program is really "hot." Here are some ways to attract preteens and keep them coming to your choir program:

◎ Always have scheduled performances, so kids know they will perform regularly. Pick performance locations that take the kids away from church.

◎ Every practice must be fun and, better yet, include food.

◎ Choose your leaders carefully. Make sure they are fun people.

◎ Select upbeat, contemporary, easy-to-sing songs. The music should feel more like youth music than children's music.

◎ Use movements that go along with the words of the song.

◎ Have kids with musical ability help lead choirs or worship sessions.

◎ Take your choirs out of town on tours. Travel seems grown-up to kids, and grown-up is "hot."

◎ Work at recruiting guys who are thought of as leaders in your group to join choir. This is the secret to getting the rest of the boys to think it's cool enough to join.

Making Drama Teams Preteen-Friendly

One way to simplify drama and make it more enjoyable for your students is to teach them to ad-lib. Choose a published script and read the script to your drama team. Next, guide the students through identifying the major ideas in the script and specific key lines. Once the big picture is identified, have your kids get on their feet and act out the skit. With this approach, you should be able to get a skit ready with one or two simple, painless rehearsals.

Now make this group important! Have them perform for the younger children in Sunday School. Four-year-olds through second graders are especially appreciative and their awe of these older actors will not go unnoticed by your egocentric preteens!

Making Puppet Teams Preteen-Friendly

Puppetry is an old standby that is often forgotten in today's preteen ministries. Early adolescents enjoy playing characters and being creative without having to stand up in front of their peers.

To start your team, ask two or three adults to prepare and present a truly top-notch puppet show to the preteens. (Or ask the puppeteers from another church in your area to perform for your kids.) Use this performance to promote your puppetry group, and be ready to take sign-ups immediately after the performance.

Selecting a published script from a puppetry or drama book is the simplest way to prepare a puppet show. Have a few people (either kids or adults) record the script on a tape recorder. Amplify the voices so that they can be heard and understood. Have your voices speak slowly enough for the puppets' mouths to be able to keep up!

Your team will be ready to perform for younger children immediately. As long as the words can be heard, it doesn't matter for younger children how well the puppeteers manipulate their puppets.

Special Events for Preteens

Preteens have reached an age when they need more than just weekend services and weekday clubs at church. These students have the need and desire to spend time together. Remember that socialization is critical to preteens. Special events can help fill this need. When designed specifically for the early adolescent, they also serve as a transition between children's ministries and youth ministries, preparing the late-elementary child to be an active youth group member of the future.

Disability Awareness Weekend

Make this a special weekend for your preteens and the community by hosting a disability awareness weekend. Get help from a church in town that has a significant ministry to people who have disabilities.

Include in your weekend some or all of the following:

❂ Ask a guest speaker who has a disability to share his or her testimony. Contact Christian colleges or campus clubs for leads.

❂ Lead music in your church service or youth group with overhead transparencies purposely projected out of focus (as one with a visual impairment might see them) or with the letters of various words scrambled (as one with a reading disability might see them).

❂ Establish a maze or obstacle course in a safe environment. (Remove sharp corners or things that could trip someone.) Then blindfold participants, and have them feel their way through the course.

Turkey Bowl

Around Thanksgiving, gather all of your preteens together for the Turkey Bowl, at which students, sponsors and even parents join to play flag football. The girls (young and old) get to run full force, but have the guys hold one foot behind themselves with one hand while hopping on the other foot. After the game, plan on gathering everyone together somewhere warm for hot cocoa and cookies!

Here are some tips for different situations:

❂ If you don't have a big enough crowd, challenge another church's preteen youth group to a game.

❂ If you only have a muddy field to play on, be glad! This improves your annual Turkey Bowl! You may even want to water down a dry field to

make your own mud. Be sure to tell your kids to dress appropriately.

Almost any activity in this chapter can become an evangelistic event for preteens and their friends or families. Make every preteen activity so much fun that you can promise kids that they will never be embarrassed to bring a friend. Never place your students in the awkward position of having to apologize for a poorly run, untested activity or event.

Some ideas for outreach events could be renting paintball guns to aim at youth leaders, renting inflatable bounce tanks or hiring contemporary bands—anything to attract early adolescents. Then sometime during each event, present the gospel in a positive, relevant way. In your message, focus on God's love for the preteen.

Indoors, you can have everyone hold one foot behind his or her back.

Game Nights for Preteens

Large, fun events are important for building relationships and for transitioning kids from the style of children's ministry to the youth group approach. These might be considered the "edge" between children's and youth ministries.

Dale Torry, a junior high and missions pastor, offers a game night once each month on a Friday night for his Club 56. These evenings are created completely around games and relationships, to be with preteens and to do stuff. Using the gym at church, he has done everything from whipping up 50-gallon batches of Jell-O to play games in and with to collecting refrigerator boxes for human bowling and tank wars. He always includes a meal, often pizza or hot dogs.

Laser Tag

Laser tag is not available everywhere, but it's a big enough thrill for preteens to drive a ways if you must. If you have enough kids, you can normally arrange for a private party.

This very safe activity is conducted in a dark room where participants run around in multilevel human mazes. Each person wears a vest and a helmet with electronic targets and carries a laser gun that shoots beams of light. Score is given for each hit on another player, and a computer keeps track of 20 or 30 players at the same time.

Join in with your kids. It's a great workout!

Creative New Lock-Ins for Preteens

Lock-ins are a must for your preteen calendar of events—especially in the fall. When kids are back in school and the group is up and running for the year, a lock-in is an excellent special event that helps build relationships between your preteens and staff. There's nothing like being held captive all night in a building with a whole group of sleep-deprived early adolescents and adult leaders!

Lock-ins require a lot more preparation and planning than most people realize. You should schedule every minute of the night, with at least one back-up activity or plan up your sleeve in case another activity flops. (Even the most creative leader has trouble winging it when he or she is exhausted and something goes wrong.) A few hours of nothing to do can seem like an eternity with a roomful of sleepy kids and adults.

Start lock-ins with an excursion that lets kids expend some energy, maybe bowling or an active game of walleyball at the YMCA. Then take kids to the lock-in location, and they will be better prepared to settle in for a night of quieter activity, such as movies and games. Make sure your lock-in ends early in the morning. We recommend about 7:00 A.M.

There are lots of fun places to hold your lock-ins:

🌀 **At church**—Typically there is plenty of space for all your wonderfully creative ideas. Plus, it is usually easy for visitors to find.

🌀 **In a home**—When holding a lock-in in a home, you must have additional staff. Ask the home owner to put away any special belongings, breakables or private possessions. Lock any rooms that are off-limits to students. Start the evening with all of the kids in one room. Introduce the home owners, and explain all of the rules of the house at the start of the evening.

🌀 **At a school**—Try renting or borrowing a local school for your lock-in. The MPR (multipurpose room) is an ideal place to have games, videos, food and sack time.

🌀 **At a local pizza parlor**—This is the easiest of all lock-ins! Many of the national chains will rent out the restaurant for the night. Sometime after their normal hours of operation, groups get the exclusive use of the building. A flat-rate charge per person normally covers game tokens, unlimited pizza and soda during specified hours, and the use of the televisions and VCRs. (The price also includes dishwashing and janitorial service!)

🌀 **At the zoo**—Most local zoos will provide an evening of tours and demonstrations for church and school groups, followed by a sleepover for the kids and sponsors. Contact your local zoo for details.

🌀 **At a natural history museum**—A perfect lock-in to follow a unit on creation is the lock-in at the local natural history museum. Imagine spreading your sleeping bag out under a replica of a wooly mammoth!

After the museum guides have given the secular version of all of the artifacts, have your kids spend some time talking about what they've heard that was true, false or not certain. Have them

Do not hesitate to call a parent to come pick up a child whose behavior is over the line. This will save you a lot of trouble in the long run.

rethink what the Bible says about the claims of the exhibits in the natural history area of the museum.

Here are some ideas for what to do at a lock-in at church or elsewhere:

⦿ **Host a mystery event.** Mystery games are available at party or game stores. These are especially good for a smaller group.

⦿ **Go out in your church's neighborhood in groups on a pizza scavenger hunt.** Tell kids that they must go door-to-door asking for donations of pizza toppings. Have ready-to-top pizza crusts or English muffins at church on cookie sheets or pizza stones. When the kids return, have them make their own pizzas.

⦿ **Rent a karaoke machine (or use a boom box with a microphone) and have a songfest.** Make sure that you have a knowledgeable person control the machine and screen songs before they are performed.

Special Events for the Families of Preteens

Mother-Daughter Thanksgiving Getaway

The Friday and Saturday nights following Thanksgiving are typically the lowest attendance nights of the year for large four-star hotels. Because of this, managers are ready to make deals.

Choose one of the nicer hotels or resorts in your community or in a neighboring town. You may want to consider how many amenities (such as an indoor, heated pool; Jacuzzi; exercise room; gift shop; quality restaurants) are available at the hotel or within a short walking distance.

Call ahead to set up an appointment; then ask the manager for the best possible deal he or she can give your church group. You will need to make your best guess as to how many rooms you will need. The larger the group, the better the deal that the manager will make with you, but you will most likely be asked to guarantee a minimum number of rooms with no ability to cancel.

Advertise this outing as a great mother-daughter getaway. Moms may want to just rest and relax with their daughters, they may choose to make it a Christmas shopping weekend, or they might even use this as a mother-daughter heart-to-heart.

Make several sets of Dr. James Dobson's *Preparing for Adolescence* CDs and books (see p. 183) available to moms several weeks prior to the getaway. Suggest that this would be a good time for moms to talk with their preteen daughters

about the coming challenges of adolescence.

Mother-Daughter Christmas Shopping Spree

Many women like to make one big trip to a large shopping mall or outlet center after Thanksgiving to get most of their Christmas shopping done all in one day. Why not make this a church event that can foster healthy relationships between moms and preteen daughters and between families of preteens?

Find out where the mothers of your preteens like to go; then start advertising a date for the event. Try to form carpool groups of two or three mother-daughter teams in order to facilitate friendships. Announce a time for all the women and preteens to meet at church. Offer coffee, juice, milk and

Be ready to cover for the preteen boy who would like to attend but does not have a dad active in his life. Before announcing the event, recruit men to attend with boys whose dads are not available. These may be fathers of your preteen daughters, childless men, pastoral staff, grandfathers, or even dads who bring their own son and don't mind having one extra along.

Do the same for the preteen girls who may want to participate in the mother-daughter activities but whose mother cannot attend.

To make this shopping spree extra special, arrange to have a dinner catered at your church. Tell the moms and daughters what time dinner will be served. During the dinner, have each group of shoppers share their most outrageous purchase or their best bargain. Award prizes!

donuts. Have the carpools take off together.

Spring Training for Dads and Sons

Whether your church is large or small, or whether you have facilities or not, you can do this one!

Just find a room where you can serve a dinner. Prepare a chili dinner—consider having mild, medium and macho batches—and use disposable utensils.

Rent a couple of sports blooper videos and arrange for a speaker with an athletic background to share his testimony or a message of inspiration. Even if you don't have professional sports teams in your town, standout high school and college players or coaches are well received also.

If you have a gym or multipurpose room where you can get a little messy, put peanuts in their shells out on the tables and encourage the guys to eat the peanuts and toss the shells on the floor—

Sports Clinics

Use whatever athletic resources you have in your church or Christian community to sponsor a sports clinic at your church for parents of preteens and their kids. Be ready for a crowd, because this will be a big outreach into your community.

If your church does not have the appropriate space or facilities for the sport you choose and for a crowd, consider renting a local YMCA or elementary school. Parks are also available in most communities and may often be reserved through the local parks and recreation office.

Spend a Saturday teaching the preteens (boys and girls) how to play the sport you have chosen to highlight. Teach the parents (moms and dads) how to coach the sport—whether officially or from the bleachers. Then go a step further and train the parents how to be supportive of their child, their child's teammates and, especially, the coach leading the team.

Finish the day with a sports awards banquet where every participant receives a certificate or ribbon and is given the opportunity to hear the gospel message from the very leaders who have been working with them all day.

Oldies But Goodies—
Revamped for Today's Preteens

Roller-Skating or In-line Skating

This is an old standard, and it works well every time you use it!

If you have a large enough group, reserve the whole rink for a private party and ask the rink management if you can bring your own music. If you have a smaller group, ask your local rink if they have a Christian-music night already established and take your kids to it.

Roller rinks depend on groups to fill their off-hours. Ask for a group discount in advance. If you can offer the event at a price cheaper than normal, it's easier for kids to get their friends to come.

New Twist: Because in-line skates are so popular now, many kids have their own at home. Because in-lines normally have hard nylon wheels, they are safe to use on most types of flooring. This makes it possible for you to have a free or low-cost night of skating. Just find a gym or hall that you can use for the evening, set up orange cones to mark off the rink, and have a ball!

Ice Block Relays

Buy three or four blocks of ice. (They are available in one-foot cubes at most grocery stores and ice suppliers). Hold your activity on a grassy field, near cement walkways, or in a gym with a cement floor. Have kids line up in teams as for a classic relay race.

During the relay, one student sits on the block of ice while another student pushes him or her to the finish line. Then the students switch places and return to their team.

This is a great activity for a hot summer day.

New Twist: After the races are over, have each team elect their most courageous team member to come forward and sit on a block of ice. Time the students, and see who can weather the challenge for the longest time! Give a hot water bottle to the winner!

Triple Treats

Triple Treats is an example of using childhood games in a way that preteens love. Offering the security of known equipment and physical challenge in an upbeat setting helps preteens come to life.

New Twist: There is a certain chemistry that happens when you offer preteens three different activities going on at the same time. Whatever you have planned, divide the group into three smaller groups and have each group do a different activity, all three activities going on at the same time. Blow a whistle or some other attention-getting device when it is time to switch.

Here are some great oldies that work well as Triple Treat activities:

◎ Tricycle races

◎ Roller board or skateboard races. (Have one student sit on the skateboard while a teammate pushes from behind.)

◎ Relay race using a baseball bat. (Have each participant run up to bat, put forehead on bat, turn around 10 times and run back.)

◎ Eat-and-whistle relay. (Fill a bag with small baby food jars, crackers, banana, dry bread, peanut butter, taffy and other chewy or dry foods. Have kids reach into bag, chew up whatever food they grab and whistle before returning to their team.)

Note
1. "How to Create Games Your Kids Will Love," *Jr. High Ministry* (October/November 1997), p. 20.

Chapter 11

Helping Preteens Serve the Church Family

> "With our children growing up in a 'what's in it for me?' society, how can we help them put their learning into practice? Service projects are not only the best cure for 'me-it is,' but they are the natural response to many lessons we teach . . . they allow us to take our students beyond simply hearing, talking about or even planning ways to love and obey God."
>
> -"The Big Book of Service Projects"[1]

Preteens can and should be involved in responsible ways in the life of the family of God. It is our privilege as leaders to get kids involved in serving and ministering to others in the church family. There is certainly no end to the ministry and service opportunities. And besides, some things the kids can do better than anyone else!

It's also important for early adolescents to feel included and to know that adults believe in them enough to share responsibility with them. Early adolescence is a key time for us to help young believers find their place in the Body of Christ.

Foster Cline and Jim Fay, in *Parenting Teens with Love and Logic*, tell us that the early adolescent's self-concept is built largely upon the teen's perception of the parent's negative and positive affirmations. Such affirmations from other key adults also make a significant impact. Three of the most important statements they recommend making a regular part of our speech are these: "Provide both stated and unstated messages that say, 'I value you,' 'You can think' [and] 'You have control.'"[2]

Preteens will hear these messages when they are allowed to be involved in service projects and ministries within the church. They need to experience that great feeling inside as they fulfill their responsibility to other members of the Body. Cline and Fay tell us, "Responsibility and its companion, self-concept, are passed on through covert messages that allow teens to build their character on their strengths. As we give teens opportunities to make decisions, we must also allow them to make mistakes."[3]

This chapter will offer specific suggestions on how to prepare early adolescents for success in church-related service and ministry. It will also share a number of concrete, age-appropriate opportunities that you can offer your preteens at church.

Ideas for Training
Preteen Kids for Ministry

⊚ **Use VBS as a student teacher experience.** We know that public school teachers spend several years in college studying the philosophy of education. But before they are given charge of their own classrooms, they must successfully serve as student teachers under a master teacher, whereby they are given the opportunity to practice their training. The master teacher is charged with the responsibility of mentoring and guiding the student teacher, sharing with him or her the tricks of the trade that the experienced teacher has learned over the years.

Try this same approach when you want to train early adolescents to work with young children. Use Vacation Bible School or another program filled with younger children as your exploratory classroom! Offer these preteen teachers a morning training session. In the first half of the session, model the hands-on educational style you want them to use as you cover these vital training topics:

⊚ Classroom management. How are the young teachers to positively affect the atmosphere of the classroom? What role do you want them to assume when discipline problems arise? If they are to discipline, what techniques are they to use? When should they defer to the adult workers?

⊚ The importance of being a role model. One of the cool things for early adolescents working with preschoolers is that they are really looked up to by the young children. They need to understand the responsibility this places on them for modeling the correct behavior and attitudes.

⊚ How kids learn. Explain why you use active, hands-on learning methods. Have young teachers observe you as you teach a group of preschoolers.

⊚ How to use the curriculum. If these young teachers are expected to be in charge of even a portion of the lesson, they should be trained in how to use curriculum and how to prepare a lesson or activity from the curriculum.

⊚ Your church's policies for those who work with children. Explain procedures for what to do if a child has an accident, how children are registered and dismissed, safety policies, etc.

⊚ Turn them loose—a little bit—to get some practice. Spend the second half of the morning taking the trainees to younger kids' classrooms. Let them practice with a small group of younger kids under the loving guidance of the teachers who are already working with those kids.

Be sure to prepare your adult staff by clearly outlining and casting your vision for training young people to minister in the church. Work with the teachers to decide when to bring in the teachers-in-training so as to minimize disruption of the classroom. If you have teachers who do teacher training for you, have them monitor the preteen teachers to help with any conflicts or questions that might arise.

For all those who complete the training session, have a graduation party and award cool certificates. Let them know how proud you are of them for accomplishing something big and for committing to a very important ministry.

Use Midweek Programs
to Offer Training Classes

For many churches, Wednesday night is club night or in-depth training evening for families. This can be an ideal time to train preteens to serve

in ministry. Utilize your midweek program to offer specialized classes to train kids in service, spiritual gifts and ministry opportunities.

Here's a plan for a Wednesday night training program:

◎ **Week 1—Teach on the importance of service and ministry.** Take a look at the lives of Dorcas, Moses, Paul and Stephen, among others.

◎ **Week 2—Give an overview of spiritual gifts.** With the kids, dig into Romans 12:3-8, 1 Corinthians 12 and Ephesians 4:11-13.

◎ **Week 3—Provide a spiritual gift inventory.** Administer one of the many tests available. Free tests may be downloaded from the Internet after a search on the key words "spiritual gift inventory."

◎ **Week 4—Host a ministry fair.** Have representatives from various ministries within your church create displays that will interest preteens in their ministry and educate them as well. These representatives can answer questions, educate people about their ministries and register kids who want to volunteer.

Age-Appropriate Ideas to Help Preteens Minister at Church

◎ **Organize kid-to-kid meeters and greeters.** Red Mountain Community Church in Mesa, Arizona, has a typical problem: It's hard for visitors to find the classrooms they're looking for, and having church greeters walk them to their destination, although helpful, is a lot of work. Their solution? Enlist the friendliest, most outgoing fifth and sixth graders to stand with the adults at the welcome table and then serve as runners to escort families to children's classrooms.

Church-growth specialists have long known that the first impression of a church may well determine whether a family returns. The first thing a visiting parent usually wants to know is, Will this be a good place for my kids? Young, friendly greeters will make visiting kids feel very welcome and provide a warm touch for families. It tells not only the children but also the families that there is "someone like me" at this church.

Train your kids for this ministry by making sure they know where each classroom is. Have them practice role-playing with pretend visitors. For their comfort (and to make sure the visiting children are welcomed), ask the greeters to talk with the family's children as they walk to the room. The adults will love this, and so will their kids.

◎ **Adopt-A-Grandparent.** Gather the names of the senior citizens in your congregation and start calling to see who would appreciate having a relationship with a young person. Look for those who do not have family nearby. They'll most likely want to adopt a grandchild!

Steve Case and Fred Cornforth suggest these activities that kids can do with seniors. All they take is a little time and energy and a lot of love from both parties:

◎ Introduce your friends. Ask the senior citizen to introduce the preteen to his or her friends and neighbors. Have the preteen ask these friends to tell stories about the adopted grandparent. The preteen shows interest in the older person by learning about his or her other relationships.

◎ Share your photos. What senior citizen doesn't have dozens of photo albums to share with anyone who will take the time? Ask the seniors to play show-and-tell with your preteens. This activity will be a blessing to the seniors and will help the preteens learn tons about their adopted grandparents.

◎ Go to the zoo. Here's one everyone will like. It may require the involvement of the preteen's parents, but it can become a very healthy and relational activity for the whole family. Just go to the zoo and have a good time!

◎ Go shopping. Again, this may require parents, but many older people don't have anyone to take them shopping for things they need. If parents aren't available, choose five or six preteens and arrange to pick them and their adopted grandparents up in the church van. Make a day of it at the mall together and have lunch while you're at it![4]

⊚ Train preteens to teach preschoolers, not just babysit! Preteens have a natural connection with young children. Preschoolers and preteens are good for each other! Capitalize on this and enrich your preschool and nursery ministry staff with some capable early adolescent teachers. "Our [preteens] minister on Sundays to our four- and five-year-olds and younger in our nurseries," says Corey Hooper, a junior high pastor. "They are taught not to babysit but to minister."

To make sure that the young teachers understand the importance of the ministry to younger kids, have them go through the same processes that you use to recruit adult teachers:

⊚ Ask them to pray about their decision before making the commitment.

⊚ Provide a written job description for each person.

⊚ Use the same application and screening precautions that you use with adult volunteers. One difference for preteens: Require them to have one of their parents sign their application. It will be much harder for your young workers to be successful if their parents don't understand and support their commitments.

⊚ Train them to do their ministry well. See training suggestions above.

⊚ Use preteens in the church nursery. Many preteen boys and girls love to work with babies. Don't assume that this will be a place for only the girls. In fact, this is such a popular place for early adolescents to serve at church that it is wise to make the standards high and let the kids know that the commitment is a serious one.

Some people may be concerned about using young children with babies, but here are some precautions that make it safe for early adolescents to work with the very young:

⊚ Student staff never changes diapers. A 10-year-old girl may well change a diaper better than an adult counterpart but may lack the presence of mind to remember things such as not to leave the child unattended on the table.

⊚ Workers under 12 (or so) don't carry babies. Holding a baby properly takes some skill and physical strength. One of the biggest dangers in a nursery, of course, would be a worker improperly supporting a baby's head or dropping a child. Young children are better served by having your preteen workers get down on the floor to play with babies on a blanket or to look at books with crawlers. Recent medical reports have also warned against allowing growing kids to carry

"What's your favorite thing to do at church?"

"I like to work here [at the church] with my dad [who is the church maintenance man] and in the nursery."
—Aaron, 12 Years Old

"My favorite thing about church is working in the 2s and 3s."
—Cory, Seventh Grader

excessive weights that may damage their own growing skeletal and muscular development.

I can see clearly now! Try finishing up a unit on service or on church life by having your pre-teen youth group slip out of the church building one morning with window cleaner and paper towels in hand. Clean all the windows of the cars in your parking lot while the unsuspecting owners worship or attend adult classes.

Be sure to give your kids specific instructions on how to clean the windshields well and about being gentle with the cars' wipers. Print slips of paper saying, "Someone in the preteen group loves you. Can you 'see' the results?" Slip the papers under the windshield wipers on each car after the windows are shiny clean.

After church, let your kids go back out a bit early so that they can enjoy the surprised looks on the faces of the rest of the family as they reach their cars!

Have preteens help in the church office after school. Looking for a way to minister to a couple of preteens that go home to empty houses but who are not in an after-school care program? Want to spend some time with a special student to get to know him or her better but not sure what to do together? Try having two or three of your students meet you at church after they finish school one or two days each week. Work with them on service projects for the church office, for your ministry, or just helping clean and straighten the church. Some of these jobs they can do on their own, while others you may want to tackle with them.

Have a crew of students help with the maintenance of the church each week. Depending on the interest levels of your students, this may be done as a weekly commitment, or you may want to have four separate crews each take one week a month.

One maintenance man told us that he's got his crew all figured out. One boy who works for him hates vacuuming but loves cleaning tabletops. The boy's brother would rather die than clean tabletops, but he thinks vacuuming is fun. The crew chief has a great team! Both boys help him set up tables and chairs for Sunday School on Saturdays, too.

Our senior pastor's son mows our large field of grass each week. He decided this would be a pretty cool job, even before he found out that the church had purchased a riding lawnmower!

Create a ministry team for preteens using puppets or drama. Preteen kids love to perform and they are naturals with puppet and drama ministries. One church we observed has their preteen kids prepare living statue dramas for the church patio on Easter. The kids read the various narratives telling the events of the last week of Jesus' life on Earth; then they choose parts and recreate the scenes by making living dioramas. No one moves except the audience!

Have your students write postcards to absentees, shut-ins or guests. Gather your introspective kids and your adults who have a heart for following up on absentee kids and have them make their own postcards on card stock, saying things such as "We missed you!" or "Not the same without you around here!" or "Thanks for being our guest. We hope you come back soon!" Make sure the kids decorate only one side of the card stock.

Then give the group a list of the names and addresses of various people who could use a personalized card:

Kids who have been missing from Sunday School for two or more weeks.

Church members who are homebound or hospitalized.

Last Sunday's visitors to your church.

Address the cards and write a brief note. Have lots of kids sign each card. Be sure the size of the cards conforms to postal service regulations.

Use your artists to publicize special events at church. Have lots of art supplies on hand when you gather your creative artists for this project.

Whenever you're getting ready for a big event at church that involves kids or whole families, have the early adolescents create posters, banners, flyers or even personalized invitations. Give them a list of the basics that you want included: the name of the event, who is invited, the date(s), times, cost and any other details people need to know. Then turn the kids loose to create your ad campaign! Their artwork may not be as perfect as your computerized versions, but it's bound to be more colorful and eye catching. It's just one more way to help kids know they belong to this family!

⊚ **Wash and wax the church vehicles.** Central Christian Church in Arizona has a team of kinesthetic-type kids (kids who love action) wash one of the church's vans each week. A male leader who relates well to active kids gathers the soap, sponges, buckets and hose and meets the kids at the van. They climb all over the vehicle inside and out. The van doesn't always turn out as perfect as if the paid adult staff cleaned it, but the kids learn how much work it is to keep a van clean, which helps build in them a healthy respect for the church's property and maintenance of it. Older people in the church see a new side of the early adolescents as they give back to the church in this practical service project.

⊚ **Use creative early adolescents to design and make bulletin boards or to decorate rooms for special events like VBS.** Many preteens have the time, energy and creativity that we sometimes lack as adults. Utilize these attributes to help decorate the church in ways that kids like!

When we started a new children's church program, we had our own kids come and decorate the room with a huge sign, streamers, balloons and some inexpensive posters from a Christian bookstore. It

only took a few hours, the girls felt proud of their "space," and the room looked wonderfully inviting to kids.

Consider having your whole class of preteens come to church before a major event like Vacation Bible School. Many hands make light work, and your hardest job will be keeping up with them and having enough supplies ready for them to keep working!

⊚ **Have preteens help collect the offering or otherwise minister during a worship service.** In some churches this won't be acceptable, but if there isn't a cultural or doctrinal issue forbidding it at your church, try entrusting to your students the responsibility of collecting the offering, singing in the worship choir, playing in the worship band or ministering in drama or puppetry. They will live up to the challenge, and you'll be proud of them!

Letting preteens help in the worship service has many benefits:

⊚ It makes the worship service more enjoyable for those who are involved.

⊚ It creates an interest in the service for other students who aren't involved.

⊚ It models for your congregation the place students have in the Body of Christ.

⊚ It shows those who do not minister in the church that we are never too young or too old to serve God in practical ways.

⊚ Some parents will help their children with this task, even if they wouldn't have committed to doing it alone.

⊚ You'll never have a shortage of servants to do any of those ministries again!

Notes

1. *The Big Book of Service Projects* (Ventura, CA: Gospel Light, 2001) p. 6.
2. Foster W. Cline, M.D., and Jim Fay, *Parenting Teens With Love and Logic* (Colorado Springs, CO: Pinon Press, 1992), p. 44.
3. Ibid., pp. 45-46.
4. Steve Case and Fred Cornforth, *Hands-On Service Ideas for Youth Groups* (Loveland, CO: Group Publishing, 1995), p. 20.

Chapter 12

Challenging Preteens to Minister Outside the Church

"It's easy for typically self-centered [or early adolescents] to think of no one other than themselves from dawn till dusk—and then dream about themselves at night. Ironically, these most self-centered individuals find huge satisfaction in helping other people. They just need a little nudge."

—Mark Oestreicher, "Help! I'm a Junior High Youth Worker!"[1]

Prepare Your Kids to Serve

Preteens are typically self-consumed and not very experienced in reaching out to help other people, so we need to train them and prepare them for service projects. Steve Case and Fred Cornforth tell us that "a youth group enthusiastic about serving others is the result of intentional planning that exposes them to community and world-wide needs through a diversity of methods."[2] For preteen ministry, intentional planning might look something like this:

◎ **Conduct ongoing teaching and training to expose preteens to the needs in their world and to the ways that young Christians can meet those needs.** Tell your kids about the needs in your community and the world at large. For preteens this may be done by sharing newspaper articles, video clips of television news reports or letters from organizations that help children, such as Compassion International or Samaritan's Purse. Whenever possible, have guest speakers come and share pictures with your kids, possibly directors of local homeless shelters, orphanages or children's hospitals. Ask these people to share specific, concrete ways that early adolescents could make a difference. (Note: The pastor of your church or your church denomination's missions organization can provide you with contact information for missions projects.)

Be sure to give your youth group plenty of time to debrief at this stage. Ask them questions such as these and allow them to answer completely and honestly:

◎ How did seeing the pictures of the homeless children make you feel?

◎ How would you want to be treated if you were in the hospital? If you were suffering from a terminal disease?

◎ What were you thinking and feeling when you heard the presentation?

◎ What do you wish you could do now that you've seen the needs of other people in our community? Around the world?

⊚ **Offer quarterly involvement in one-time service projects or events that almost anyone can do successfully.** None of us like to commit to a long-range project without first knowing more about it. After all, what if we say we'll do something and find out that we are unable or unwilling to continue?

The same is true of our kids. We need to give them short-term projects that they can commit to and successfully complete in a few hours on one day. These projects are especially good for preteens who have little concept of time and don't understand the long-term duration of some outreach ministries or programs. Preteens are good at coming to church for a few hours to clean up some closets, singing at a retirement home, or making one visit to another child who is sick.

Involvement in one-time projects may be the level that most of your early adolescents remain in until later in their teen years. That's OK. The idea behind a one-time involvement is to allow the student to finish and not return, without having a sense of guilt or a failure experience. If a preteen doesn't enjoy one service project, next time he or she will choose another, but only if he or she doesn't feel forced into maintaining an activity long after interest as been lost.

Offer a variety of service projects over the eight or more quarters that you will have the preteen in your ministry. It is good for early adolescents to experience a variety of ways to serve, because one may just turn out to be the right fit for them and turn into a more frequent involvement or even a lifelong ministry.

⊚ **Challenge preteens to stretch themselves annually for a several-day project away from church.** For early adolescents, these annual projects should involve one or two nights away from home. There is something important that happens when a service project requires an overnight stay. The difference between ministering to other kids in your own town before going home to your comfortable bed and minis-

tering to kids in another town where travel and an overnight stay are required is dramatic. The overnight stay will cause the service event to have a much deeper and more long-lasting impact on your kids.

Preteens are able to do a variety of projects in other regions, including construction, painting, leading VBS programs, and more.

⊚ **Launch kids into their teen and adult years with a heart for service.** The ultimate goal, of course, is to train kids to make service a regular part of life, whether you are asking them to join a church project or they are just going out into the community (or world) to find their own opportunities to serve. One of the most exciting elements of working with young people at church is this idea of developing Christlike habits in their lifestyles before they grow up. While kids are young, they are teachable and moldable. We want them to grow to be more than spectators or "pew-sitters" in the church; we want them to be truly involved in the life and ministry of the church.

Dale Torry, a missions and junior high pastor, tells us that he tries to expose kids to three different types of service and missions experiences in the two years they are in his program:

✎ Cross-cultural projects, in which kids are exposed to a culture different from their own.

✎ Work projects, in which kids use their hands and can say, "I built this" or "I cleaned this"; and

✎ Service projects, in which kids get entangled with another person's life and needs and can say, "I served this person."

Ideas for Preteen Service Projects

⟲ **Celebrate Christmas in July at convalescent homes.** Most of us eventually take our kids caroling at homes for the elderly around Christmastime. But these homes are overloaded with carolers in December. Why not take your kids to a convalescent home in July? Sing some of your favorite songs from the youth group and add in some patriotic songs (many are religion-based) that the older folks will appreciate. Have them join in and sing along! Take along a craft project that your kids have made for the senior citizens or the supplies to make the project with the residents.

⟲ **Celebrate birthdays with the kids in homeless shelters.** Case and Cornforth offer an idea your preteens can really relate to: Have a birthday party at a nearby homeless shelter for all of the kids living there.

Contact a local shelter and arrange a day and time (probably about two hours) when your kids can come and have a party. Have your kids or adult sponsors talk to local grocery stores or toy shops to gather all the typical party goods: cakes, ice cream, party favors and toys for the birthday kids. Prepare games for the kids like Pin-the-Tail on the Donkey, Break the Piñata and Drop the Clothespin in the Bottle.

Then arrive at the shelter full of merriment and ready to celebrate in a way that your kids understand and the shelter kids will appreciate![3]

⟲ **Have a canned-food drive for community food banks.** Many churches involve kids in canned-food drives to stock the local food banks and to replenish their church's emergency food pantry. But don't just ask your kids to bring cans to church. With preteens, the more hands-on you can make the project, the better.

Have the kids gather the food at church. Then announce a day and time when the kids themselves will box up the food and transport it to the food pantry or to the families that need it. If possible, have the kids carry the food right into the community food bank and stack it on their shelves.

It's important for the kids to see tangible evidence of the difference they have made. Early adolescents are worried about hunger and poverty, and this is a practical way for them to make an impact in their communities. Help them feel and see the impact of their donations.

⟲ **Feed the hungry.** Find a soup kitchen or homeless shelter that will allow kids to help feed the hungry. Some will allow kids to actually help serve food; others will at least let the students work in the back, loading food boxes for distribution.

Whenever you plan to take kids into inner-city neighborhoods, across international borders, or into any unknown situation, it is wise to make the trip yourself first to check it out!

⟲ **Work to help others and to raise funds for church.** Try having an annual day of service in the community that also helps raise funds for your preteen ministry. The students ask their friends and family to pledge an amount (of their choice) for each of the eight hours that they will work in the community. Once the pledges are all in, have your group hit the road, some going to impoverished churches and doing repairs, some showing up at the homes of elderly people in the community to do yard work and odd jobs, and others cleaning the litter off of the city's roadways. After the workday, have your students go back and collect their pledges and turn them in at church.

⟲ **Minister to and serve mentally disabled adults or kids.** There are a number of group homes, camps and schools near you that you've never heard about. Do some research through your denomination or your state's social services or health department to find them. Contact them to find out what they need and how your preteens might help them. Then take your kids to do whatever is needed! You will be blessed!

◉ **Have students participate in weeklong work camps for preteens.** Early Teen SERVE is a work camp for kids who have completed sixth grade or are 12 years old. These camps are typically five days and four nights long. Youth Unlimited sponsors these camps in various parts of the country and involves early adolescents in painting, yard work and local missions help.

Making a Mission Trip Mega-Important to Kids

It is a mega-important responsibility to go on a mission trip, representing both the sending agency (in this case, your church) and God! So let the kids experience the importance of what they are signing up to do.

◉ **Have a formal application and interview procedure.** Preteen kids like to be treated like adults. The more official you make the application process, the better, as far as your students are concerned. The applications themselves can also help you prepare for the trip by getting better acquainted with some kids. (See p. 111 for a sample reproducible application you can use with your students.)

After receiving the applications, you may want to have personal interviews as well. This time can be used to cast the vision for the trip and to remind kids of the great privilege to represent the church and Christ. Then review rules and expectations for the trip. You may also want to review some of the answers given by the students on their written applications. Offer a lot of affirmation, and explore the questions more deeply if you feel it is necessary.

Use this time to share the gospel with students who do not seem to understand what being a Christian means. If applicable, discuss problem behavior that you have observed in the young person that could be a particular problem on the trip. You may want to include parents in this interview so that everyone understands what is expected,

especially if problem behavior is being discussed.

◉ **Require kids to raise at least a portion of the required funds.** Whatever the cost of your mission trip, it will be more meaningful if the kids understand the costs and are responsible for raising at least a portion of the funds needed. After helping them create a budget for their trip (see the budget worksheet sample on 112), share with them a few ways to raise their own funds.

◉ Show them how to write and submit a formal request to your church's missions board or committee requesting support. (Let the board know that the kids are requesting only partial provision.)

◉ Have the kids write and mail support letters to their parents, friends and relatives asking for additional financial support and sharing the purpose of the trip.

◉ Finally, at least a portion of the money should come from the kids themselves, whether from their odd jobs, such as babysitting and lawn jobs, or from group fund-raisers such as car washes. The work will make the trip that much more meaningful. Make it clear to the kids and their parents that this portion of the funding must be earned, not given to them by parents or others.

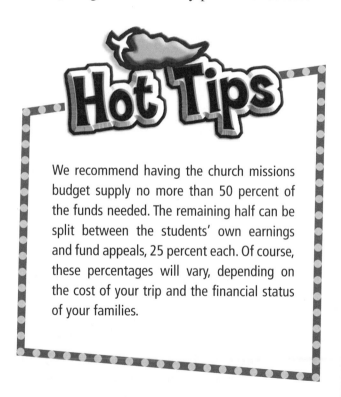

We recommend having the church missions budget supply no more than 50 percent of the funds needed. The remaining half can be split between the students' own earnings and fund appeals, 25 percent each. Of course, these percentages will vary, depending on the cost of your trip and the financial status of your families.

APPLICATION FOR MISSION TRIP

Student's Name_____ Phone _____

Address_____ City and State_____ Zip_____

E-Mail Address_____ Date of Birth_____ Age_____ Grade_____

Please complete the following questions to the best of your ability:

1 Why do you want to attend this mission trip?

2 What do you hope to get from attending the trip?

3 What do you hope to offer the other students and those to whom we will be ministering?

4 What are your biggest fears about attending this trip?

5 How do your parents feel about your participation in this trip?

6 In your own words, what is a Christian and how does someone become one?

7 Are you a Christian? If so, tell us how you became one and what differences it has made in your life. Use the back of this paper if necessary.

Please sign your application and have at least one parent sign it also. Return your completed application to the church office.

_____   _____   _____   _____
Student's Signature   Date   Parent's Signature   Date

MISSION PROJECT BUDGET WORKSHEET

Number of People Expected to Attend _____

Cost of Travel, Food and Lodging

Transportation _____/Person x _____ People = _____

Food _____/Meal x _____ Meals x _____People = _____

Lodging _____/Person x _____ People = _____

Total Cost of Travel, Food, Lodging _____

Cost of Project

Craft Supplies _____   Cost _____

Building Materials _____   Cost _____

Curriculum/Resources _____   Cost _____

Fees/Permits _____   Cost _____

Miscellaneous _____   Cost _____

Total Cost of Project _____

Total Funds Needed

Cost of Transportation, Food, and Lodging   _____

Cost of Project   _____

Emergency Fund _____ (10 percent of the above two)   _____

Total Funds Needed _____

Source of Funds

Church Budget   _____

Student Contributions   _____

Youth Group Fund-Raisers   _____

Individual Contributions   _____

◎ **Ask your church leaders to commission those who are going.** Finally, before the big day comes, ask your church leaders to hold an official commissioning for students who will take part in the mission trip. If possible, do this in front of the whole church, perhaps during a church service. If not, make it a special evening, and invite parents, families and friends. Ask your senior pastor to pray for the kids and all of your pastors, elders or missions commission members to stand with the student missionaries.

This would be a great time to present the kids with a token gift, like a Spanish New Testament (if going to Mexico) or a bottle of suntan lotion (if doing a work project somewhere hot)!

Train Kids for Missions

Bill Russell, a junior high pastor, says that he uses training for ministry opportunities as a way to keep churched kids excited about learning. "Today's fifth and sixth graders need a solid foundation of biblical knowledge to deal with tough issues, but at this age many of our churched kids are ready to check out."[4] He keeps sixth graders on track in discipleship programs by the goals he sets before them in his Kids Quest program.

Kids Quest works similarly to some of the other guidelines we've presented:

◎ Both the kids and their parents must sign a commitment form.

◎ A specific training program prepares kids for service. Kids Quest is 17 weeks long, one hour each week.

◎ Involvement in Kids Quest is considered a privilege. Kids must attend all meetings, be involved in the class discussions, do homework assignments and memorize assigned Scripture verses. They earn membership!

Russell explains how he uses the hour each week. The first half hour is a large-group discussion led by Russell and covering key doctrinal issues that he wants sixth graders to know: the end times, sacraments and the truth of Scripture. The second half hour is accomplished in small groups of no more than seven kids with a leader who helps quiz them on memory work and reviews their homework with them.

The successful students who complete all of their assignments and attend all of the meetings get to go on a one-week ministry trip at the end of the course. This is a real draw for many of the kids. Located near Mexico, Russell is able to take his kids across the border to do construction work, experience the culture and minister to orphans.

The Kids Quest program has "helped kids discover solid answers to tough questions and understanding that the Bible is relevant to their lives. Kids get excited about God's Word. . . . The outreach trip opens kids' eyes to a biblical worldview."[5]

Dale Torry describes the missions experiences in which he involves early adolescents as introductory missions. His goal is to stretch kids beyond their comfort level but still have the trip be enjoyable enough that they want to come back and experience more through their later teens years.

Torry's training takes place for five weeks prior to a trip and focuses on building community among the kids who are participating. He attempts to prepare kids' hearts and attitudes by having them write encouraging notes to the pastors and others who will be attending. Teams are created and spend time preparing for specific responsibilities needed for the individual trip or project. Kids are reminded that there will be hard times, even between close friends as they live, work and "smell" together for a number of days!

Ideas for Preteen
Missions Projects and Trips

◎ **Collect school supplies and books for missions organizations to distribute or to use in their ministry.** Jeanne Scheetz, an assistant pastor for junior age children, has kids gather school supplies and books to send to missionaries that the church supports in Hungary, Honduras and

Indonesia. She finds that pictures taken by the missionaries (especially of kids) really help get her preteens excited about the ones they are serving with their gifts.

🌀 **Have a special offering in your youth group just for missions projects.** Choose a project the kids can identify with, such as supporting a child through Compassion International, and provide regular reports to the group about how much they have raised and how the money has been used.

Some Southern Baptist churches have a birthday offering once each month when each person in the church who has had a birthday that month is encouraged to contribute a dime for each year of his or her life. The money gathered goes to their denomination-wide missions fund. Consider using something fun like this for your own gathering of money for missions projects.

🌀 **Host a fund-raiser to send a short-term missionary out in the field.** Sometimes early adolescents feel that they can't be involved in the big picture of the church. Here's a way to help them feel connected and valued.

Lois Sherwin in La Mirada, California, has her fifth and sixth graders host an annual spaghetti dinner to raise funds for missions. The kids advertise the meal to the congregation, making visits to each of the adult fellowship groups, and they help prepare and serve the meal.

The first year the church held this dinner, 64 people bought advance tickets and 230 showed up to eat! One year, the funds were used to send the church's high school group on a short-term mission trip. When the teenagers returned and reported to the church, they also had their young sponsors come forward and be honored for their contributions to the ministry.

🌀 **Encourage missionaries with food, cards, audiocassettes and videos.** Ask the missions leaders at your church or in your denominational headquarters to put you in touch with missionaries in the field who have preteen kids. Then write to the family and ask what kinds of food from

home they miss or what kinds of movies they like. Many missionaries tell us that one of the most touching care packages they receive from home is the one that contains peanut butter, candy or something else they enjoy but can't get in the area of the world where they are serving. Preteens especially like to keep up on the latest movies in the American theaters or replays of major sporting events, and surprisingly, many missionary families do have access to VCRs, even in the most remote areas. In one college town where we lived, missionaries got regular installments of the basketball season (even when the home team lost)!

Make a list for your youth group and put together a package of treats for the missionary family. Make sure to have the kids write personal letters or cards to the family, too. Or you can have the whole group record an audio- or videocassette greeting!

🌀 **Ministry to inner-city churches.** Try establishing a sister-church relationship with a church from a needier part of your town or the inner city. Ask the church leadership what service your kids could provide in a few hours one afternoon. There are a variety of projects that may be needed:

🌀 Painting and cleaning the facilities

🌀 Weeding the yard and trimming bushes or trees

🌀 Washing toys for the church nursery (or perhaps you could have a toy drive and take new toys to the church)

🌀 **Ministry to Native Americans living on reservations.** One of the largest unreached people groups in the United States really isn't just one people group—it's all the various groups of Native Americans around the country.

If your church happens to be anywhere near a Native American reservation, contact a church or missions group that serves the reservation to see if your kids are able to come lead outreach services for other kids and their families. You may also be able to do a variety of work projects on the reservation or for the church.

One advantage of a service project or mission

trip to a Native American reservation is that it provides preteens with a cross-cultural experience without necessarily requiring a long trip or a team of translators.

🌀 **Organize missions trips to Mexico.** Mexico is an excellent place for short-term missions trip for preteens. On past trips to children's homes in Mexico, we have had kids serve in a variety of ways:

🌀 Repainting the children's bedrooms and playrooms in the home

🌀 Clearing rocks from a soccer field and installing goals

🌀 Constructing a new chicken coop

🌀 Making lunch and dinner for all the kids from both countries

🌀 Leading an evangelistic VBS, including testimonies, crafts and music

If you choose to cross an international border with kids, be sure that you take the following precautions:

🌀 Contact a missionary who is making the crossing regularly in your area to see what the latest concerns may be. He or she will have helpful tips for you.

🌀 Drive the route yourself to see where the stopping points are and to gather the appropriate forms before hand. Normally, you will need a set of paperwork for each vehicle you are taking across the border.

🌀 Make sure that you bring a passport or birth certificate and a notarized permission form from each child's parents. (Both custodial parents must sign.) Keep them in your possession for safety.

🌀 If any of the vehicles have liens against them currently noted on their title, you must have a notarized letter from the lien holder authorizing the vehicle to leave the United States. (We learned this one the hard way!)

🌀 Tow trucks are not allowed to cross the border in either direction. (We learned this one the hard way, too.) So it is wise to have at least one vehicle with a sturdy bumper and tow cables in case another vehicle needs help returning to the United States.

Involve Whole Families in Missions and Service Projects

🌀 **Plug parents into your project.** A number of years ago, we were taking fifth and sixth graders across the border into Mexico to minister to abandoned children in a foster home. Our 30 kids would travel about five hours to sleep on a hard cement floor, use crude plumbing and eat food prepared in a kitchen overrun with flies. They would wash the lice out of the hair of close to 100 children and teens and then do their best at providing free haircuts. In the evening, the kids would sing songs (some of them in Spanish), share other musical talents, lead a craft and share testimonies with the help of translators.

Taking large groups of young kids across an international border is tricky and involves a lot of work on the part of the church leaders. However, over the years we noticed that sometimes the parents who went along liked the trip even more than the kids did. Many of these parents wanted to keep coming after their sons or daughters had gone on to junior high. This gave us an idea.

We turned the trip into a family event in which parents were required to attend with their child. This automatically involved more adults who were willing helpers and who provided their own vehicles for the trip, making crossing the border safer and easier. Children whose parents couldn't or wouldn't attend were "adopted" into a family unit that was willing to have an extra person.

Kids and parents were blessed by being able to experience this life-changing event together, and we were blessed by all the additional adult workers who ended up taking over and running the trip for the sake of their own kids.

🌀 **Help families find their own projects.** Other churches have had success in involving families by gathering parents and kids at a pizza night or other social setting. At this initial gathering, they've had several families share their past experiences with service or missions projects as a family. They present blessings that the project brought them as a family along with the real-life view of the headaches and hassles. The leaders or visiting guests then present a variety of different options for families, everything from beginning, exposure-level activities to life-long ministries.

Before the evening is over, the families are challenged to pick a project and commit to doing it as a family or as a team of families. Another meeting date is set that night. This provides a deadline for the projects to be completed and a debriefing victory celebration for all the families to reconvene and share their experiences with one another.

Reaching Out to Others Isn't Always Fun— But That's Part of the Lesson

In fact, we don't believe the Bible even pretends it's going to be fun. But we hear great stories at conferences or from peers at other churches about how God miraculously blessed one leader's efforts or how another group saw great changes in its kids and in those it was seeking to serve. Don't get discouraged if this doesn't happen on every trip!

Case and Cornforth remind us that "warm fuzzies aren't guaranteed. Although people often talk about how good they felt because they served, it's quite possible that the service activity [or missions project] you're involved with may result in hard work but not necessarily warm feelings of appreciation. In fact, you may end up feeling sour or angry. Here's a great opportunity to truly test your motivations for service. Bring on the debriefing!"[6]

One leader recalls a time when an early adoles-

cent girl took part in a trip to San Francisco's inner city. One of the crew's outreach events for the week was to serve a spaghetti dinner to the homeless people in the area. During the day, as the dinner was prepared, the kids went out in small groups, each with an adult leader, to pass out flyers and invite the men and women on the streets to the dinner.

In this neighborhood full of prostitutes, homeless people and drug dealers, this young gal handed a flyer to a man sitting on the street. Before she could walk away, the man asked her if she was a Christian. She said yes.

He continued, "I want to ask you a question and if you'll be 100 percent honest with me, I'll be 100 percent honest with you. I'm a homosexual. I'm dying of AIDS. And I'm an alcoholic living on the streets. Does your God still love me and forgive me?"

The girl said, "Yes, of course He does."

"Then I believe you're a Christian." The team then circled around the man and prayed for him. As they started to walk away, however, he said, "Stop!" He then proceeded to pray for each member of the team, one by one, and to quote a verse of Scripture from memory for each student. He had more Scripture memorized than any of the students did. He knew the Bible, but he wanted someone to be compassionate and loving—no matter what.

The dying man touched these kids. They went out to offer love and acceptance. They returned with a blessing.

When we expose kids to the realities of the world in ways that they can truly reach out and touch those around them, they are changed for life. They learn that there is a dying world that

Notes

1. Mark Oestreicher, *Help! I'm a Junior High Youth Worker!* (Grand Rapids, MI: Zondervan Publishing House, 1996), p. 50.
2. Steve Case and Fred Cornforth, *Hands-On Service Ideas for Youth Groups* (Loveland, CO: Group Publishing, 1995), p. 10.
3. Ibid., p. 26.
4. Bill Russell, "Kids Quest," *Children's Ministry* (July/August 1998), p. 51.
5. Ibid., p. 52.
6. Case and Cornforth, *Hands-On Service Ideas for Youth Groups*, p. 18.

ISSUES FOR PRETEEN MINISTRY

Discipline and Preteens

> "Children and teenagers may be conceptualized as mirrors. They generally reflect rather than initiate love. If love is given to them, they return it. If none is given, they have none to return. Unconditional love is reflected unconditionally, and conditional love is returned conditionally."
>
> —Ross Campbell, "How to Really Love Your Teenager"[1]

Over the years of working with volunteers in our own churches and after discussing our hypothesis with a number of children's leaders across the country, we are convinced of this:

More volunteers quit teaching kids at church due to their frustration and feelings of inadequacy brought on by student discipline problems than for any other issue.

It is natural for a teacher who spends many hours preparing a lesson to be discouraged when he or she feels as though the students are completely out of control, disrespectful and not wanting to be in class. Even though the problem may not be the teacher's, the volunteer is left feeling like a total failure and, eventually, finds a polite way to quit.

Whether you are a leader of teachers, an experienced teacher yourself, or a novice just getting into preteen ministry, you will need to be ready for some unique behavior challenges that arise in groups of early adolescents. (If you are a parent of one, you are already quite aware of these challenges!) This chapter will look at those challenges and some creative ways to prevent discipline problems before they happen and to consistently help students understand and assume the responsibility for their own choices.

"I've Got to Be Me!"

Just as the singer in the 1968 Broadway musical *The Golden Rainbow* belted out "I've Got to be Me!" on the Broadway stage, the behavior of early adolescents cries out to all who will listen, too. Our job is to understand what the student's behavior is saying. Here are some of the lines that you may hear your students performing:

"I'm unique." Each early adolescent is completely unique and is maturing socially, physically, emotionally, mentally and spiritually at his or her own rate. This means that we have the challenging task of treating each child individually as we determine what we can rightfully expect of him or her and what guidance would be most beneficial to the student and the situation.

There are few cut-and-dried methods that apply for disciplining kids at these ages. While a boy in your class may be into puppies and frogs, the girl sitting next to him may be thinking about make-up, boys and the latest teen idol. We are dealing with kids all across the developmental spectrum. Our discipline methods, whatever they may be, must recognize each child's uniqueness.

⊚ **"I'm misunderstood!"** Early adolescents truly believe that they are so different from anyone else in the world that no one could possibly understand their problems, the reasons they do what they do and their feelings. Subsequently they easily fall into a whining and complaining mode concerning home, school and church. Though adults may think the appropriate response is to fix these things, they must realize these named externals are not the true battle. The battle is actually within the early adolescent.

As teachers (or parents), we need to realize that we should listen to kids through a filter. For most of our kids, their parents, siblings, teachers, homework load, chores and the rest of life could not possibly be as bad as they would have us believe! The wise leader will listen intently, realizing that the child is sharing an important, emotional message with us, however inaccurate or exaggerated it may be. The leaders should focus on helping the student learn to deal with disappointments and frustrations and to handle their problems in a Christlike manner. The currently popular "WWJD" (What Would Jesus Do?)

bracelets offer a great tool for early adolescents to use to work through their episodes of self-pity.

⊚ **"I'm changing."** Early adolescence is a period of change; so on any given Sunday, the student you thought you had all figured out last week could suddenly show up as a completely different kid. What the child likes one week, the adolescent will not put up with the next. Emotional roller coasters are a normal part of the preteen's life. And peer pressure and constantly changing fads will further complicate things.

This is why we urge preteen ministries to focus their energies on small groups. What a large-group leader cannot possibly know about the mass, a small-group leader will discover almost instantly. We cannot overstate the importance of getting to know your students and what makes them "tick"!

⊚ **"I'm tired."** Preteens are experiencing so many physical changes that they are often truly fatigued. They need more rest than they have needed for years. Overly tired kids have a very difficult time controlling their emotions and therefore their behavior.

Be ready to cut your kids some slack on big holiday weekends when you know they will have stayed up too late. When you're involved in activities, make sure to plan in some downtime to let kids rest. They probably will not admit that they are tired if they are doing something fun, but you need to insist on rest. It's the adult who must make decisions about schedules in order to avoid overtiring kids and creating attitude and discipline problems.

At camp, where kids are active all day, we follow the guidelines (or requirements) set by many states and plan in an hour of bunk time after lunch each day. Planning cabin discussions or individual journal projects keeps this time from seeming like a nap time, which preteens would rebel against. Our experiences over the years have consistently shown that the afternoon and evening behavior patterns are significantly improved if this rest time is enforced.

◉ **"I'm fragile."** A preteen will do almost anything to avoid being trapped in an embarrassing situation. The trapped student may become a clown or an angry aggressor to protect him- or herself from a perceived threat. When a student behaves in an unusual manner, stop to evaluate whether he or she is feeling insecure about something going on in your classroom.

One place this behavior may show up is when you are dividing kids into teams, small groups, or vehicles. At this age level, we want to stretch kids to meet others and to learn to be social with the opposite gender. However, we must not force them into a social setting that they do not have the skills to handle.

Try to group kids so that each student has at least one friend with him or her. Be sure to have at least two kids of the same gender in each group. A boy or girl who feels alone in a group will get little out of the discussion or activity and may become a discipline challenge.

Early adolescents are vulnerable emotionally, so they need protection from others. The wise teacher will not allow students to inflict pain on one another. Nor will the teacher engage in put-downs, sarcasm or other hurtful remarks disguised as humor. (See chapter 6 for tips on getting the right leaders for your preteen ministry.)

◉ **"I'm supercharged."** Preteens are full of energy that needs to be channeled. Girls will be particularly susceptible to the effects of hormones as exhibited by mood swings. Boys will be especially rowdy and physical.

It is normal for kids to have a lot of energy. The physical changes that result in these characteristics are part of God's design for their growing bodies. It is up to us to work with these givens of early adolescence as we design programming.

Physical energy needs to be channeled into movement within lessons and activities. Let the kids get up and change seats, move to a different part of the room, form groups of various sizes and play games or be involved in activities that help illustrate the point of the lesson.

Emotional energy needs to be expressed in the context of relationships. Learn to listen to kids. Help your kids learn to listen to each other. Create an environment that says it's okay to share emotions. One practical tool is to reflect to the student what he or she has shared without showing any approval or disapproval, just acceptance of the reality of the emotions.

When students do get emotional or physical, our best response is to remain calm and even-tempered. This self-discipline models for the students the behavior we desire (appropriate self-control) and it keeps us from further escalating the behavior. Challenging or punishing kids who are being "hormonal" will only lead to more severe discipline problems.

◉ **"I'm angry and afraid. I need to be loved and forgiven."** Two common emotions that can both result in behavior problems are anger and fear. These are dual emotions. When the preteen is fearful, he or she often reacts in anger to protect him- or herself. Fatigue, feelings of inadequacy and fear of rejection are all common elements of the preteen's life and all can lead to "acting out" behaviors.

If the teacher ministers to the preteen's needs, he or she can help prevent behavior problems. Affirm your student's sense of personal worth by praising the student personally and frequently. Make the preteen feel secure in your classroom by using his or her name, giving nonverbal acceptance such as smiles, eye contact and appropriate touch. Make unconditional love the basis of your relationship with each child. Even when they do act out, make sure that you express your forgiveness, acceptance and understanding (none of which requires you to approve of their behavior).

◎ **"I'm bored."** Rest assured. Preteens are supposed to say this. It's in their contract with God! Early adolescents are supposed to go around saying, "I'm bored." Many leaders lose their confidence when their kids start spouting that age-old complaint. After all, we kill ourselves to entertain these kids and they still say, "This is boring!"

Walt and Diane Pitman shared some of their struggles in this area. "As exciting and as 'youthy' as you make it, some will still feel they are too grown-up and want to go to junior high or ditch or complain that the games are dumb. It's part of the age. I tell my kids in a joking way to watch out for 'sixth grade-itis' and describe all these characteristics to them. At the beginning of the year, I address ditching and attitudes using cartoon overheads because it is common with this age even if you have the most fantastic program. It's hard not to take it personally when you do all this hard work to make it cool and upbeat and still hear that some kid is bored. You just do your best, pray and thank the Lord for those lives that are letting the Lord touch them."

The Pitmans describe "sixth grade-itis" as that belief that the pasture is greener on the other side of the fence (that is, in the youth ministry). Many sixth graders can't wait to get to the junior high program, often encouraged by older siblings or parents to act older than they really are, and they end up missing out on the fun that they should be having in the programs actually designed for their age level. Symptoms of this malady include ditching programs and complaining of boredom or that everything is too babyish.

Don't lose your confidence. Just smile. Listen to them. Don't react to them. Just keep on doing what you know is right for them. There's no use trying to get them to violate their contract with God!

◎ **"I'm too cool."** The preteen is saying to himself or herself, *Everyone is looking at me*. So the logical conclusion is for the preteen to do what he or she thinks all these other people want him or her to do, to be what they want him or her to be. The preteen's perception of his or her peers will greatly influence the preteen's behavior. The preteen's insecurity with his or her own identity and the desire to be accepted by peers will make it important for the preteen to follow the behavior of others. Rather than addressing the symptoms, make sure that what you are doing *is* cool:

◎ Your activities and classroom need to be fun and what kids think is cool.

◎ Make sure that you (or your adult leaders) are perceived by the students as being a fun person. Don't be uptight.

◎ Have both male and female leaders in your room. Boys, especially, have a need to see male role models who prove that it's possible to be a cool adult male Christian.

◎ Build strong relationships with your students—especially the kids who you see as leaders. They will lead others into accepting your activities.

◎ Have fun yourself, and get involved in your own activities to set the example. Kids will follow the lead of an adult to whom they are able to relate.

◎ **"I don't want to."** This is another common attitude problem that you will eventually experience in preteen ministry. If you give an early adolescent enough time to think about it, he or she will come up with a reason not to do *whatever* you have planned—no matter how wonderful it may be.

So, rarely tell preteens what is coming next, at least not everything. Don't announce all the details of your program in advance. Just tell the kids the basics of what they need to know, such as where to meet and what to bring, and then let them be surprised! (This also gives you an "out" in case you have to switch gears midstream.)

This principle works especially well at a lengthy retreat or camp. They need to know where to meet and how much it costs and what to bring, but they don't need to know what they'll be eating, what games they'll play, or if they'll see videos or not. Make sure your event staff knows not to tell the kids what's coming up next. (The kids will love bugging you to try to get the information!)

◉ **"I'm learning to think for myself."** Don't be shocked, angry or defeated when your students question the existence of God or the truth of the Bible. They may even temporarily claim to not believe at all. More commonly, preteens will question morality and value choices. They'll want to know:

◉ Is it really wrong to steal?

◉ What's so terrible about cheating?

◉ Is it OK to lie? (Especially if you can get away with it?)

Some of these questions may be an attempt to shock you. But others are a necessary part of the child's search to internalize values that were once automatically accepted from parents and other authorities.

These questions are not meant as challenges to your beliefs and are not meant to put you on the spot. Students this age are simply challenging their own beliefs as they rethink what they have learned from their parents and other adults. We should embrace this process, since it is a necessary step that the child must take in order to move toward independence and adult faith.

Always welcome and honor the student's faith and morality questions. Enthusiastically receive them and respond to them respectfully. Let them know that asking questions is good. The more unconditional love students feel while they are searching, the more likely they are to come through the process spiritually healthy on the other side.

Intellectually, preteens are transitioning from concrete thinking to abstract thinking. Like most of the changes in early adolescents, these modes of thinking will advance at irregular and individual paces. Be prepared for a variety of cognitive levels and answers that reflect them.

Use open-ended questions to help all of your learners be involved. Encourage the questioning inherent with the maturing thought processes of preteens as they rethink their faith. Stretch them to think more and to ask more questions. We want to walk closely with preteens through this time of internalizing faith and values.

◉ **"I want to sit with my friends."** Friendships are important to preteens and fitting into the group becomes a high priority. Kids will do whatever it takes to make friends and keep them. They are far more interested in their social standing than in your lesson, so allowing kids to sit with a friend removes one obstacle to creating a good environment for learning.

As an early adolescent rethinks his or her beliefs, the influence of peers will weigh more heavily on decisions than ever before. And though the preteen's parents will influence him or her less, the parent still has a profound influence on the child. For these reasons, we don't want to fight the preteen's desire to be with friends at church, even though these friendships may at times appear to create discipline problems.

The way you group boys and girls at this age can either create or prevent behavior problems. We normally give kids a chance to be with one or two friends during any small group, class or activity. Occasionally, being with a friend causes problems, but this privilege can also be used as an incentive to motivate the kids toward good behavior. Explain that if sitting with a friend causes a disruption, the friends will be separated. The desire to be with friends is so powerful that most students will be strongly motivated to behave!

If you are wondering if boys and girls are compatible in the same group, you're not alone! As adolescence approaches, girls tend to mature more rapidly than boys. So a group with both fifth and sixth graders is likely to have noticeable differences in maturity levels between older girls and younger boys. Some leaders choose the path of least resistance and completely separate girls and boys. However, if both girls and boys are involved in an interesting activity, they are unlikely to create a disturbance over who happens to be working alongside them.

There are exceptions to the rule, of course. Some leaders do better with mixed-gender groups, others with same-gender groups. Know yourself and your kids.

🌀 **"I want to talk and talk and talk!"** Recently, following a discipline workshop that we presented at a regional convention, a woman who taught sixth-grade girls approached us, frustrated that she couldn't keep her girls from talking while she was presenting the lesson. She said that she was already giving the girls time to discuss the key points as we had suggested in the workshop, but she still couldn't keep them on track while she was trying to teach the rest of the lesson.

After a bit of exploration, we finally discovered what the problem was: Her discussion time was saved for the end of the class after all of the important material that she wanted to present was done. Kids need frequent opportunities to talk sprinkled throughout the session. These chat breaks actually help the students learn and apply the lesson, and they reduce extraneous talking that arises from those kids who simply can't sit still that long without talking.

If you are trying to use a lecture style of teaching and do not adequately account for the social needs of your students, you create an atmosphere ripe for discipline problems. Be sure to plan in regular neighbor nudges and small-group discussion in which all of your students have the opportunity to talk. They will talk anyway, so plan for this time to be profitable by telling them when they can do it and what they will discuss.

Prevent Discipline Problems by Filling Your Students' Emotional Tanks

In *How to Really Love Your Teenager*, Ross Campbell gives an insightful look at the behavior of early adolescents and teens: "Teenagers [and preteens] are *children* emotionally. To illustrate this, let's look at how a teenager is like a two-year-old. Both a teenager and a two-year-old have drives for independence and both have emotional tanks. Each will strive for independence, using the energy from the emotional tank. When the emotional tank has run dry, the teenager and the two-year-old will do the same thing—return to the parent [or other significant adult] for a refill so they can again strive for independence."[2]

The emotional tank that Campbell describes is how a child or teen feels about him- or herself and the world. It must be full for the preteen to behave his or her best. Yet the very developmental processes that are occurring in the preteen's life drain his or her tank. (Other events drain it as well, such as fatigue, hunger, name-calling by peers, parents' divorce, and so on.)

We have seen the difference that a teacher can make in the filling of a preteen's emotional tank over the past few years of the preteen school life of our daughter, Ashley. In third grade, Ashley had a teacher who was a true emotional tank filler, and she had a fantastic year educationally. In fourth grade, she had an excellent teacher who, unfortunately, didn't connect with her emotionally. It was a good year educationally, but not a fantastic one. In fifth grade, Ashley and her teacher shared a love for writing and literature. This teacher went out of her way to encourage, support and challenge Ashley's skills in this area.

Her teacher said, "I just consider them my kids. They will always be my kids. I just talk to them like they're people!"

Some time ago, this teacher helped Ashley enter a districtwide writing contest, which she won. As if the success was not a big enough tank filler on its own, the day after the results were announced, Ashley arrived at school to find a special certificate that her third-grade teacher had made and left on her desk. Tank filling has a lot to do with relational bonds, many of which will last for years after our kids leave our programs.

So the first job of a preteen leader or teacher is to do whatever he or she can do to fill early adolescents' emotional tanks. There are many ways to do this:

⊚ Listen carefully and sensitively to them when they want to share.

⊚ Encourage them to be their best.

⊚ Encourage them when they feel their worst.

⊚ Accept them just the way they are.

⊚ Phone them during the week.

⊚ Remember their birthdays.

⊚ Write notes to them "just because."

⊚ Honor special achievements.

⊚ Spend time together doing things kids like to do.

⊚ Attend special functions, such as games, concerts and award ceremonies.

⊚ Pray for their special needs.

Our second job is to avoid draining the emotional tanks of our preteen students. Again, we can learn from Ross Campbell: "When your [student] tests you by striving through inappropriate behavior to be independent, you must be careful not to overreact emotionally. This does not mean condoning the misbehavior. You need to express your feelings honestly but appropriately; that is, without extreme anger, yelling, name-calling, attacking the child verbally, or otherwise losing control of yourself . . . . The more a parent [or teacher] loses self-control in a teenager's presence, the less respect a teenager will feel for his parent [or teacher]."[3]

One volunteer fifth-and-sixth-grade teacher that we observed used her quick wit and motherly demeanor to her advantage. Watching her, it was obvious that nothing much could get under her skin. She did not, however, let the kids get away with bad behavior. When one boy continued to disrupt the small group she was leading, she looked at him with a smile and said, "John, since you seem to need some attention, why don't you come and sit right here next to me?" John was quiet for the rest of the session.

Of course, as we have already mentioned, with preteens there is a fine line between having a sense of humor and putting kids down. We need to keep our smile, but we must never embarrass these fragile egos. In the case of John, the teacher seemed to know him well enough to know he could take the teasing. Her joke let the whole group know that she was serious about their behavior, but her lack of ridiculing language also left John with his dignity. He got the message without getting destroyed.

Prevent Discipline Problems by Making Your Boundaries Clear

⊚ **Kids want and need boundaries.** Lawrence Crabb, Christian psychologist, author and speaker, tells us that children need both boundaries and love. In his book, *Understanding People,* Crabb gives a prescription for avoiding discipline problems: "Children, I suspect, would become more manageable and infinitely more lovable if parents would answer, properly and with some consistency, a few elementary questions that all kids ask. First, 'Am I loved?' Correct answer: 'Yes, deeply—and here's the unmistakable evidence of my rich, committed involvement with you.' Second, 'Can I get my own way?' Correct answer: 'No, not without cost—and here is a sample of the painful consequences that result from bucking against God's plan.'"[4]

This is just as true of the students in your classroom or other activities. If a child never pushes against the boundaries, the child never gains the security he or she needs. Expect kids to test you. Those who have never had the two critical questions answered at home (or have not had them answered appropriately or consistently somewhere else) will be looking for some adult who will give them Crabb's two correct answers.

Sometimes when kids are pushing the limits and complaining about rules, they are truly asking you to show them love by *not* giving into their requests or demands. In their attempt to relate to the cool early adolescents, some leaders mistakenly think that they must remove all or almost all of the boundaries. This is simply not true. Removing boundaries causes insecurity that leads to further acting out as the preteen desperately searches for some boundary further away from normal behavior.

Whether at home or in the classroom, Ross Campbell tells us that an early adolescent "will strive for independence in typical adolescent ways—doing things by himself, going places without family, testing parental rules. But he will eventually run out of emotional gasoline and come back to the parent for emotional maintenance—for a refill. This is what we want, as parents [or teachers] of teenagers. We want our adolescent *to be able* to come to us for emotional maintenance when he needs it."[5]

Part of our role in the classroom is to be the solid rock that kids can test, push away, and then come back to when they need to be loved and filled up again. When we do not consistently enforce limits, we lose our ability to be the secure foundation that kids want and need.

◎ **Expect the best.** A number of years ago we consulted with a church that was concerned about its youth ministry. Although the youth group was growing, the regular attenders from church families and other kids who had been excited about their involvement in spiritual growth were dropping out in record numbers.

After evaluating what was going on, it became evident that the leadership was the problem. The youth pastor preferred to spend time with the non-Christian kids. He didn't expect any of the kids to be very interested in spiritual things. He programmed almost exclusively for the spiritual seeker and, therefore, offered almost no serious studies or discipleship programs.

When we interviewed young adults who had weathered this leader's ministry, we discovered that as young teens they were convinced that they were expected to behave like non-Christian youth, with little interest in spiritual things and not much respect for authority. The kids themselves told us that they were faced with two alternatives:

1. Live up to the leader's expectations, and show little to no interest in spiritual things to fit into the group, or

2. Drop out and find a place that encouraged spiritual and social maturity.

As mentors and disciplers of preteens, we need to have the highest of expectations for the early adolescents we lead. These kids desperately want to know how to live and they want to know how to please us. Our expectations will subtly show through in all we do. The students pick up on these expectations and consciously or subconsciously attempt to live up to them. Therefore, if we believe the best and hope for the best, we're more likely to get the best!

◎ **Tell the kids what you want.** Some discipline problems exist not because there are no boundaries but simply because we have never made clear to the kids what those boundaries are. We must remember that our kids have different adults with different expectations in every sphere of life: school, home, Mom's house, Dad's house, the babysitter, coaches and even Sunday School and midweek programs.

Leaders and teachers of the various ministries for preteens at your church should discuss and come to some agreement on what the behavioral expectations will be for your kids. These expectations must then be clearly spelled out from time to time so that your students will be aware of what the game plan is at your church. Key times to review the expectations are at the start of a new year, at the beginning of a new program, after a major break or holiday and whenever kids seem to be forgetting what you want them to do.

Prevent Discipline Problems by Loving Kids Unconditionally

Much of our discipline of preteens is discipleship with lots of loving patience. Just as Jesus patiently loved His disciples (and us) through their failures and shortcomings, we must do the same with our students. We are loving them to maturity in their Christian faith and walk. When leading preteens, look at every discipline challenge as an opportunity to be Jesus in their lives. Every problem is in reality an opportunity to help our students see where they must become more like Christ and how to do so.

In order to do this, we must be focused on the kids and what is of benefit to them. We must be selfless in our leadership and ministry.

Recently, we had a fifth-and-sixth-grade skating party and invited a junior higher from the church to play Christian CDs for us. He had the music turned up a little loud but not to an unreasonable level. (After all, we asked a junior higher to help because we assumed he would play the type of music that the fifth and sixth graders would like and in a way that they would like it.) The preteens were having a great time and were loving the music, the recreation and the fellowship with their peers.

It was just then that one of our leaders came to Gordon and asked, "Shouldn't we turn the music down? It's so loud. I don't like it!"

Thinking this was a good teaching opportunity, Gordon responded with the question, "Would we be turning it down for our comfort or for the benefit of the kids?" She got the point.

We cannot serve preteens with the focus still on ourselves. These kids will know instantly if we are more concerned about ourselves or about them. They are so focused on themselves already that they can tell if we aren't! We must be ready to have tough skin, to receive little thanks and to grin and bear some rudeness from time to time. Of course, we also need to not show our shock when the next day our kids give us a huge hug, are sweet and gentle and exhibit the spiritual sensitivity of David.

When we feel loved by someone, it is much easier for us to obey that person and to cooperate with him or her. This is true, to a lesser degree, even with people that we just like. As adults, we experience this on a regular basis. When our boss treats us well, it's no big deal to do him or her a favor or to work a little harder to meet a deadline. When a good friend asks us to go out of our way for him or her, it doesn't seem like such an imposition.

The same is true of preteen kids. If our students have really experienced our love, even when they know they are being unlovable, they will find it much easier to behave appropriately in our programs.

As mentioned by Lawrence Crabb earlier in this chapter, when a child feels loved, he or she is more manageable and more lovable! It's a self-fulfilling cycle. A child who feels loved will behave better. A child who behaves better will experience more love and acceptance. A child who feels loved and accepted feels better about him- or herself and life and, therefore, behaves better, and so on.

This means that some of the hardest to love and hardest to discipline kids may be the ones who are not experiencing unconditional love at home. (Not experiencing unconditional love does not necessarily mean that it is not present. Some children have loving parents but for one reason or another just don't receive their love.) These kids need some extra love and acceptance from us. Give the workers in your preteen ministry a copy of Loving Preteens to Good Behavior (see p. 128).

LOVING PRETEENS TO GOOD BEHAVIOR

♥ Preteens are not mature adults.

♥ Preteens tend to do immature and irresponsible things.

♥ Some of the irresponsibility and immaturity of preteens will be unpleasant for me.

♥ I am the mature adult. Therefore, God's expectation of me is to act like a mature adult. This includes loving these young kids, no matter what.

♥ If I am consistent in my unconditional love for my students, I will set the stage for them to grow and mature, since they will feel good about themselves and will learn to take responsibility for themselves.

♥ If I am inconsistent in my love and love them only when they make me happy, I will harm them by making them feel insecure and even unlovable.

♥ Therefore, my role in whether or not my students mature and grow into responsible adulthood is critical.

Prevent Discipline Problems by Building Positive Relationships

We asked quite a number of early adolescents whether or not they liked school and why or why not. It was fascinating to hear, over and over, that their perceived relationships with their teachers were key to their answers. One 10-year-old was consistent with the opinion of many other kids: "It's cool. . . . The teachers are nice."

This truth was understood by many of the successful preteen teachers we interviewed as well. We asked Lori, a volunteer fifth-and-sixth-grade teacher and mother of grown children, this question: What discipline tip would you give a new preteen teacher? Her answer was insightful: "For me, it's been a process of getting to know the children so that they have a reason to behave when they're in my class. And it's just not a lot of orders and discipline given out. It's a relationship that's built over time, a long-term relationship, of the kids' trusting you."

When we first started working at our present church, Becki stepped in to lead one session of the fifth-and-sixth-grade Sunday School that had been without a regular teacher for more than eight months. Different substitutes had worked for one-month periods and then moved on. No one had spent enough time with the kids to develop relationships, and the behavior of the class showed it. Becki's first few mornings with the kids were difficult (OK, very difficult). Even as a veteran ministry leader and a credentialed middle school teacher with several years of experience in public schools, she was discouraged. After Becki was with the group long enough to prove to them that she was there to stay, that they could count on her for the long haul, the kids' resistance started to fade and she was able to start developing relationships with them. It was an amazing transformation that followed. Once a few kids felt like their teacher was also a friend, the behavior of most of the kids changed dramatically.

Our preteens want to know if we love them and if they can get their own way!

Prevent Discipline Problems by Programming for the Needs of Preteens

Many of the discipline problems that we experience in preteen ministry could be prevented or at least minimized if we programmed to meet the needs of our students. When working with preteens, it is imperative that we understand who we are dealing with (see chapter 1) and that we program for their characteristics and needs (see chapter 2).

Eric, a ministry leader of fifth and sixth graders, told us how he strives to prevent discipline problems before they happen. "I think the best discipline is preventative. I would advise making the lessons and the classroom setting always a surprise. Never do the same thing at the same time from Sunday to Sunday. Make it so the kids are always on their toes."

Quick Tips for Correcting Problem Behaviors After the Fact

No matter how much work you do preventing discipline problems, you will undoubtedly experience a few challenges that will require your appropriate and timely response. Here are some quick dos and don'ts for disciplining early adolescents:

◎ Do smile and take a deep breath.

◎ Don't lose your temper, yell, scream, or belittle the child.

◎ Do speak directly to the student.

◎ Don't embarrass him or her in front of his or her peers.

◎ Do have the student verbalize what the inappropriate behavior was.

◎ Don't ask why he or she did it.

◎ Do help the preteen understand why the behavior was inappropriate.

◎ Don't threaten consequences that you are unwilling to carry out.

Do maintain a sense of humor.

Don't think that it's the end of the world.

Do talk with the student after you discipline him or her to make sure that the student knows you still care about him or her.

Don't be inconsistent in applying the rules.

Do ignore inappropriate behavior when it seems the child is just looking for attention.

Don't ignore behaviors that disrupt the class or might hurt someone or something.

Get Preteens to Take Responsibility for Their Behavior and Choices

Early adolescents need to understand the impact their behaviors have on other people. Recently, one of our sixth-grade boys had to be disciplined for hitting a girl in Sunday School. In talking with him, he was quick to say the right words: "I'm sorry." Something didn't click, though. With the boy's mother present, Gordon asked him why he was sorry. He said he was sorry because he knew it was wrong.

After several more questions, it was apparent to both Gordon and the boy's mother that his sorrow was consistently connected with getting caught, not with the harm he had done. The boy had great difficulty in understanding that he had hurt another student and that his behavior had made the girl cry and had upset her parents, his parents and the class leaders.

Empathy is a quality that we must continually teach early adolescents. As they move from concrete thinking to abstract thinking, they are able to think beyond punishment to consequences and impact on others. We teach empathy by identifying it, talking about it and modeling it whenever possible.

Early adolescents need to experience real consequences that appropriately help them take responsibility for their decisions. An important part of our discipline and discipleship of preteens is to help them learn that their behavior has consequences. Kids must learn to take responsibility for their decisions, contrary to what they are being taught in our society and in the media. We must treat them as responsible agents, not victims, so that they learn to own their mistakes and enjoy their successes.

A mother just shared with us that she would not be attending an awards ceremony at which her daughter would be receiving a presentation, because the daughter forgot to give her parents the invitation to the ceremony until the last minute. The mother wanted to teach the girl a lesson.

Yes, this is a realistic consequence, but, no, it will not help the child in an appropriate way. The consequence of the mother's behavior has a far greater impact on making her daughter feel unloved and unimportant than it will have on teaching her to bring papers home to Mom and Dad.

The mother was attempting to punish *childlike behavior* (forgetfulness) as though it was *wrongful or disobedient behavior*. In the last story about the boy who hit the girl, it would have been inappropriate to discipline the boy if he had hurt her while playing a game. We would have disciplined him in a different manner had he hurt her because of a thoughtless or careless event. But he deliberately chose to swing and hit her out of anger. Consequences must never diminish the child's self-worth or damage the relationship between the adult and the child, but they must be painful enough (such as loss of privileges or extra chores) to help the child understand the seriousness of his or her actions and choices.

Another boy recently came to Gordon and asked, very politely, if Gordon would sponsor him on a junior high work-a-thon to raise money for the youth group. Gordon agreed to sponsor him. For the next few Sundays, the same boy got into a series of situations in which he chose to be extremely rude and disrespectful to Gordon. Then one Wednesday night he came back to Gordon and, very politely, asked him for the money he had pledged.

Gordon shared with the boy and his parents that it seemed the boy was using good manners just to get what he wanted. When he didn't want anything, his manners would slip. The issue at hand was that the boy needed to learn to be polite and respectful to other people and especially to adults *all the time*.

Instead of giving the money as pledged, Gordon gave twice the pledge directly to the junior high group and explained to the boy that he would not get credit toward the incentives given by the group for pledges gathered. He needed to know that using good manners to manipulate an adult would not benefit him in the long run. He also needed to see that an adult would follow through on a promise in spite of his behavior.

It can be hard work, but we must take our own focus off punishing or rewarding kids. We need to teach them, train them to be responsible young people and to help them understand that what they do will affect other people and themselves.

Notes
1. Ross Campbell, M.D., *How to Really Love Your Teenager* (Wheaton, IL: Victor Books, 1981), p. 28.
2. Ibid., pp. 28-29.
3. Ibid., p. 30.
4. Lawrence J. Crabb, Jr., *Understanding People* (Grand Rapids, MI: Zondervan Publishing House, 1987), p. 18
5. Campbell, *How to Really Love Your Teenager*, p. 29.

Reaching Out to the Whole Family

"In order to have a committed young person at this age, his or her parents must be just as committed; otherwise the young person isn't there on time or doesn't show at all."

—Corey Hooper, junior high pastor

God's Plan for Families

There's no debating it. God plans for healthy, mature God-fearing parents to raise their kids to love and know God through their consistent, daily exhortations and demonstrations of the truth of God's Word:

> Hear, O Israel: The Lord our God, the Lord is one. Love the Lord your God with all your heart and with all your soul and with all your strength. These commandments that I give you today are to be upon your hearts. Impress them on your children. Talk about them when you sit at home and when you walk along the road, when you lie down and when you get up. Tie them as symbols on your hands and bind them on your foreheads. Write them on the doorframes of your houses and on your gates (Deuteronomy 6:4-9).

But those of us who work with kids at church know that, all too often, parents aren't living up to this passage. Some are doing all they can to live up to it but don't know how. Some are unable to do so, because of other life problems or disabilities. And some just aren't around anymore. Those of us parents who are trying to nurture our kids spiritually will be the first to say we could use all the help the church has to offer!

Instead of becoming the prime source for spiritual nurture for preteens, churches need to start partnering with parents for the sake of our kids. If we want to have maximum impact on preteens, we must work with their families. As leaders we can provide kids with excellent age-appropriate ministry at church *and* help to make parents and families more successful in their God-given responsibilities.

Ben Freudenberg and Rick Lawrence reported the results of Search Institute's 1995 study on the factors that nurture faith in kids. "There is little debate about the importance of family in shaping people's lives, including their physical, intellectual, emotional, psychological and social development. But we sometimes forget that the family is just as important in the area of spiritual or faith development. This study examined several ways families express faith in the home—each of which is extremely important for nurturing a dynamic faith. Four family practices are particularly important in helping young people grow in faith (both in childhood and adolescence):

1. Talking about faith with your mother.

2. Talking about faith with your father.

3. Having family devotions or prayer.

4. Doing family projects to help other people.

"Fewer than one-third of youth report that any of the above activities happen often—either in their past or present—and adults are even less likely to remember these experiences in their childhood and adolescence. It is hardly surprising, then, that parents—most of whom did not experience nurturing of their faith in their own growing-up years—need help nurturing their children's faith."[1] So how can we help the families of preteens? First, we need to understand what the families are up against.

The State of the Family

"After the surge in church membership in the 1950s, about 50 million baby boomers left the church—intending never to return. But now about 43 million of them are back. And 60 percent of these 'prodigals' have kids—many of them regulars in your group. . . . That means your ministry . . . necessarily includes ministry to their parents."[2]

Here are some startling statistics that show the state of the American family today:

☉ In 2002, there was a total of 72.9 million children in the United States, with a projected total of 80.3 million in the year 2020.[3]

☉ In 2003, 68 percent of all children in the United States lived with two parents (down from 1980's 77 percent), 23 percent lived with their mothers only, 5 percent with their fathers, and 4 percent with neither of their parents.[4]

☉ The percentage of children who live with both parents is continuing to decline in every racial and ethnic group in the United States.[5]

☉ In 2002, 44 of every 1,000 unmarried women (ages 15 to 44) gave birth (up from 29 per 1,000 in 1980).[6]

☉ In 2001, 61 percent of all three- to six-year-olds in America were cared for in a child-care center.[7]

☉ Child care is not necessarily hooked to financial need for parents to work. In 2001, 59 percent of children from families above poverty level were enrolled in an early childhood care and education program.[8]

☉ In 2002, 16.3 percent of our children lived in families that had incomes below the poverty line (the national standard of poverty). Nine percent of the kids in two-parent homes were in poverty, while 40 percent of the female-parent-only households were in poverty.[9]

☉ In 2002, 30 percent of the two-parent homes in America had both parents working full-time, up from 17 percent in 1980.[10]

☉ Thirty-six percent of the families with children in 2002 had inadequate housing, overcrowded housing, or housing that exceeded 30 percent of the household income.[11]

☉ In 2003, 9.7 percent of eighth graders reported having used illicit drugs in the previous 30 days, compared with 19.5 percent of tenth graders and 24.1 percent of twelfth graders.[12]

Our Families Are Facing More Complex Issues

Not only is the structure of the family more complicated than ever before, but the family's environment and social setting are more complex as well. The hot topics that we hear on the news are realities for our families. And the issues our preteens who attend church are facing aren't too different from the ones the unchurched families in our neighborhoods are grappling with. (See p. 134 for a list of some of the significant issues that families of preteens, whether churched or unchurched,

FORTY ISSUES

AFFECTING FAMILIES WITH PRETEENS

1. Divorce

2. Remarriage

3. Single parenting

4. Stepparenting

5. Blended families

6. The influence of television

7. The impact of media, movies and music

8. Need for discipline of kids

9. Harried family lifestyle

10. Rush for kids to grow up

11. Alcoholism within the home

12. Drug abuse within the home

13. Physical or sexual abuse within the home

14. Drug, alcohol or tobacco use by children

15. Financial problems

16. Unemployment

17. Marital infidelity

18. Nominal or unbelieving spouses

19. Live-in couples or unwed parents

20. Never-wed single moms

21. Grandparents raising grandchildren

22. Dealing with in-laws

23. Caring for aging parents

24. Multigeneration households

25. Two-career families

26. Stay-at-home mom's well-being

27. Choice of schools: Home? Private? Public?

28. Chronic illnesses of adult or child

29. Disabilities—physical or mental

30. After-school care for kids

31. "De-parenting" or preparing to launch kids

32. Family friendships

33. Gangs, crime and shoplifting

34. School problems

35. Friends of children

36. Leisure activities

37. Vacation choices

38. Prodigal children

39. Homosexuality in society

40. Emotional intimacy in marriage

are facing.)

So if our families are dealing with all of these issues, we need to realize that our church is (or should be) dealing with the same issues. If you've taken this list seriously, it should be a bit overwhelming. Let's take a look at a way to break down the needs into bite-sized chunks, and then we'll look at some practical ideas for meeting these needs as we partner with parents.

What Do Parents Hope to Find at Church?

Jean Grasso Fitzpatrick, author of *Something More*, suggests several questions that parents should ask before placing their child into your ministry. We have adapted those questions here:

⊛ Are the leaders and teachers friendly and loving? Do they appear happy to be working with kids this age?

⊛ Are the workers trained to work with kids the age of my child?

⊛ Will my child get affirmed for participating?

⊛ Is the goal of this ministry one that will encourage my child's spiritual development?

⊛ Will I, as a parent, be informed of the happenings of the group? How will I know what the kids are doing if my son or daughter doesn't tell me?

⊛ Does it seem that my son or daughter would find a good friend in this group?[13]

Look at the Seasons of Family Life

Several researchers have popularized the notion of family life having developmental seasons or, as Elizabeth Carter and Monica McGoldrick term it, "stages of the family life cycle."[14] Families with preteens would fall in the early years of Carter and McGoldrick's "family with adolescents" stage, which they characterize as being a period of increasing flexibility of family boundaries to include children's independence. For the parents, this is the beginning of a shift in the parent-child

relationship to permit the adolescent to move in and out of the family system.

This way of looking at families, and their needs, in cycles or stages of development is extremely helpful for ministering to families, especially if you are primarily responsible for just one segment of family life, such as the preteen years.

Don Hebbard, author of *The Complete Handbook for Family Ministry in the Church*, recommends doing research to discover the felt needs of our families and then designing programming to meet those needs. "Programming is an ongoing process . . . described as a rational-purposive process designed to access, address, and evaluate the needs of a system with the overall goal of effecting a desired change."[15]

"The needs of families in our churches and communities are far too great to be ineffective in meeting them. Most churches do not have the luxury to throw people and dollars at ministerial hunches. Since we do not have the ability, as Luke said of

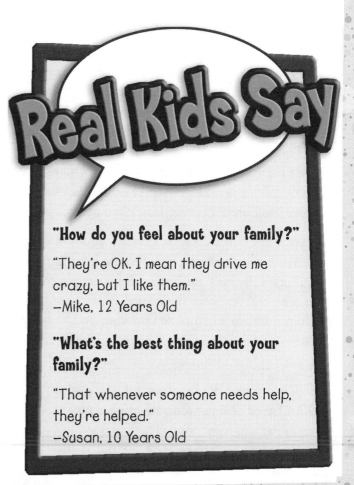

"How do you feel about your family?"

"They're OK. I mean they drive me crazy, but I like them."
—Mike, 12 Years Old

"What's the best thing about your family?"

"That whenever someone needs help, they're helped."
—Susan, 10 Years Old

Jesus, to know the hearts of all (see Acts 1:24), we must rely on more mundane methodologies.

"Congregational family need analysis is one of the tools in our tool kit. It is a multifaceted effort to determine what is going on in our congregational families. It allows us to focus our attention on meeting real human needs,"[16] Hebbard says.

How do you accomplish this needs analysis? Start out by reading any one of the many family life cycle developmental textbooks that will help you project the typical needs of families at this stage of development. But then personalize your research by reading the latest articles and books, by listening to the news and, most of all, by talking with (and listening to) your families, whether through surveys or interviews, focus groups or random chats.

What Do the Parents of Preteens Need?

The following are a few of the basic needs that you can assume your families and parents of preteens are feeling:

◎ **They need new friends.** As parents see their child (especially their firstborn) approaching the teen years, they are motivated to get to know other parents going through this same confusing and sometimes frightening transition. Parents of early adolescents also want to know the parents of their child's friends to see what kinds of influences they are receiving from their peers.

Have open houses in your preteen youth room (or someone's home) for your kids and their families. Parents will show up just so they can meet other parents and see who their kids' friends are. Lead parents and kids in one or more fun get-acquainted games to break the ice and help start relationships among the family members.

◎ **They need to understand their child and what he or she is going through.** Once the kids reach school age, parenting doesn't have any major new challenges for a while—that is, until early adolescence hits. All of a sudden, parents

are ready to be taught again. They want good, practical information on the following:

◎ Dealing with early adolescent children, their mood swings, their challenges to authority and what else to expect in the future

◎ Understanding the differences among childhood, early adolescence and the teen years

◎ Specifics about the church programs to be offered in the immediate and coming teen years

Try having an in-service time for parents to help them connect with one another and receive the information they are looking for. Ask middle school teachers in your congregation to help do the training, or assemble a team of the children's ministry and youth ministry leaders to cohost a seminar or workshop on early adolescence.

◎ **They need skills to talk to their children about sexuality and drugs.** Due to constant media bombardment, parents have gotten the message that they need to discuss sex and drugs with their kids. Parents of preteens are realizing that their days of opportunity on these issues are quickly fading. They want to know how to handle these touchy topics in ways that their kids will respect and respond to appropriately.

At church, we can either take over the parent's job and address these issues for them, or we can provide the training and resources (and encouragement) that they need to handle the responsibility themselves.

◎ **They need to be spiritual leaders for their kids.** Many parents of preteens have a renewed desire to be spiritual leaders in their homes. They realize that they do not have many years left with their children under their roof and that, as teen years approach, life decisions are becoming more and more critical. It is important for kids to know that church is important to their parents. Parents need to know how to share their faith with their own kids and need opportunities to model their involvement with God and His church.

Provide a variety of opportunities for parents to be involved in ministry so that their kids can see that they are active and involved. Design ways for families to serve together: team teaching in a preschool classroom, coleading a portion of the all-church worship service or a youth-group meeting, doing service projects together, or ministering to another family in need. Kids need to see their parents in action.

🌀 **They need to be connected as a family.** Many of our churches do such a good job of programming for each individual age group that church becomes a time to separate family members from each other. At this developmental stage, parents are hungry for ways to connect with their kids in positive activities. Most don't want more reasons to be separated.

Ross Campbell wisely counsels, "As children enter adolescence, they need more time with family, not less. It is so easy to assume that since teens are rapidly becoming more independent and seem to want more and more time away from the family, that you should spend less and less time with them. This is one of the most devastating mistakes parents make today. As their children enter and progress through adolescence, parents often use their free time in ways which meet their own pleasure needs. Every teenager I've ever known interprets this as rejection, feeling that their parents care less and less about them."[17] Let's not continue this mistake at church!

Think about all the different activities you do for preteens and consider which ones could be family events in which you do the same activity but invite the whole family. Later we will also share several ideas for adding programs that encourage family togetherness.

Making the Church Family-Friendly

Is your church helping families, or is it hindering their efforts to be healthy? We can program in the name of family and actually be working against family life! Check your church to see if you may be unwittingly hindering healthy family life with some of these common practices:

🌀 Sending kids one way and parents another

every time families come to church

🌀 Having so many wonderful activities for your preteens that they're never home with their families

🌀 Talking about parents in preteen meetings in ways that subtly undermine their authority or the respect they should be receiving from their kids

🌀 Giving parents and kids the message that the church will take care of all the Christian education of kids

Here are some tips for making your church a little more family-friendly for your preteens and their parents:

🌀 **Streamline the church calendar.** Have everything at church on one night—or at least, have one night of the week when nothing happens at church. From the pulpit, encourage families to use this free night as Family Night to spend time together doing anything they want!

🌀 **Provide reduced rates for whole families to attend activities.** Whenever you have an all-church dinner, social, retreat, or any other activities where participants must pay to be involved, consider having a flat rate for whole families. In many cases, the more kids a family has, the less extra money they have for recreational activities. With normal methods, these are the very families that get hit the hardest for paid church activities.

🌀 **Encourage the church leadership to support preteen ministry.** Those of us who work with early adolescents know that this can be a forgotten corner of the church. Help your leaders understand the critical period of family development that is represented in the preteen years. Encourage them to give this ministry the respect, finances and manpower it so richly deserves.

Adapt Current Preteen Events to Include Families

🌀 **Encourage intergenerational activities.** A number of years ago, a study showed that the highest SAT scores were earned by kids who often spent time with their families doing things like going camping and having dinner together regularly. Spending time together is good for families.

Try turning the fun things you are already doing with preteens into activities for the whole family. Look for opportunities to host socials that involve the preteens, their siblings, their parents and even their grandparents! Try picnics, going to the zoo or family film nights at church.

You may also want to have special family groupings, like mother-child or father-child events. Just account for kids who don't have the type of parent your event calls for by either having surrogate parents ready to sponsor a child or by offering enough events that missing one won't matter.

◉ **Turn VBS into a family activity.** Use a curriculum that offers suggestions for an intergenerational or family VBS at which the whole family learns, plays and grows together. Then plan your VBS for a week of summer nights or once a week for 5 or 10 weeks. Have families sign up together and place the whole family in a small group. Let Mom or Dad be the small-group leader and everyone in the family have a job for the week.

Ben Freudenburg, coauthor of *The Family-Friendly Church*, had great success at his church with this format in his "5 for the Family" program, in which the families all come together to enjoy meals with one another and the educational times are woven around these fellowship times.

Lois Sherwin, director of children's ministries at a church in La Mirada, California, created a family VBS called "S.T.A.R.T." (Summer Time Activities, Recreation and Teaching). Moving her traditional VBS to five consecutive evenings allowed whole families to attend. It also helped those kids who are normally in day care and wouldn't have had a ride to VBS otherwise. Advertisements in the newspaper, leaflets handed out by her preteens, and local radio station spots all help bring in unchurched families from the community.

◉ **Have a Birds and the Bees workshop.** Instead of getting permission from your preteens'

parents to have your annual sex education talk with the kids, have a workshop for your parents and give them the tools to talk with their own kids. Give this responsibility back to the willing parents, but equip them to do the job.

In your training session include information on what to cover with their kids and when. Brainstorm creative, comfortable ways to bring up the subject, and use your parents who have older kids to share ideas and first-person anecdotes whenever possible. Be sure to include time for the parents to share in small groups and to pray for one another.

Here are some tips for talking with an early adolescent about their teen years:

◉ Start early. The topic isn't as important as the habit of communicating frankly and easily with your kids.

◉ Don't wait to be asked. Middle schoolers are shy—they might be waiting for you to bring up the subject.

◉ Avoid lecturing. Instead, use a casual approach. If you're embarrassed, admit it. Use humor to ease any awkwardness, and talk about your own stormy emotions during adolescence.

◉ Keep talking. Junior highers need different information at different times. . . . Talk about your own values and religious beliefs that relate to sexuality."[18]

Purchase copies of several resource books that you believe would be helpful for your parents and make them available for check out.

◉ **Involve parents in missions trips and service projects.** Kids learn best from the example of loving parents, so consider involving parents in the planning and execution of any missions trip or service project that you would normally offer for preteens. (For more ideas on missions and service projects, see chapters 11 and 12.)

◉ **Initiate family worship Sundays.** If the schedule at your church has preteens attending Sunday School while their parents attend the worship service, try calling off your preteen Sunday School one week and encouraging your families to worship together. Work with your worship team to include your preteens and their families in the worship service in a variety of ways:

- Taking the offering as a family

- Reading Scripture as a family

- Greeting as a family

Your leaders will love this idea, too! Maybe they can even worship with their own families for a change!

Add Family-Focused Activities and Ministries

Hold family camps and retreats. Consider joining your denomination, a regional Christian camp, or some other churches in your area for a weekend family retreat or a summer vacation camp that the whole family attends. Retreats often work for most families, because the camps can become quite costly and it's easier to get the whole family away together for a shorter period of time.

Plan family campouts. Reserve a national forestry group campsite and announce the date. Then families can do all the work themselves! Most group sites will accommodate tents, tent trailers or RVs all in the same area.

Red Mountain Community Church in Mesa, Arizona, started their own annual family campout a few years ago when they discovered that very few of their families wanted to spend the money that the denominational family retreat was costing. They believe their success comes from not overloading anyone with lots of planning and activity. Families are brought together and then allowed to come up with their own recreational options together. The only planned activities are one group potluck and a Sunday-morning worship service before breaking camp.

Have preteen youth group meetings in private homes. Have your preteen youth group in different homes where the parents are able to socialize with the kids. It will be good for both parties! One church calls these meetings "H.O.B.B.I.T.S." or Homes Open by Believers in the Savior. Use the church bus to take all the kids or ask parents to drop them off at a prearranged location. Ask the host or hostess to provide snacks and drinks for the night.

Consider family Sunday School. Sharon Hovanic, a children's and family pastor, shared with us her plan for classes for whole families she holds once each month. She alternates holding these on Sunday mornings and Friday nights, in order to allow families with different schedules to take part.

When the preteens arrive with their families, they enter a room to the sounds of contemporary Christian music and notice a variety of different activities waiting for them. These often include food or craft projects designed to be done by members of several generations at the same time. All the families are gathered together for large-group singing, praise and worship, and enjoyable preteen selections; then they're off to a fun large-group game or opening activity such as a scavenger hunt.

Her program includes fun, hands-on activities that the whole family can do together, each designed to illustrate one point for the evening. Sharon will present an idea and then have parents discuss prepared questions with their children.

At some point in the lesson, the kids are sent to their own age-appropriate activities for about 20 minutes while Sharon leads a discussion with the parents about parenting issues and the biblical insights into them, including family devotions, creating family mission statements, how to deal with teenage rebellion, statistics on and methods for developing greater family unity, prayer and family activities. The atmosphere is kept casual and not "churchy," since Sharon wants this to be an outreach and advertises the program in the local papers.

Organize mother-daughter and father-son activities. Although we must be careful not to

leave out kids who do not have the same-gender parent available, kids still need special times with their parents. Don't be afraid to have father-son or mother-daughter programs. Just be ready to have surrogate moms or dads ready to fill in for kids who need them.

Granada Heights Friends Church in La Mirada, California, has a father-son club called "Eagles." The dads meet at the beginning of the year and plan their own craft projects, games, outings and special events—normally each having something to do with a hobby or special interest of one or more of the fathers involved. The children's ministries leaders then weave devotionals around the themes

the fathers have picked and provide the leaders with these materials.

Look for Opportunities to Equip Parents of Preteens

When you are trying to teach adults how to parent, we have found that "soft" accountability helps. Challenge parents to be involved and to work hard, but don't be controlling or demanding. We need to understand the demands that are already realities in the lives of the families in our church-

most popular. Quarter-long, 13-week courses are no longer the preference of most parents. Parents struggle to fit long-term commitments into their already-packed schedules. They also tend to become overwhelmed when they receive more information week after week and are still trying to apply the first things they learned. Instead, try intense, brief seminars, perhaps on a Friday night and all-day Saturday. Include workshops on the needs of children and creating healthy family relationships, guidelines on disciplining early adolescents, whether in the classroom or at home, and helping parents learn to lead family devotions. Experienced leaders in your denomination, your church or your community may lead these sessions.

Training your preteen teachers is also a great way to train parents. Many workers are parents and can therefore apply teacher training to their own homes. And you can equip your children's workers to be leaders in training parents both formally and informally as they build relationships with the parents of your early adolescent students.

☺ **Minister directly to mothers of preteens.** Sharon Hovanic shared with us the ways that she attempts to reach the mothers of her preteen students: "We realized that unless there was continuity between the home and church, there was no application. Anytime we started with kids, we were starting at a negative. Unless modeled in the home, the preteens were not very receptive to what we were teaching. They get an 'attitude' at that age."

In order to combat that attitude, Sharon went to the mother's group at her church to begin equipping them to model the faith at home. She gave ideas for incorporating faith into home in simple ways. After a trip to the local Christian bookstore, she shared plaques and sayings that could be hung in prominent places around the house as reminders.

One of her major goals in doing this was to develop cooperative teamwork between her ministry and the parents. "The parents need the backup from a 'youth minister' type person. One girl told me, 'You say a lot of the things my mom says but in a better sort of way. I always wondered if what my mom said applied today.'"

🌀 **Try educating whole families.** Ben Freudenburg has created family workshops in which the whole family gathers over a meal and is instructed in specific life skills, including good manners and family worship. Sometimes the kids leave during part of the instruction for their own class, but at other times they remain with their parents. Try this format with lots of interactive times for parents and preteens to discuss the issues. The leader becomes a third party that can bring balance to family discussions and lead them into positive sharing.

🌀 **Have parent-teacher conferences.** This is a family connection that we can pick up from our local schools. Most public schools have individual parent-teacher conferences (sometimes with the student, sometimes without) about twice each school year. Try the same personal approach with the parents of your students!

Schedule individual meetings with the parents of your preteen students. Use this meeting to further build a bond between the church and home. Tell the parents that you desire to partner with them in nurturing their child spiritually. Ask open-ended questions about how you can help:

🌀 Does Susan seem to enjoy coming to our preteen programs? Why or why not?

🌀 What have been some of her favorite activities?

🌀 What could you share with me that you think would improve Susan's experience at church?

🌀 Are there any ways that the church could be of help to you or your family?

Minister to Preteen Families with Special Needs— The Single Parent Family

Ministry to single-parent homes is a given in preteen ministry. In fact, according to Dr. Greg Cynaumon, approximately 75 percent of the kids who show up in a counselor's office for post-divorce counseling are in the age span of 10 to 12 years.[19]

Cynaumon explains, "One possible reason that children between the ages of 10 and 12 are likely to experience more emotional struggles is because of their prepuberty 'transitional stage' in life. These changes during the preteen years can cause children to feel less stable and sometimes out of control."[20]

George Barna tells us this: "Almost without exception, single parents hurt from their broken relationships, their economic hardships, and their bouts with self-doubt. And increasingly, we hear from single parents that the Church is not a place of healing but of condemnation.[21]

How can we design our ministries to preteens and their families so that we consistently show single-parent families God's love?

🌀 Avoid making your ministry appear to be designed only for two-parent families. Make sure your language is inclusive and that registration forms allow for a variety of family units.

🌀 Track multiple addresses in your church records, because you will probably need to correspond and communicate with multiple sets of parents.

🌀 Offer socials and workshops for single parents only, catering to their unique needs and interests, but always be sure the same people feel included in all parent or family events.

🌀 Be sensitive to the financial needs of single-parent families. Don't just offer scholarships; seek out those who you know have need, and help them personally.

🌀 Offer counseling or financial assistance for single parents and their kids to find counseling in your community.

🌀 Be a friend.

Make Families the Lifeblood of Your Ministry

The church and the family must work together for the sake of the kids. We must always listen to parents; they are the experts on their own kids. But we must also remember that families are looking to the church for help.

Don Hebbard says: "Church families are in desperate need of teaching, training, discussion, clarification, analysis, questioning, reading, demonstration, argumentation, and confrontation on the family issues of the day. They have placed the church in the resource provider role, and I think too many churches have remained silent." [22]

Don't let your preteen ministry remain silent any longer! Work at equipping parents, supporting families and creating a partnership in which early adolescents will thrive and have their faith nurtured consistently at home and at church.

Notes

1. Ben Freudenberg and Rick Lawrence, *The Family-Friendly Church* (Loveland, CO: Group Publishing, 1998), p. 17.
2. Jolene L. Roehlkepartain, "What Parents Want From Your Ministry," *Jr. High Ministry* (February/March 1992), p. 19.
3. U.S. Census Bureau, quoted at "America's Children 2004," *ChildStats.gov*. http://www.childstats.gov/ac2004/summlist.asp (accessed December 29, 2004).
4. Ibid.
5. Ibid.
6. Centers for Disease Control and Prevention, quoted at "America's Children 2004," *ChildStats.gov*. http://www.childstats.gov/ac 2004/summlist.asp (accessed December 29, 2004).
7. U.S. Department of Education, quoted at "America's Children 2004," *ChildStats.gov*. http://www.childstats.gov/ac2004/summlist .asp (accessed December 29, 2004).
8. Ibid.
9. U.S. Census Bureau, quoted at "America's Children 2004," *ChildStats.gov*. http://www.childstats.gov/ac2004/summlist.asp (accessed December 29, 2004).
10. U.S. Bureau of Labor Statistics, quoted at "America's Children 2004," *ChildStats.gov*. http://www.childstats.gov/ac2004/summ-list.asp (accessed December 29, 2004).
11. U.S. Census Bureau and the U.S. Department of Housing and Urban Development, quoted at "America's Children 2004," *ChildStats.gov*. http://www.childstats.gov/ac2004/summlist.asp (accessed December 29, 2004).
12. National Institute on Drug Abuse, quoted at "America's Children 2004," *ChildStats.gov*. http://www.childstats.gov/ac2004/summ-list.asp (accessed December 29, 2004).
13. Jean Grasso Fitzparick, quoted in Jolene L. Roehlkepartain, "What Parents Want From Your Ministry," *Jr. High Ministry* (February/March 1992), p. 19.
14. Elizabeth A. Carter and Monica McGoldrick, eds., *The Expanded Family Life Cycle: Individual, Family, and Social Perspective* (Paramus, NJ: Prentice Hall, 1998), n.p.
15. Don W. Hebbard, *The Complete Handbook for Family Life Ministry in the Church* (Nashville, TN: Thomas Nelson, 1995), p.93.
16. Ibid., p. 110.
17. Ross Campbell, *How to Really Love Your Teenager* (Wheaton, IL: Victor Books, 1981), p. 35.
18. "How to Talk About Puberty," *Jr. High Ministry* (October/November 1997), p. 21.
19. Dr. Greg Cynaumon, *Helping Single Parents with Troubled Kids* (Colorado Springs, CO: David C. Cook Publishing, 1993), p. 52.
20. Ibid., pp. 52-53.
21. George Barna, *Ministry Currents*, April-June 1992.
22. Hebbard, *The Complete Handbook for Family Life Ministry in the Church*, p. 31.

Getting the Most Out of Your Curriculum

> "They're teachable. You get them before they're in junior high and you can get their attention and they don't act so cool that they can't learn something."
>
> —Kevin, fifth- and sixth-grade team leader

Recently, Sarah, one of our preteen teachers, told us about her first Sunday on the job with fifth- and sixth-grade Sunday School. (It also happened to be our first Sunday at the church, so we claim no credit nor responsibility!) It was Easter Sunday and another teacher was working alone with about 25 fifth and sixth graders. Sarah was invited to join the lone teacher to assist with what was expected to be a bumper crop of kids on Easter Sunday.

That morning a crowd came and the class was pretty unruly. Much of their behavior was blamed on the sugar intake from the candy they had undoubtedly eaten before church. At the end of class, Sarah told the other teacher that "she wasn't sure she was cut out for this age level." She didn't come back for six weeks! (She smiles about it now and says she loves preteens!)

That story is all too common at this age level. We throw workers into a classroom when they don't understand the kids and they don't have the right tools to do their job. (The curriculum the classroom was using at the time was a primarily teacher-centered, lecture-based style of education.) If you're not ready for preteens, they can be difficult! But if you understand them and you have the right tools to work with them, this can be the most exciting ministry you've ever experienced! This chapter will look at how to choose and use tools that will work.

Choose Curriculum and Resources That Will Work for You and Your Teachers

Let's be real—and practical. We would all list good Bible teaching as the number one priority in evaluating curriculum for our ministries, but there are some basic considerations that must be met before a teacher will even pick up the teacher's guide and use it. And, realistically, if the teachers won't use the books, it really doesn't matter how significant the Bible education inside is!

Here are some practical considerations that will make or break your curriculum choice:

◎ **Both the student papers and the teacher's guides must be attractive.** Look inside the books. Is there enough white space to make the page look inviting to the reader? Too much print is overwhelming to most people and will end up intimidating untrained teachers. Do you need an orientation class just to read the book or is the layout clear and easy to follow?

Is artwork age appropriate (that is, cool) and colorful? As we age, we find it more and more helpful to look to our youth pastor friends for help in evaluating this. We even have our junior high pastor (who is more than 10 years younger than we are) take a look at brochures and letters to make sure we're hitting the mark. Remember that the art on student pages or resources needs to appeal to preteens, not adults.

◉ **A good curriculum will provide more ideas than you could possibly use in the amount of time you have.** Some people get frustrated that they can't get through the whole lesson in the time allotted for their class. This is far preferable to getting through the whole lesson and still having time left over!

Good lessons will provide extra ideas, so teachers can pick and choose. If you don't like a particular activity, you'll be able to skip it without having to come up with your own material. If you have a church with services that occasionally (or regularly) run long, you will also want to make sure that your curriculum has games that can be extended by playing additional rounds or other easy time-stretching activities that you can pick up and do on the spot with little or no preparation.

◉ **It must be easy for teachers to use.** Try to find a curriculum that does not require tons of teacher time to prepare materials and supplies. You want your teachers focusing on the kids and the point, not cutting out crafts and shopping for supplies.

Look for teacher tips to be included in the lessons. Does the publisher provide practical guidance on how to do each activity? These tips are signs that the curriculum has been field-tested and had its bugs worked out. The tips will often be things that the field testers discovered.

Good curriculum will provide not only what to do in the lesson but also how to do it and what to say while you're doing it. Make sure that the newest teacher can follow the lesson and be successful. Conversation suggestions should be age appropriate and sound natural for an adult to say verbatim.

◉ **It must be affordable.** Compare cost realistically:

◉ How many teacher guides will you need?

◉ What other support tools will you need to purchase?

◉ To do the activities, do you need to purchase lots of unusual supplies that aren't readily available in your church's supply room?

◉ Is the curriculum reusable or dated? (Some publishers publish curriculum in a cycle that allows churches to reuse it every two years.)

Choose Materials That Meet the Physical Needs of Early Adolescents

◉ **Each lesson must provide ideas for movement and activity.** Preteens learn best when they are able to move. Therefore, the curriculum you use with preteens should have an active-learning style of education. Think of it this way: For many early adolescents, if their bodies are not moving, their brains are not switched on.

Read through several lessons, and evaluate how often the students are encouraged to get up and move, discover, interact and discuss. When this is done well, the movement will be a natural outgrowth of the activities rather than just an occasional stretch break.

◉ **The lessons should shift focus at least every 10 to 12 minutes.** The attention span of 10- to 12-year-olds is 10 to 12 minutes long. Our lessons need to account for this by shifting focus frequently. This does not mean that there has to be a new activity every 10 minutes, but the focus needs to change.

In addition, activities that last for short chunks of time will help the preteen's need for movement and change of physical activity. These will make the class much more desirable and successful for both teacher and student.

Choose Materials That Meet the Emotional Needs of Early Adolescents

🌀 **The lessons should be fun, both for the student and the teacher.** Preteens learn best when they are having fun. Teachers teach best when they're having fun. The ultimate goal is for the kids to go home thinking they played the whole time, while the adults realize they taught the whole time!

Deborah G. Estes in her seminar on brain research comments that "emotions play an important role in the enhancement of learning. . . . Anything you do which engages students' emotional . . . interest will naturally . . . result in stronger memories."[1] We're always concerned when we are asked to evaluate a church's ministry and we see rows and rows of kids sitting quietly in straight lines of chairs. How boring! It's not politically correct in some churches; but the louder the laughter coming from a children's classroom, the better the chances that good ministry and good education are happening!

In their book, *The Learning Revolution,* Gordon Dryden and Jeannette Vos tell us, "Make [learning] outlandish, funny and preferably emotional—because the 'filter' in the brain that transfers information to your long-term memory is very closely linked with the brain's emotional center."[2]

🌀 **The teaching style should allow preteens to feel secure in the classroom.** Make sure the curriculum you choose sets up a comfortable environment in which everyone is welcome to share and be a part of the community. The questions provided should include a significant number of open-ended questions so that students are encouraged to think out loud and enabled to expand their concepts and explore their thoughts without fear of being put down if they give a wrong answer.

Choose Curriculum That

Meets the Social Needs of Kids

🌀 **Each lesson should provide frequent opportunities for kids to discuss the focus of the lesson.** This is called interactive education. Preteens learn best when they are able to talk while learning.

A few years ago, we had a 10-year-old boy in our fifth-and-sixth-grade worship time who always sat in the front row. Harry, as we'll call him, was a nice boy. In fact, his family and our family spent a lot of time together as friends. So we couldn't figure out why he was so disrespectful in class, always talking and distracting Gordon as he tried to lead the devotion time.

Then a lightbulb went on for us. He wasn't trying to be disruptive; it's just that he truly needed to talk. In fact, that's why he sat in the front row, so he could "discuss" the lesson with Gordon as it was being taught! Once we realized what was going on, and planned in more frequent opportunities for Harry to chat with purpose, the frustration level dropped considerably for both leader and student!

Choose Curriculum That Meets the Intellectual Needs of Preteens

🌀 **The scope and sequence of the curriculum should be made up primarily of topics relevant to the preteen's world.** Some of the topics that interest or concern these kids and that you will want to address at various times throughout your years with them include the following:

🌀 Friendships and Relationships

🌀 Setting Priorities

🌀 Peer Pressure

🌀 Death and Eternal Life

🌀 Fear

🌀 Popularity and Success

🌀 Substance Abuse (Drugs, Alcohol, Inhalants)

🌀 Justice, World Hunger and Poverty

- ◎ Violence and Gangs

- ◎ Respect for Parents and Other Authorities

- ◎ Self-Esteem and God's View of Us

- ◎ School, Grades and Handling Pressure

- ◎ The Future

- ◎ Dating, Love, Marriage and Sex (in that order!)

This is the time to talk about these hot topics. Preteens are close enough to being involved with the opposite gender to be interested but far enough away to be open to discussing them. We need to establish correct standards before they are involved in the activities. They're already seeing more than they are ready to see on TV, so they need to know what God says about this issue. They don't need to hear all the specifics to learn about God's standard for these important topics.

◎ **Each lesson should attempt to teach only one major Bible truth or concept.** Some of us believe in the old jingle, "Ram it in, cram it in, students' heads are hollow. Ram it in, jam it in, there's always more to follow!" After all, don't we have an awful lot of Bible to teach to our preteens?

Well, that kind of logic will backfire on us. We will have students who rebel and who forget most everything we try to teach! Better retention comes from looking at one key Bible truth over and over in different ways throughout an entire session.

If we can get our kids to enjoy church enough to attend fairly regularly (say, 30 to 40 times each year) and if we can get them to understand and apply just one Bible concept each time they come, they will still end up having more than 30 spiritual principles added to their lives annually. That's a lot better than most adults who attend church can claim!

◎ **Every aspect of the lesson should help reinforce, explain or make application of the one Bible concept.** We don't have enough time with our students to add lots of extra stuff. We need to make sure that the music, the art projects, the prayers, the activities and the games all help repeat, reinforce, explain and explore the Bible concept. Repeated exposure to one point throughout the session will cause our students to learn and retain what is taught.

◎ **Good lessons will include thought-provoking questions that cause kids to use higher order reasoning skills.** We want to challenge our students intellectually. Good questions will do that. But we must plan our questions (or have them planned for us in our curriculum).

Questions are much harder to ask than most of us know. Beginning teachers will especially need help in this area. Don't minimize the value of purchasing good questions found in the right curriculum!

Questions should move students to higher orders of thinking (as described on p. 32). The questions also need to be open ended so that students are made to think about and analyze the information before answering. Yes or no answers, or simple repeating of information that has been presented, will prove whether the student was listening and has some short-term memory of what was said, but they don't advance the student's thought process and understanding of the material.

◎ **Make sure that each lesson accounts for the various learning styles of your students.** You may not be able to utilize every learning style in each lesson, but each style of learning should be included regularly and all should be accounted for within each two- to three-week period.

The Eight Ways People Learn

Howard Gardner, a professor at Harvard, tells us that there are eight (or more) different intelligence constructs, or ways, that each of us learns best. No one has just one learning style. Most of us dominate in one or two of these intelligences or routes to our brains. It is natural for us as teachers to teach to our own preferred learning styles, so we must work at incorporating the other intelligences to meet the needs of the kids who learn differently from the way we do. (See the chart on p. 147 for a brief description of Gardner's eight

THE EIGHT WAYS PEOPLE LEARN

LEARNING STYLE	TYPES OF ACTIVITIES THAT HELP LEARNER	TIPS FOR CONNECTING WITH LEARNER
LINGUISTIC	The linguistic learner learns best when involved in ◎ Reading and writing activities, using words creatively ◎ Talking, discussing and storytelling	Use discussion and creative storytelling. Challenge these kids to memorize.
LOGICAL	The logical (or mathematical) learner learns best when involved in ◎ Experiments, analyzing topics ◎ Problem solving, answering tough questions	Help students challenge and defend the faith. Stretch their thinking by asking open-ended questions.
VISUAL	The visual (or spatial) learner learns best when involved in ◎ Drawing, building things, art projects, mapping ◎ Visualizing and then creating things or doodling ideas	Provide activities in which students create visual representations of what they've learned.
MUSICAL	The musical learner learns best when involved in ◎ An environment with musical mood setters ◎ Singing and listening to Bible words set to music	Have your students help supply popular Christian CDs from which you can choose appropriate mood music for before and after class. Play and sing along with CDs of Bible passages set to music.
KINESTHETIC	The kinesthetic (bodily) learner learns best when involved in ◎ A variety of short learning activities ◎ Moving, touching, playing, acting, running	Minimize furniture in your room so that you may quickly, easily and frequently shift the activity from one part of the room to another. Have kids role-play Bible stories and applications of lessons.
INTERPERSONAL	The interpersonal learner learns best when involved in ◎ Leading, building friendships, talking ◎ Small groups, teams, social settings, projects	Make cooperative learning a regular part of your learning environment (including pair shares and small groups). Allow get-acquainted times each session.
INTROSPECTIVE	The introspective (or intrapersonal) learner learns best when involved in ◎ Meditation, reflection, prayer ◎ Self-study projects, one-on-one times with teachers and other students	Allow for some quiet reflection in each class and don't assume quiet kids are shy.
NATURALIST	The naturalist learner learns best when involved in ◎ Outdoor activities in God's creation and natural surroundings ◎ Activities utilizing plants, animals, nature items	Take your class outdoors or plan outings, camps and retreats. Have windows in your rooms.

intelligences or learning styles with adaptations by the authors for ministering to preteens.)

Choose Curriculum That Meets the Spiritual Needs of Kids

⊙ **The lessons must be doctrinally and theologically acceptable to your church or denomination.** Ask the publisher for a copy of its curriculum scope and sequence. Most have a printed brochure or chart that tells you what stories or Bible concepts are taught at what age levels. If you need help in evaluating the scope and sequence, ask a church or denominational leader to sit down with you as you look at specific lessons that might be of concern to your church.

⊙ **Each lesson should have the kids opening God's Word for themselves.** We want our preteens to see that the Bible is practical and usable for them in their own lives. Choose a curriculum that gets them to look up verses, read short passages and even search for truths in the Scriptures on their own. Help kids establish a habit of using the Scriptures, actually touching the Book!

⊙ **Lessons must be practical and must emphasize life application.** Early adolescents want to know "What's in it for me?" They no longer are interested in the stories that younger Sunday School classes emphasized. Now they want to talk about real issues, meaning how these stories can help them and how they can apply them to what is happening in their lives.

An elder at one church used to listen to his father, the preacher, during these years and write in his notes or in his Bible "YBH"—"Yeah, but how?" Early adolescents aren't very interested in theory; they want to know how to apply this to their lives and what will happen when they do.

⊙ **Lessons must be relevant to the student's search for a more abstract understanding of faith and God.** As a preteen moves into the realm of abstract thinking, he or she wants and needs to rethink faith in God. The purpose of the preteen's search is to make God real in his or her new ways of thinking.

Will the Curriculum Work with Our Kids?

It's important that the leader is excited about the curriculum, or it won't work. At one training meeting we had a husband and wife each come to us to talk about an upcoming lesson. They both taught fifth- and sixth-grade Sunday School.

The wife came with the concern that the upcoming lesson had several skits for the kids to do. She said, "This won't work. The kids hate skits." The husband came a bit later, not knowing his wife had been to us, and said, "I'm so excited about this lesson. The kids love to do skits!"

We mentioned the discrepancy to the husband. His response was insightful: "Oh, no, the kids don't hate the skits. My wife hates them."

Preteens are very capable of picking up on our likes and dislikes and they are easily influenced to follow suit. If you try something that we've shared with you in this book or something that a teacher's guide tells you to do and it doesn't work, make sure that you're presenting it to your students with the attitude that says, "This will be fun and exciting." (Keep in mind that some teachers have a tendency not to use a curriculum the way it was designed and then are surprised by the fact that the curriculum doesn't work.)

Should I Write My Own Curriculum?

One of the most common questions we hear at Christian education gatherings is, Do you know of anything that works with fifth and sixth graders? Because it may seem like such a struggle to find a workable curriculum, some churches have chosen to write their own curriculum for preteens. Before you undertake this task, consider the pros and cons of writing your own material.

The pros for writing your own curriculum for preteens:

◎ You'll be in complete control of what you are teaching kids.

◎ You can include lessons to cover your church's or denomination's doctrine and traditions.

◎ You are the best one to understand the special needs of your specific students and your lessons will reflect this.

◎ Your culture is slightly different from anyone else's and you can address this in your writing.

◎ There is a certain creative energy in designing your own materials that will be reflected by those involved in the process.

◎ You won't have to pay someone for the materials.

The cons for writing your own curriculum for preteens:

◎ You'll be amazed at how much work writing your own curriculum is. Some larger churches have actually hired full- or part-time curriculum writers to accomplish this task. It is almost always easier to adapt a published curriculum rather than to write a curriculum from scratch.

◎ Even the most creative individual eventually runs out of ideas. (Producing one creative, well-written lesson is a lot of work. Producing the thirteenth or the fifty-second lessons seems almost impossible at times.)

◎ The hidden costs of photocopying and distributing lessons may match or exceed the cost of buying published curriculum.

◎ The time it takes for a person (or team) to write curriculum (even if the person is an unpaid volunteer) does come out of some other area in which this gifted individual (or these several team members) might have been serving in your church. (This person might be the right person to pull together a variety of ideas from published resource books to liven up the published curriculum you select.)

◎ You will not have the benefit of field-testing that most publishers use to see if a lesson will actually work before it gets distributed.

◎ Unless you are a professionally trained educator, you may not realize how much you need to know to produce a good lesson that others can follow easily and that meets the needs of a variety of learning styles and interests.

◎ Very few of us can match the colorful artwork and support materials that publishers are able to offer to make their resources shine for preteen kids.

How to Get Your Curriculum to Work for You

Many of us need to augment what we're doing with some extra ideas and excitement. Whether you're stuck with a curriculum you didn't pick and don't like or you just want to jazz up one you're pretty happy with, there are some tricks to making your lessons work without overworking yourself!

Step 1: Use the curriculum evaluation guide on pages 151 and 152 to help your church find the

best curriculum available for your situation. Instead of focusing on what's wrong with "all those publishers," find the one that comes closest to meeting your needs and desires and go with it as your starting point. If, for some reason, you are not able to select a curriculum different from the one you are currently dissatisfied with (perhaps your leader or your denomination wants you to use this one), adjust your focus to recognize that it's the best one you've got and go on to step 2.

Step 2: Decide what you need to do to adapt your curriculum. Have frank, open discussions with all of the people involved in using the materials. Ask positive, solution-oriented questions, such as:

◎ What would make our lessons better?

◎ How could we have more fun?

◎ How could we help kids learn more?

◎ What do we need to add to our lessons?

Include kids in this discussion by asking them open-ended questions, such as How do you feel about Sunday School? What would make it better? Then really listen to them! (You may not, or possibly should not, do everything they ask, but their desires should be thoroughly considered and they should be able to recognize the impact of their suggestions in your final program plans.)

Use the evaluation guide on pages 151 and 152 to help identify areas in your curriculum that need improvement.

Step 3: Take steps to make the correct changes. Buy the resource books that will help where you need help. If your lessons need more artistic activities, buy craft books. If you need more active learning, buy game books, learning activity books and skit books. You get the idea! Then have one or two people search these extra resources for ideas that will give your curriculum the spark it's missing.

Advanced Curriculum Punch-Up Ideas

Whether you decide to write your own curriculum (which many of us do for some weekday programs, even after selecting a published curriculum we like for Sunday School) or you decide to supplement a published curriculum, here's an effective way to have a team of workers minister from their areas of strength:

◎ **Create one folder for each unit of curriculum and label it with the topic for the unit of lessons.** These file folders will serve as your idea banks for the year. Whenever you or one of the team members comes across a joke, a story, a visual, or any great idea for the topic, simply make a photocopy and slip it into the file. When the time comes to work on creating or refining a month's lessons, pull the appropriate file and you'll have a bunch of ideas ready to go.

◎ **Choose eight different people to help you.** Find people who each have as their own learning style a different one of Gardner's eight intelligences. Then have each person look through various resource books, specifically looking for activities that utilize their own learning style and could be used for the different topics you need for the year.

Have the team members photocopy a specific project or activity and pop it into the file for the unit that it best corresponds with topically. Make it your goal to have each person come up with at least two ideas for each unit.

Notes

1. Deborah G. Estes, Ed.D., *Strengthen Your Students' Learning by Using the Latest Brain Research* (Bellevue, WA: Bureau of Education
and Research, 2004), p. 24.
2. Gordon Dryden and Jeannette Vos, *The Learning Revolution* (Torrance, CA: The Learning Web, 1999), p. 169.

CURRICULUM EVALUATION GUIDE

As you review each curriculum piece, use the following questions to rate your likes and dislikes of the resource from 1 to 5, with 1 meaning home run; 3 meaning a characteristic that you could live with if you had to; and 5 meaning unacceptable (and would on some issues, disqualify the curriculum, no matter how the rest of the questions are answered).

Is the curriculum teacher friendly?

Are learning goals clearly stated, measurable and attainable?

1   2   3   4   5

Are the teacher's materials attractive and is the student artwork age appropriate for preteens?

1   2   3   4   5

Are there more ideas in each lesson than you could use during one session?

1   2   3   4   5

Is the teacher's guide user-friendly?

1   2   3   4   5

Are the lessons and activities fun for the teacher?

1   2   3   4   5

Does the guide give teaching tips that are helpful for use with preteens?

1   2   3   4   5

Are the suggested activities easy to prepare?

1   2   3   4   5

Are the necessary materials readily available to the teacher?

1   2   3   4   5

Is the curriculum within the budget of your church?

1   2   3   4   5

Does the curriculum meet the emotional needs of preteens?

Do the activities and experiences affirm kids and make them feel secure?

1   2   3   4   5

Are the lessons and activities fun for the students?

1   2   3   4   5

Does the curriculum meet the physical needs of preteens?

Is the curriculum based on active learning?

1   2   3   4   5

Are there sufficient ideas for noncompetitive games that preteens would enjoy?

1   2   3   4   5

Do kids get opportunities to get up and move frequently throughout the lessons?

1   2   3   4   5

Does the curriculum meet the social needs of preteens?

Do the lessons help build relationships among preteens and between students and teachers?

1   2   3   4   5

Are students encouraged to engage in discussion at various times during each lesson?

1   2   3   4   5

Are students in small groups frequently in this curriculum?

1   2   3   4   5

Are a variety of cooperative learning techniques suggested (small-group discussion, pairs work together on an art project, etc.)?

1   2   3   4   5

Does the curriculum meet the intellectual needs of preteens?

Do the lessons challenge preteens to think?

1   2   3   4   5

Are questions clear and meaningful for student discussion?

1   2   3   4   5

◎ Do questions move kids to higher levels of reasoning and thinking?

1   2   3   4   5

◎ Will the lessons interest early adolescents?

1   2   3   4   5

◎ Does each lesson focus on one major biblical truth or concept?

1   2   3   4   5

◎ Do all of the activities in each lesson help teach the Bible truth of the lesson?

1   2   3   4   5

◎ Does the focus of the lesson shift every 10 to 12 minutes?

1   2   3   4   5

Does the curriculum meet the spiritual needs of preteens?

◎ Are the lessons based on biblical principles that are relevant to preteens?

1   2   3   4   5

◎ Do the students open the Bible for themselves?

1   2   3   4   5

◎ Is the curriculum acceptable to your church theologically and doctrinally?

1   2   3   4   5

◎ Do the lessons help preteens apply the point of the lesson personally?

1   2   3   4   5

◎ Is each lesson application oriented and appropriate for early adolescents?

1   2   3   4   5

Does the curriculum utilize all eight learning intelligences?

◎ Are activities that would appeal to the linguistic learner included?

1   2   3   4   5

◎ Are activities that would appeal to the logical learner included?

1   2   3   4   5

◎ Are activities that would appeal to the visual learner included?

1   2   3   4   5

◎ Are activities that would appeal to the musical learner included?

1   2   3   4   5

◎ Are activities that would appeal to the kinesthetic learner included?

1   2   3   4   5

◎ Are activities that would appeal to the interpersonal learner included?

1   2   3   4   5

◎ Are activities that would appeal to the introspective learner included?

1   2   3   4   5

◎ Are activities that would appeal to the naturalist learner included?

1   2   3   4   5

Overall, how do I feel about the curriculum?

◎ How excited are you about this curriculum?

1   2   3   4   5

Leading Preteens to Christ

> "Make the Christian life contagious. Remember, many a child has learned first to love his teacher, and then his teacher's God. Your own Christian life must be genuine and real if you are to be a convincing teacher. Your pupils sense this every time."
>
> —Henrietta Mears[1]

Many adult Christians look back to their upper elementary years as the time when they accepted Christ as Savior. For those who have grown up in the Church and have previously made commitments to Christ, the preteen years often become an opportunity to reaffirm the commitment or to deepen their understanding. Not only are preteens able to understand the difference between right and wrong and their own personal need of forgiveness, but also they are interested in Jesus' death and resurrection as the means by which God provides salvation. In addition, students at this age are capable of growing in their faith through prayer, Bible reading, worship and service.

However, preteens are still limited in their understanding and inconsistent in following through on their intentions and commitments. Therefore, they need thoughtful, patient guidance in coming to know Christ personally and continuing to grow in Him.

Pray

Ask God to prepare the students in your group to receive the good news about Jesus and prepare you to communicate effectively with them.

Present the Good News

Use words and phrases that students understand. Avoid symbolism that will confuse these literal-minded thinkers. Remember that 10- to 14-year-olds bounce between literal thinking and abstract thinking and each child's learning will be at different places on the spectrum of understanding. Discuss these points slowly enough to allow time for thinking and comprehending.

a. God wants you to become His child. Do you know why God wants you in His family? (See 1 John 3:1.)

b. You and all the people in the world have done wrong things. The Bible word for doing wrong is "sin." What do you think should happen to us when we sin? (See Romans 6:23.)

c. God loves you so much, He sent His Son to die on the cross for your sins. Because Jesus never sinned, He is the only One who can take the punishment for your sins (see 1 Corinthians 15:3; 1 John 4:14). On the third day after Jesus died, God brought Him back to life.

d. Are you sorry for your sins? Tell God that you are. Do you believe Jesus died to take the punishment for your sins? If you tell God you are sorry for your sins and tell Him you do believe and accept Jesus' death to take away your sins, God forgives all your sins (see 1 John 1:9).

e. The Bible says that when you believe in Jesus, God's Son, you receive God's gift of eternal life. This gift makes you a child of God. This means God is with you now and forever (see John 3:16).

Give students many opportunities to think about what it means to be a Christian; expose them to a variety of lessons and descriptions of the meaning of salvation to aid their understanding. Allow preteens to share the message with their peers, too.

Talk Personally with the Student

Talking about salvation one-on-one creates the opportunity to ask and answer questions. Ask questions that move the student beyond simple yes or no answers or recitation of memorized information. Ask what-do-you-think kinds of questions.

"Why do you think it's important to . . . ?"

"What are some things you really like about Jesus?"

"Why do you think that Jesus had to die because of wrong things you and I have done?"

"What difference do you think it makes for a person to be forgiven?"

When students use abstract terms or phrases they have learned previously, such as "accepting Christ into my heart," ask them to tell you what the term or phrase means in different words. Answers to these open-ended questions will help you discern how much the student does or does not understand.

Offer Opportunities Without Pressure

Preteens are still young and normally desire to please adults. This characteristic makes them vulnerable to being unintentionally manipulated by well-meaning adults. A good way to guard against coercing a student's response is to simply pause periodically and ask, "Would you like to hear more about this now or at another time?" Loving acceptance of the student, even when he or she is not fully interested in pursuing the matter, is crucial in building and maintaining positive attitudes toward becoming part of God's family.

Give Time to Think and Pray

There is great value in encouraging a student to think and pray about what you have said before making a response. Also allow moments for quiet thinking about questions you have asked.

Respect the Student's Response

Whether or not a student declares faith in Jesus Christ, there is a need for adults to accept the

student's action. There is also a need to realize that a student's initial responses to Jesus are just the beginning of a lifelong process of growing in the faith.

Guide the Student in Further Growth

There are several important parts in the nurturing process.

a. Talk regularly about your relationship with God. As you talk about your relationship, the student will begin to feel that it's OK to talk about such things. Then you can comfortably ask the student to share his or her thoughts and feelings, and you can encourage the student to ask questions of you.

b. Prepare the student to deal with doubts. Emphasize that certainty about salvation is not dependent on our feelings or doing enough good deeds. Show the student places in God's Word that clearly declare that salvation comes by grace through faith (see John 1:12; Ephesians 2:8-9; Hebrews 11:6; 1 John 5:11).

c. Teach the student to confess all sins. This means agreeing with God that we really have sinned. Assure the student that confession always results in forgiveness (see 1 John 1:9).

Note

1. Henrietta Mears, quoted in Eleanor Doan, *431 Quotes* (Ventura, CA: Regal Books, 1970), p. 37.

Ready-to-Use Forms

Use the forms on the following pages to help you in your ministry to preteens and their families.

Assessment: Reasons and Recognition

Teacher Assessment Tool

Parent Assessment Tool

Church Office Notification Injury Report

Making Dinnertime Connections

Helping Teachers and Families Connect

Medical and Liability Release Form

Preteen Ministry Job Descriptions

Preteen Questionnaire

Safety Policy and Introductory Letter

Volunteer Application Form

ASSESSMENT

Reasons and Recognition

How can we recognize the milestones of a preteen's spiritual growth?

Every so often, parents, teachers or children's pastors suddenly realize that although the preteens in their care are graduating to the next grade, they have passed no test that confirms a certain amount of spiritual growth or Bible knowledge. Sometimes panic ensues and a flurry of testing measures are tried. (Can they repeat the Lord's Prayer? Psalm 23? John 3:16? Can they find verses in the Bible? Can they pray aloud? Can they recite the catechism?)

It is admirable to be intentional when it comes to teaching our preteens. When we have clear objectives in mind, we are better able to think about the bigger picture of their spiritual growth. We can ask ourselves, *What kind of spiritual growth would I hope to see in these kids 10 years from now*? and *What can I do today to help make that happen?* This kind of thinking keeps us on point as teachers, parents or children's pastors.

However, when we try to test kids for spiritual growth, we often work from a school model of testing, grades and scores. Many of us have taken a test when we were not at our best and discovered that the test was not a highly accurate reflection of our knowledge or ability! Also, within school systems, such testing forays are not only related to measuring intellectual achievement, but also they more usually are related to gaining greater funding. That isn't our purpose for children's ministry. It's not likely that we can show our church boards our children's test scores ("Look! Thirty-six kids can say the Lord's Prayer!") and expect to gain a higher percentage of the church budget! Instead, let's consider a biblical model.

Jesus said, "What shall I compare the kingdom of God to? It is like yeast that a woman took and mixed into a large amount of flour until it worked all through the dough" (Luke 13:20-21). If you have ever tried to make bread without first having seen it done, you know how difficult it was to understand what the recipe meant by the words "sponge" or "elastic." However, once you had seen, smelled and touched bread dough in those stages, the terms became quite clear. Since it was Jesus Himself who compared the growth of God's kingdom (societal change growing out of spiritual maturity and understanding) to microscopic yeast, perhaps we need to look beyond the school system's method and consider Jesus' methods for ways to most accurately assess the kids we love.

We recognize that Jesus had far more insight than any of us will ever have. He is the master teacher of all time! First notice that Jesus preached to thousands yet selected only a small group to be trained. How did He train them? He walked with, ate with and spent time with His disciples. In this way, He modeled in everyday life the behavior He wanted them to imitate! He taught them by His words, but more than that, He modeled those words by His actions.

Second, Jesus built a close relationship with each one. There were three with whom He spent the most time—Peter, James and John. Then there were nine more with whom He had very close relationships. (Does that tell us how important it is to have good teacher-to-child ratios?) He knew these men well. They were not once-a-month, casual acquaintances. He carefully observed each one in every situation so that He would know his strengths and weaknesses.

Third, He asked masterful questions. As He and His disciples walked to Caesarea Philippi, He asked them, "Who do people say I am?" (Mark 8:27)—a nonthreatening, open-ended question that revealed both what they had heard and what they understood. They responded freely. Then Jesus moved to a personal question of the same kind: "'But what about you?' he asked. 'Who do you say I am?'" (Mark 8:29). In the context of a well-established loving relationship, He asked open-ended questions (questions that have no right answer but are an effective way to find out what people do or do not understand). He asked and answered many other kinds of questions, too; but moving from open-ended questions that revealed His friends' hearts and minds to questions that made them personally respond to the truth were far more effective than parroting right answers or memorized facts.

Fourth, Jesus the creator already knew something we are just now learning about the brain: Most learning takes place not while people are taking in information; rather, different learners learn differently. And much learning takes place in everyday living out of Bible truths, not just in the classroom. Application of Bible truth may not be able to be measured in the same way for all children—especially when application takes place outside the classroom setting. For a preteen, more learning may happen while walking to school on Monday, thinking about something that happened on Sunday. How can that be measured?

Only with these ideas in mind is it then appropriate to offer an assessment tool.

Modeling, relationship, careful observation, the right kinds of questions and respect for the work of God's Holy Spirit must guard any assessment we make.

The rate at which the kingdom of God works through a life cannot be measured in any standard way. We cannot gauge the numerous factors that affect any preteen's life outside of our relationship with him or her.

In the same way, we must realize not only that high marks on any kind of assessment are subject to the mind-set of the assessor but also that high marks cannot guarantee a preteen has reached some level of complete (or even moderate) spiritual maturity or understanding. But even as we keep these things in mind, we can use an assessment tool as an effective part of our relationship building and our loving observation. (Note: Some parents may prefer that teachers not be involved in the assessment process. Provide parents with the parent assessment tool on pp. 163-165.)

These assessment tools are merely tools. Because these tools are not modeled on a school test, there is no pass-fail connotation. The concepts included are basic core truths about God, Jesus, the Bible, prayer, the Church and Christian living. The tools are designed to evaluate a preteen's current place along a spectrum of understanding these core truths that ranges from some awareness to the ability to put that core truth into action. The tools may be adapted to meet the needs of a particular church. Other concepts to consider when evaluating a preteen's spiritual understanding can be found in the age-level characteristics described in chapter 1. You may also suggest that, instead of using the assessment tools to measure a preteen's progress, teachers and parents use the tools as lists of goals for their teaching and put into practice the suggested action steps.

The goal of the tools is to help us focus our desire to be intentional in the ways we teach the preteens we love. However, if you have experienced seeing the yeast work through the dough, you know how it feels to knead it. You know how it feels, smells and looks when it is ready.

In the same way, the most important thing you can do for each preteen is to lovingly encourage him or her on toward maturity—that will always be "kneaded"!

Action Steps for the Preteen's Ministry Coordinator/Director

From Jesus' model of assessment and action, we can see the imperatives:

1. Provide programs that allow for large amounts of small-group and relationship-building time as a norm, not an occasional focus. (Regardless of the entertainment-type ministry programs advertising that they require fewer adults, such programs cannot by themselves provide for close relationships that nurture spiritual growth.)

2. Communicate to teachers and helpers the vision of your children's ministry and the mission of what you want to accomplish and how you plan to get there. Take good care of these fellow visionaries by providing the training that will give them the skills they need (how to ask questions, how to talk and listen to children, how to weave God's Word into conversations, etc.). Provide support that helps them know that they are doing vitally important work in the church.

3. Distribute the assessment tools to parents and/or teachers, taking care to review the information presented in this article.

TEACHER ASSESSMENT TOOL

Action Steps for Teachers

1. Focus on building relationships! During the time you are teaching, stop to recognize the importance of simply listening to children. Prayerfully consider whether God would direct you to invest more time with these children through occasional or regular times to talk and pray together.

2. Children will imitate what you do. Children learn more by what they see you do than by your words alone. Modeling kindness, patience, gentleness, self-control and a sense of humor will teach them far more than words alone.

3. Understand that because you see children on such a limited basis, you cannot expect even your best evaluation or assessment to be completely accurate. Don't make any final conclusions or take too much personal responsibility. Rather, use this assessment to understand the best ways you can pray for and help children. Remember, the church's goal is to support parents in nurturing spiritual growth in their own children.

4. Taking time to assess children's spiritual growth provides a wonderful reason to connect with parents or other family members. Talk about ways you and they can work together to help the children grow spiritually.

CHiLD iNFORMATiON

Child's Name _____

Child's Address _____

Child's Phone Number _____

Child's E-Mail Address _____

Child's School _____

Child's Instant Message Address _____

Mom's Name _____

Mom's Address _____

Mom's Phone Number _____

Mom's E-Mail Address _____

Mom's Church Involvement

High   Medium   Low

Dad's Name _____

Dad's Address _____

Dad's Phone Number _____

Dad's E-Mail Address _____

Dad's Church Involvement

High   Medium   Low

Who brings child?

Mom   Dad   Grandparent   Child's Friend

Other _____

Child's Attendance Pattern

Weekly   Two Times a Month   Irregular

Comments _____

EVALUATiON

1. How well do you know child's parents?

Not at all   Acquaintances   Friends   Close Friends

Comments _____

Action Ideas

◎ Introduce yourself to parents at all-church events

◎ Telephone parents at beginning of term

◎ Visit child at home

◎ Invite parents to attend youth group events and to observe in class

2. How would you evaluate the child's desire to be at church?

High   Medium   Low

Comments _____

Action Ideas

◎ Call, e-mail or write to child at home

◎ Plan fun relationship-building event during the week

3. Does the child bring a Bible to class?

Yes   No

Comments _____

Action Ideas

◎ Provide Bible for child

◎ Provide classroom Bibles

4. How comfortable is the child in locating Bible references?

Action Ideas

◎ Put up a Bible book poster

◎ Provide bookmarks

◎ Play games to learn books of the Bible and develop Bible skills

5. How would you evaluate the child's understanding and demonstration of the following core Bible truths?

	Awareness/Recognition (can state the core truth)	Understanding/Verbalization (can restate the core truth in his or her own words)	Demonstration (puts the core truth into action)	Action Ideas
	No 1 2 3 4 5 Yes	No 1 2 3 4 5 Yes	No 1 2 3 4 5 Yes	Incorporate Action Ideas into your small-group time.

God
- ◎ God created the world and He loves and cares for all people. — 1 2 3 4 5 | 1 2 3 4 5 | 1 2 3 4 5
- ◎ We can praise God for His power and love. — 1 2 3 4 5 | 1 2 3 4 5 | 1 2 3 4 5

Action Ideas
- ◎ Give examples of ways you see God's power shown in the world today.
- ◎ Invite students to describe things for which they wish to thank God.

Jesus
- ◎ Jesus is God's Son and was sent by God to be our Savior. — 1 2 3 4 5 | 1 2 3 4 5 | 1 2 3 4 5
- ◎ When we choose to follow Jesus, believing that He died to take the punishment for our sins and is alive today, we become members of God's family. — 1 2 3 4 5 | 1 2 3 4 5 | 1 2 3 4 5

Action Ideas
- ◎ Tell students when and how you became a Christian.
- ◎ Describe one or two reasons you continue to follow Jesus.
- ◎ Invite students to become members of God's family.

Bible
- ◎ The Bible is true and is God's Word to us. — 1 2 3 4 5 | 1 2 3 4 5 | 1 2 3 4 5
- ◎ We can read the Bible to discover ways to love and obey God. — 1 2 3 4 5 | 1 2 3 4 5 | 1 2 3 4 5

Action Ideas
- ◎ Tell students about ways that knowing God's Word has helped you in everyday life.
- ◎ Connect Bible verses to current news stories and situations in students' lives.

Prayer
- ◎ Prayer is talking to God. — 1 2 3 4 5 | 1 2 3 4 5 | 1 2 3 4 5
- ◎ We can talk to God anytime, praising Him and asking His help for others and ourselves. — 1 2 3 4 5 | 1 2 3 4 5 | 1 2 3 4 5

Action Ideas
- ◎ Invite students to share prayer requests.
- ◎ Help students form prayer partners.
- ◎ Pray individually with student who shares a concern.
- ◎ Keep a prayer journal, listing prayer requests and answered prayers.

Church
- ◎ The Church is made up of everyone who believes in Jesus as Savior. — 1 2 3 4 5 | 1 2 3 4 5 | 1 2 3 4 5
- ◎ Everyone who believes in Jesus as Savior is part of the Church and can worship and serve God together. — 1 2 3 4 5 | 1 2 3 4 5 | 1 2 3 4 5

Action Ideas
- ◎ Share examples of ways your church family helps and encourages others.
- ◎ Lead students in completing a service project to help others in your church family or your community.

Christian Living
- ◎ God's followers respond to God's love by loving Him and others. — 1 2 3 4 5 | 1 2 3 4 5 | 1 2 3 4 5
- ◎ We can show our love for God through attitudes and actions (kindness, honesty, patience, etc.) that please Him. — 1 2 3 4 5 | 1 2 3 4 5 | 1 2 3 4 5

Action Ideas
- ◎ Recognize and thank students for loving actions you observe.
- ◎ Regularly invite students to tell situations in which they find making right choices difficult and brainstorm ways to obey God in these situations.

PARENT ASSESSMENT TOOL

Action Steps for Parents

1. Don't be overwhelmed by anyone's expectation that you must rear children to be spiritual superstars. Rearing your children is your responsibility, but it ultimately rests in God's hands—and He loves them more than you do! So pray diligently for your children as you set the tone for your family by loving and worshiping God and putting Christ first in your everyday life.

2. Always remember that your children will do more of what they see in your life than of what you say. Your words must match your actions. Preteens adopt the values of the significant adults in their lives by whom they feel loved.

3. Consider ways to support your child's learning at church: Get to know his or her teacher, help in the classroom or invite the teacher to your home. Make sure your child attends often enough to make friends and then help your child cultivate those friendships through social times with other families and invitations to your home. Talk with your child regularly about what he or she enjoys about programs at church. Talk also about parts he or she dislikes and brainstorm ways to help your child adjust; share that information with teachers as appropriate.

4. Think of one action you can take every week to help your child grow spiritually. Repeat that action at least three times during the week.

INFORMATION ABOUT YOUR CHILD   Child's Name _____   Age _____

How would you evaluate your child's understanding and demonstration of the following core Bible truths?

Core Bible Truth	Awareness/Recognition (can state the core truth)	Understanding/Verbalization (can restate the core truth in his or her own words)	Demonstration (puts the core truth into action)
God	No 1 2 3 4 5 Yes	No 1 2 3 4 5 Yes	No 1 2 3 4 5 Yes
☺ God created the world and He loves and cares for all people.	1 2 3 4 5	1 2 3 4 5	1 2 3 4 5
☺ We can praise God for His power and love.	1 2 3 4 5	1 2 3 4 5	1 2 3 4 5
Jesus			
☺ Jesus is God's Son and was sent by God to be our Savior.	1 2 3 4 5	1 2 3 4 5	1 2 3 4 5
☺ When we choose to follow Jesus, believing that He died to take the punishment for our sins and is alive today, we become members of God's family.	1 2 3 4 5	1 2 3 4 5	1 2 3 4 5
Bible			
☺ The Bible is true and is God's Word to us.	1 2 3 4 5	1 2 3 4 5	1 2 3 4 5
☺ We can read the Bible to discover ways to love and obey God.	1 2 3 4 5	1 2 3 4 5	1 2 3 4 5

Incorporate Action Ideas into family discussion time.

God — Action Ideas

- ☺ In everyday situations, look for "teachable moments" when you can talk about ways you see God's power shown in the world today.
- ☺ In a family prayer time, invite your child to describe things for which to thank God. Tell characteristics of God for which you are grateful.
- ☺ Memorize a verse together about God's power and love (e.g., Psalm 106:1).

Jesus — Action Ideas

- ☺ Talk with your child, asking questions such as What questions do you have about who Jesus is? Why do you think it's important to know about Jesus' death and resurrection? What are some things you really like about Jesus?
- ☺ Share with your child how you became a Christian.
- ☺ Purchase (or obtain from your church) an age-appropriate booklet on how to become a Christian. Read it with your child and then talk together about it.
- ☺ As the Holy Spirit leads, ask your child if he or she would like to become a member of God's family. Help him or her pray, asking for God's forgiveness, declaring faith in Jesus' death and resurrection, and asking to become part of God's family.
- ☺ Encourage your child to tell the pastor or a teacher at your church about having joined God's family.
- ☺ Memorize a verse together about Jesus and salvation (e.g., Romans 5:8).

Bible — Action Ideas

- ☺ Provide a Bible and/or youth-friendly devotional for your child.
- ☺ Regularly read the Bible with your child.
- ☺ Regularly read the Bible yourself. Briefly share with your child what you have learned from your reading.
- ☺ Tell your child stories of everyday situations in which knowing God's Word has helped you.
- ☺ Connect Bible verses to current news stories and situations in your child's life.
- ☺ Memorize a verse together about the benefits of reading and knowing God's Word (e.g., Psalm 119:105) and keep a journal of Bible verses memorized together.

How would you evaluate your child's understanding and demonstration of the following core Bible truths?

	Awareness/ Recognition (can state the core truth)	Understanding/ Verbalization (can restate the core truth in his or her own words)	Demonstration (puts the core truth into action)	Incorporate Action Ideas into family discussion time.
Prayer				**Action Ideas**
☺ Prayer is talking to God.	No 1 2 3 4 5 Yes	No 1 2 3 4 5 Yes	No 1 2 3 4 5 Yes	☺ Invite your child to pray with you daily or weekly, focusing on issues of interest to your child.
☺ We can talk to God anytime, praising Him and asking His help for others and ourselves.	1 2 3 4 5	1 2 3 4 5	1 2 3 4 5	☺ Share with your child ways you have seen God answer prayer.
				☺ Keep a family prayer journal: List prayer requests and then note the dates and answers as they come.
				☺ Memorize a verse together about prayer (e.g., Philippians 4:6).
Church				**Action Ideas**
☺ The Church is made up of everyone who believes in Jesus as Savior.	1 2 3 4 5	1 2 3 4 5	1 2 3 4 5	☺ Share examples of ways people in your church family help and encourage each other.
☺ Everyone who believes in Jesus as Savior is part of the Church and can worship and serve God together.	1 2 3 4 5	1 2 3 4 5	1 2 3 4 5	☺ Plan and complete a family service project to help others in your church family or your community. Consider making such projects a regular family activity.
				☺ Demonstrate ways to care for others by your own actions; invite your child to offer his or her help to others as well.
				☺ Memorize a verse together about ways God's family helps each other (e.g., Galatians 6:10).
Christian Living				**Action Ideas**
☺ God's followers respond to God's love by loving Him and others.	1 2 3 4 5	1 2 3 4 5	1 2 3 4 5	☺ Recognize your child for loving actions he or she demonstrates.
☺ We can show our love for God through attitudes and actions (kindness, honesty, patience, etc.) that please Him.	1 2 3 4 5	1 2 3 4 5	1 2 3 4 5	☺ Invite your child to tell situations in which making right choices is difficult. Brainstorm ways to obey God in these situations.
				☺ Model right actions, occasionally connecting your actions with a Bible verse that describes the reason you acted as you did.
				☺ Pray with and for your child, asking God's help for him or her to make right choices.
				☺ Memorize a verse together about Christian living (e.g., Ephesians 5:1-2).

CHURCH OFFICE NOTIFICATION INJURY REPORT

Date of report _____

Name of child who was injured _____

Age of child who was injured _____

Gender of child who was injured _____

Address _____

City _____

Zip _____

Name of parent(s) with whom child lives and /or who brings child to church

_____

Phone _____ Date and time of accident _____

Describe in detail how the child was injured, including location, names and actions of all children and adults involved.

_____

_____

_____

Describe the child's injuries and what action was taken to treat the injuries.

_____

_____

How and when was the parent notified?

_____

List names and phone numbers of witnesses to the accident.

1. _____

2. _____

3. _____

Additional Comments _____

_____

_____

_____

Your Name _____

Address _____

Phone Number _____

MAKING DINNERTIME CONNECTIONS

Moving Family Conversation Beyond TV, Sports and Weather

A Few Tips for Asking Questions

☺ Cut apart the questions on page168 so that each is on a separate strip. Add additional questions of your own. Place the question strips in a container; then family members take turns, either drawing questions they will answer or ones they will ask of another family member.

☺ Share your own answers to the questions you ask.

☺ Avoid "grilling" family members. Your conversation time should be relaxed and enjoyable, not a test that becomes an ordeal.

☺ Let all family members ask questions of each other.

☺ Encourage children to have any take-home papers handy to refresh their memory and to stimulate further questions.

☺ Preteens may resent any prying into their affairs and respond to any question with thrilling answers such as "I don't know," "OK," or "I forget."

☺ Try writing three or four questions on a sheet of paper; then let the preteen select the one he or she will answer out loud in 50 words or more. Then count the words. (There is no guarantee that this will work with every preteen, but it's worth a try.)

Two Questions to Avoid

1. What did you learn at church today?
   Children especially have little awareness of when they are learning. If they know something, they tend to assume they've always known it. Instead, ask, "What did you do in youth group today?"

2. What was your lesson about?
   This question usually just draws blank stares. Try asking, "What did the leader talk about in youth group today?"

QUESTIONS FOR
MAKING DINNERTIME CONNECTIONS

1 What was one thing that happened in your class?

2 What was one thing you liked about your class?

3 Who did something helpful in your class and what did that person do?

4 What was one thing someone said that would be good for our family to remember?

5 What kind of problems did your class talk about?

6 What person in the Bible did something our family would not like? What did that person do?

7 What person in the Bible did you hear about who did something our family would like? What did that person do?

8 When we pray together, who is someone in your class that we can thank God for? Who can we ask God to help?

9 When have you seen something happen that was a lot like what happened in the Bible story or verses your class learned about?

10 Which of your friends was not in your class this week? What would be a good way to show that you missed him or her?

HELPING TEACHERS AND FAMILIES CONNECT

PRETEEN MINISTRY COORDINATOR

1. Provide all teachers with up-to-date rosters that list each student's name, address, phone number, e-mail address, birthday, and names of family members. Also provide regular attendance information to teachers.

2. Encourage teachers to get to know family members of their students, focusing on students who might need support (i.e., absentees, irregular attendees, those whose family does not attend, etc.).

3. Encourage family members to get to know the preteen teacher and leaders. Particularly in large churches where no one knows everyone, it is usually easier for parents to approach a teacher than for a teacher to approach parents. A few ideas:

   ◎ Publish a list of all classes and where they meet and the names, e-mail addresses and phone numbers of the teachers and leaders. Include an invitation to call or write a teacher for information about a particular class.

   ◎ Outside every class, mount a sign with the name(s) of the teacher(s). Also mount (outside or inside the class) a poster with candid snapshots of teachers in action with students. Add labels with the names of the people pictured and update the photos periodically.

   ◎ Distribute blank note cards to the parents of preteens. Invite everyone to write a note to a teacher telling how his or her ministry has helped their family.

   ◎ Invite family members to be prayer partners with a preteen teacher.

   ◎ Encourage families to invite a teacher and his or her family for Sunday dinner, a backyard barbecue or for dessert and coffee after an evening event.

   ◎ Suggest that parents volunteer to provide and serve a snack for the preteen class near their child's birthday.

   ◎ Form a parent support/prayer group that meets together periodically to pray for the preteens and their teachers and for each other. Invite teachers to attend or submit requests and praises for parents to pray.

   ◎ Encourage class members to invite a teacher and his or her family to participate in a family activity (picnic in the park, overnight camp out, hike in the woods, etc.).

TEACHERS

1. In class, talk informally with students about their families. Share information about your own family and invite students to tell you about theirs. (**Note:** Avoid prying or making judgmental comments about family activities of which you disapprove.)

   ◉ Take advantage of the times when students arrive early to ask them about their week and how family members are doing. When asking questions during the lesson, periodically pose the question: "How do you think your mom (or dad or brother or sister) might answer that? Why might their answer be different from yours?"

   ◉ When preteens start to become embarrassed that they even *have* parents or siblings, they may rarely (if ever) volunteer any information about their families. As young people move toward increased independence, teachers who earn their trust often become "stand-in parents" and are able to say things to the teen that might not be accepted from a parent.

2. Pray regularly, by name, for your students and their families. Share with your students that you do this and invite them or their family members to share items of concern about which you can pray. Keep a prayer journal on your class, updating it with new family information.

3. At church, look for opportunities to talk to family members of your students.

   ◉ Before and after services, use the free time to greet family members.

   ◉ Instead of sitting in your usual place during worship services, look around for students and their families that you do not know well. Sit near them and take advantage of opportunities to speak to them.

4. When family events are planned by your church or when students are involved in community events (sports games, band concerts, parades, etc.), make it a point to attend even if you aren't expected to be there. Your presence speaks clearly of your interest, encouraging students and their families.

5. At least once per quarter, make a personal contact (conversation at church, phone call, home visit, etc.) with each student's family. Share positive comments about the student and invite feedback on what the student likes most or least about the class.

MEDICAL AND LIABILITY RELEASE FORM

IMPORTANT: *This is a sample form, not intended to be reproduced.*
Ask a lawyer who is familiar with your state's church liability laws to evaluate this form.

Parent Permission/Release Form

(Church Name)

(Address)

(Phone Number)

Child's Name _____

Birth Date _____   Grade _____

Address _____

City _____   Zip _____

Phone _____

Date(s) of Activity _____

Authorization of Consent for Treatment of Minor

I, the undersigned parent or guardian of _____, a minor, do hereby authorize any duly authorized employee, volunteer or other representative of the (church name), as agent(s) for the undersigned, to consent to any x-ray examination, anesthetic, medical or surgical diagnosis or treatment, and hospital care which is deemed advisable by, and is to be rendered under the general or specific supervision of, any licensed physician and surgeon, whether such diagnosis or treatment is rendered at the office of said physician and surgeon or at a clinic, hospital or other medical facility.

It is understood that this authorization is given in advance of any specific diagnosis, treatment or hospital care being required, but is given to provide authority and power on the part of our aforesaid agent(s) to give specific consent to any and all such diagnosis treatment or hospital care which the aforementioned physician in the exercise of his or her best judgment may deem advisable. It is understood that the cost of all medical emergencies and/or treatments will be paid by the parent.

This authorization shall remain effective from_____to _____ .

Signature_____

PRETEEN MINISTRY COORDINATOR

Task: To plan and develop a program of Bible learning through loving adult relationships, Bible lessons and learning activities for preteens each Sunday morning

Term: One year, beginning in June

Supervisor _____

Responsibilities

- Recruit leaders, teachers and helpers for all preteen classes and programs.

- Plan and lead a regular program of training for all staff.

- Observe, evaluate and affirm teachers in order to note strengths to encourage and areas where improvement is possible.

- Pray regularly for preteen leaders, teachers and helpers.

- Lead regular planning meetings for teachers and leaders that include training and opportunities for spiritual growth.

- Oversee the purchase, distribution and use of all equipment and supplies (curriculum, snacks, art supplies, etc.).

- Communicate the church's approved safety policy to all staff, regularly evaluate its use and take necessary steps to put the policy into practice.

- Plan a staff get-together at least twice a year in order to build a sense of teamwork among all workers.

- Express appreciation to the staff, including an end-of-the-year event.

- Communicate with parents regarding the purpose, value and procedures of preteen programs.

- Communicate regularly with supervisor and leaders of related programs (midweek clubs, second-hour coordinator, etc.).

Note: This position may be held by a volunteer or paid staff person. In a small church, one or more of these tasks may be the responsibility of the supervisor (Christian education committee member, children's ministries elder, etc.).

PRETEEN MINISTRY TEAM LEADER

Task: To prayerfully support and build relationships with both teachers and preteens in order to ensure effective Bible learning

Term: One year, beginning in June

Supervisor _____

Responsibilities

- Coordinate teacher tasks, including use of supplies and room setup.

- Greet preteens as they arrive and guide them to an activity.

- Assist teachers as needed (discipline, activity completion, etc.), maintaining the time schedule for the session.

- Observe, evaluate and affirm teachers in order to note strengths to encourage and areas where improvement is possible.

- Lead the large-group time (Bible study and/or worship), involving other teachers as appropriate.

- Pray regularly for others on the preteen ministry team.

- Work with your supervisor to enlist qualified people to join your ministry team.

- Lead regular session planning meetings, including training and opportunities for spiritual growth.

- Plan a team get-together in order to build friendships once a quarter.

- Communicate regularly with supervisor.

Note: In a class with just two teachers, the leader responsibilities may be informally shared. When three or more people are on the team, one person should be designated as the Team Leader.

PRETEEN MINISTRY PUBLICITY COORDINATOR

Task: To communicate all preteen programs and events

Term: One year, beginning in June

Supervisor _____

Responsibilities

- Determine the ongoing publicity needs for student programs, including mailed publicity, displays at church, bulletin and/or newsletter inserts.

- Oversee the production and distribution of all preteen and parent letters, flyers, posters, etc., working with others as needed (office staff, preteen ministry leaders, etc.).

PRETEEN MINISTRY TEACHER

Task: To prayerfully build relationships with preteens and guide them in life-changing Bible learning

Term: One year, beginning in June

Supervisor _____

Individual Responsibilities

- Maintain a personal relationship with Jesus Christ.
- Desire to grow in faith and commitment to God and participate in personal Bible study and prayer.
- Worship regularly with the church family.

Team Responsibilities

- Pray regularly for each child and others on your preteen ministry team.
- Participate in scheduled ministry team meetings.
- Participate in at least one training event during the year to improve teaching skills.
- Express needs as a teacher to your supervisor.

Teaching Session Responsibilities

- Arrive at least 15 minutes before session begins.
- Arrange materials and room to create an effective learning environment.
- Greet each preteen upon arrival and involve him or her in conversation and meaningful activity.
- Model the love of Christ by getting to know preteens and sharing their concerns, needs and joys.
- Guide Bible learning by
  1. Being well prepared to use Bible lessons, verses/passages, questions and comments appropriate to preteens in order to accomplish the lesson aims;
  2. Selecting a variety of Bible learning activities and encouraging each student to actively participate in each lesson;
  3. Participating with preteens in learning activities and in large-group times.

Student Follow-Up Responsibilities

- Follow up on visitors and absentees with mailings, phone calls and/or personal visits.
- Care for each class member with prayer, telephone calls, birthday cards, etc.
- Communicate individual student needs to parents.

PRETEEN MINISTRY CAMP COORDINATOR

Task: To plan and reserve summer and/or winter camp reservations, publicize the camp program and oversee all details (counselors, registration, transportation, etc.)

Supervisor _____

Responsibilities

- In coordination with supervisor, reserve date and number of campers at (name of camp). Coordinate camp dates with school schedules.

- Request and display camp brochures in the appropriate classrooms and in other well-traveled areas of the church facility.

- Write bulletin notices for camps and send publicity materials with parent letters well in advance of registration due dates.

- Set up and oversee procedures for accepting registrations and fees.

- Mail all checks and registration to the camp registrar.

- Plan and coordinate scholarships and fund-raisers as needed.

- Two weeks prior to camp, send an information letter to each camper. Include information about final payment of all camp fees, transportation arrangements, luggage, address at camp, medical release forms, etc.

- After camp, ask several campers to write an article for church newsletter and/or arrange for several campers to be interviewed in church service.

- Communicate regularly with supervisor.

PRETEEN FAMILY OUTREACH COORDINATOR

Task: To plan, organize and direct family ministry efforts.

Term: One year, beginning in June

Supervisor _____

Responsibilities

- Provide up-to-date student/family rosters for all preteen ministry staff.

- Encourage leaders to get to know, pray for and communicate with family members of students.

- Coordinate family-education efforts.

- Evaluate the manner in which families are cared for by the preteen ministry leaders.

- Plan special events or programs for families.

- Communicate regularly with supervisor.

PRETEEN MINISTRY WEEKNIGHT PROGRAM COORDINATOR

Task: To oversee planning and development of a youth group program for weeknight (mid-week, Saturday night) preteen ministries

Term: One year, beginning in June

Supervisor _____

Responsibilities

• Recruit teachers and helpers for weeknight-program positions.

• Pray regularly for each member of weeknight-program staff.

• Answer questions and give practical tips for solving problems.

• Observe, evaluate and affirm teachers and helpers to help them understand their strengths and to encourage them in areas where improvement is possible.

• Coordinate regular planning and training meetings for team members that include both teacher training and opportunities for spiritual growth.

• Oversee the purchase, distribution and use of all equipment and supplies (curriculum, snacks, art supplies, etc.).

• Communicate the church's approved safety policy to weeknight-program staff, regularly evaluate its use and take necessary steps to put the policy into practice.

• Lead in planning a weeknight-program staff get-together at least twice a year in order to build a sense of teamwork.

• Express appreciation to weeknight-program staff with an end-of-the-year event.

• Communicate with church leaders and the congregation regarding the purpose, value and procedures of weeknight ministries.

Note: This position may be held by a volunteer or paid staff person. In a small church, one or more of these tasks may be the responsibility of the pastor, Christian education committee member, children's ministries elder, etc.

PRETEEN QUESTIONNAIRE

Name _____ Date _____

1. What's your favorite thing to do every day after school?

2. What do you and your friends like to do on weekends?

3. What's your favorite music group?

4. What advice would you give to the teacher of this group?

5. What's something you'd like to know about God?

6. Who are your three best friends?

7. What three activities would you like to do for a youth group event or outing?

SAFETY POLICY

IMPORTANT: *This is a sample form, not intended to be reproduced. Adapt to your specific needs.*

We desire to protect and support those who work with our preteens. These policies to prevent child abuse, neglect or any unfounded allegations against workers or teachers address three major areas:

1. Worker selection
2. Worker practices
3. Reporting obligation

Selecting Preteen Workers

• All paid employees, full- or part-time, including clergy, and all volunteer workers who work directly with or around minors should complete a Volunteer Application Form.

• A personal interview will be included as part of the selection process.

• Where circumstances merit, personal references listed in the application will be checked to further determine the suitability and character of the applicant. The reference check shall be documented.

• All workers with children should normally be members of First Church or have been attending First Church for a minimum of six months.

Safety Policies for Preteen Ministries

• Volunteers and other workers are encouraged to be in public areas where both the preteen and teacher are visible to other people.

• All drivers transporting preteens on out-of-town activities shall be a minimum age of 25 and maximum age of 65 and shall complete and have approved a Driver Form. (Ask your church's insurance agent to read and evaluate the Driver Form.)

• The desirable minimum age for all drivers for in-town activities is 25. No one under age 18 will be permitted to drive for any church-sponsored activity.

• Preteen workers should not provide transportation to and from church on a regular basis.

• For overnight outings and camps, whenever both genders are present as participants, both genders need to be present in leadership.

• For outdoor activities, participants are to be in groups of at least three.

• Counseling is to be by a leader of the same gender and is to be done in public areas where both the preteen and leader are visible to other people.

• Each group of preteens should have at least two workers who are not related to each other, at least one being an adult, present at all times.

• Window blinds and doors are to be kept open (or doors should have windows). A supervisor or designated adult representative will circulate where preteen activities are occurring.

Reporting Obligation and Procedure

1. All workers are to be familiar with the definitions of child abuse (see below).

2. If a worker suspects that a child has been abused, the following steps are to be followed:

   - Report the suspected abuse to your supervisor.

   - Do not interview the child regarding the suspected abuse. The interview process will be handled by trained personnel.

   - Do not discuss the suspected abuse. It is important that all information about the suspected child abuse (victim and abuser) be kept confidential.

3. Workers reporting suspected child abuse will be asked to complete the Suspected Child Abuse Report (available from your state's Department of Social Services). Confidentiality will be maintained where possible. This report must be completed within 24 hours.

4. Once a suspected child abuse case has been reported by a worker to a supervisor, it will be reported to the designated reporting agency.

Definitions of Child Abuse

Defined by the National Committee for Prevention of Child Abuse. (Contact appropriate law enforcement officials for your state's definition and laws.)

Physical Abuse

Nonaccidental injury, which may include beatings, violent shaking, human bites, strangulation, suffocation, poisoning or burns. The results may be bruises and welts, broken bones, scars, permanent disfigurement, long-lasting psychological damage, serious internal injuries, brain damage or death.

Neglect

The failure to provide a child with basic needs, including food, clothing, education, shelter and medical care; also abandonment and inadequate supervision.

Sexual Abuse

The sexual exploitation of a child by an older person, as in rape, incest, fondling of the genitals, exhibitionism or pornography. It may be done for the sexual gratification of the older person, out of a need for power or for economic reasons.

SAFETY POLICY INTRODUCTORY LETTER

IMPORTANT: *This is a sample form, not intended to be reproduced. Adapt to your specific needs.*

(Date)

(Church Name)

(Address)

(Phone Number)

Dear _____ ,
             (name)

Here at First Church we believe that having a well-thought-out Safety Policy is part of the wisdom to which Christ calls us. We are aware that even with such a policy in place, we remain dependent on Christ and His ultimate protection. However, this policy will give us confidence that our preteens will have a safe environment in which to learn and grow in their Christian faith.

We are asking that everyone in preteen ministries complete the required forms and attend a training session about the Safety Policy. The next training session is scheduled on (date). We thank you for your help and cooperation in advance.

Our efforts in this area are a bit like a CPR class. You never expect to have a problem, yet you take all the precautions you possibly can. You train in order to know how to respond if there is a situation calling for action, believing and praying that it will not be needed.

Thank you for caring about preteens and helping them grow in the nurture and admonition of the Lord.

Sincerely,

_____

(name)

_____

Pastor

VOLUNTEER APPLICATION FORM

IMPORTANT: *This is a sample form, not intended to be reproduced. Adapt to your specific needs.*

First Church has a safety policy founded on respect and love for the preteens of our church and community. This safety policy gives preteens, parents and all preteen ministry staff a sense of confidence and peace. We ask your cooperation in completing and returning this application.

Personal Information

Name_____ Social Security #_____

Addresses for the past 10 years _____

_____

Phone_____ Cell phone _____ E-mail _____

Best time to call: Morning _____ Afternoon _____ Evening _____

Day and month of birth_____

Occupation_____

Where employed_____

Phone_____

Can you receive calls at work?   ❑ Yes   ❑ No

Do you have a current driver's license?   ❑ Yes   ❑ No

License number _____

Children   ❑ Yes   ❑ No

Name(s) and age(s)_____

Spouse   ❑ Yes   ❑ No

Name_____

Are you currently a member of First Church?   ❑ Yes   ❑ No

If yes, how long? _____

Please list other churches and locations where you have regularly attended over the past five years.

_____

1. Are you currently under a charge or have you ever been convicted of any crime?   ❑ Yes   ❑ No

2. Are you currently under a charge or have you ever been accused or convicted of child abuse or of any crime involving actual or attempted sexual misconduct or sexual molestation of a minor?

❑ Yes   ❑ No

If yes, please explain_____

_____

Are you currently under a charge or have you ever been accused or convicted of possession/sale of controlled substances or of driving under the influence of drugs or alcohol?

❑ Yes   ❑ No

If yes, please explain_____

_____

Have you served in the military?   ❑ Yes   ❑ No

If yes, what was the method of termination?_____

Is there any other information that we should know?_____

_____

Church Activity

1. Please write a brief statement of how you became a Christian.

   _____

   _____

   _____

2. In what activities/ministries of our church are you presently involved?

   _____

3. Experience:

   a. What volunteer or career experiences with preteens have you had in the church or the community?

   _____

   b. List any gifts, calling, training, education or other factors that have prepared you for ministry to preteens.

   _____

4. Preferences: In what capacity would you like to minister? Explain your choice.

   _____

   _____

5. Concerns: What causes the greatest feelings of apprehension as you contemplate this ministry?

   _____

Personal References

(One reference must be a relative)

Name _____ Phone _____

Address _____

Name _____ Phone _____

Address _____

Name _____ Phone _____

Address _____

Applicant's Statement

The information contained in this application is true and correct to the best of my knowledge. I authorize any of the above references or churches to give you any information that they may have regarding my character and fitness to work with preteens. I authorize a professional social security screening for the purposes of this volunteer position.

I hereby certify that I have read and that I understand the attached provisions of (insert title of your state's penal code regarding the reporting of child abuse and neglect).

Signature _____ Date _____